IN SEARCH OF
REFUGE

IN SEARCH OF REFUGE

Yvonne Dilling with Ingrid Rogers

Foreword by Jim Wallis

Photographs by Mike Goldwater

HERALD PRESS

Scottdale, Pennsylvania

Kitchener, Ontario

1984

Library of Congress Cataloging in Publication Data

Dilling, Yvonne, 1955-
   In search of refuge.

   Bibliography: p.
   1. Church work with refugees—Honduras. 2. Refugees—Honduras. 3.
Refugees—El Salvador. 4. Dilling, Yvonne, 1955-   I. Rogers, Ingrid. II.
Title.
BV4470.D54   1984   972.84'052   84-9012
ISBN 0-8361-3364-1 (pbk.)

Copyright © 1984 by Herald Press, Scottdale, Pa. 15683
   Published simultaneously in Canada by Herald Press,
   Kitchener, Ont. N2G 4M5. All rights reserved.
Photographs © Mike Goldwater/NEWORK, London
Library of Congress Catalog Card Number: 84-9012
International Standard Book Number: 0-8361-3364-1
Printed in the United States of America
Design by Alice B. Shetler

90 89 88 87 86 85 84 10 9 8 7 6 5 4 3 2 1

In memory of my co-workers—
Elpidio,
Lucio, and
Rafael.

Contents

Foreword

For years Central America, though geographically close to us, seemed far from our conscience. Unknown to most of the rest of the world, its people suffered brutal violence and poverty under the boot of military dictators and the bulldozer of large corporations.

But Central America is no longer hidden. As our government has turned new attention to the region, news from Central America has begun to fill the pages of our newspapers and the screens of our television sets. The people of the United States are left grasping for an understanding of the Central American situation.

In this book Yvonne Dilling and Ingrid Rogers offer help in understanding all of Central America from the most important perspective—that of the people. In her 18 months in Honduras, Yvonne was able to identify with the people there to a remarkable degree and to begin to see things through their eyes, their feelings, and their experience. And that is what she helps us to do.

This is a warm, personal, and at times intimate account of the sufferings and hopes of the people of Central America. The people whose perspective she shares are the refugees. To be a refugee is to be the poorest of the poor. Telling about their lives, Yvonne gives us a view of Central America from the bottom up.

From the point of view of the Bible, this perspective is always the most important to understand. It is the perspective of the poor with which the Bible is most concerned. And in fact it is the refugee—the stranger or sojourner—who deserves special treatment and hospitality. The Bible invites us to welcome the stranger and warns that the well-being of the stranger is central to our own.

The perspective that emerges from this book is directly contrary to the perspective on Central America held by the United States government. The reason for that has little to do with politics in the usual categories of left and right, liberal and conservative. The United States government views the Central American situation not from the bottom up, but from the point of view of the regional military, which it supports, and the wealthy elites, whom it sponsors. It sees the situation from the perspective of an ideology that views Central America as an arena for a global East-West confrontation, and consistently bends, distorts, and even lies about the actual reality to fit the situation into that preconceived ideological framework.

The two perspectives are as different as night and day, and the conclusions they reach are equally opposed. But it is not hard for us to see which perspective is most biblical. The human cost and consequences of the United States ideology and policy become painfully clear in the stories of the many people Yvonne came to know. She paints vivid portraits that give us a clear picture of the life of the refugees.

These are the victims of United States policy. Yvonne has told us their names and has shown us their faces. Most of all, she has introduced them as brothers and sisters.

Christ comes alive among the refugees in this powerful plea from the heart. And through the faith of the people, the simple gospel faith of the poor, Yvonne's faith comes alive too. These are people who trust God in their suffering and find hope in Jesus, because nothing else offers hope.

Yvonne's deep compassion for the refugees pervades the book. So does her courage. She is humble about the many courageous things she did and even embarrassed at all the attention they have brought her. But her faith and strength and willingness to risk even her own life for the sake of the gospel and the people she grew to love stand as a moving testimony.

The strength of the peace church tradition from which she comes is also evident in the book. And yet her pacifist convictions were shaken to their foundation by the brutality and violence that surrounded her. She discovered that a detached North American pacifism proved utterly inadequate for dealing with the suffering she encountered. She emerged out of the inner turmoil and questioning with a commitment to a deeper kind of nonviolence—an active, engaged, and costly way of battling against injustice.

A change is occurring in the United States churches. Confronted with the faith of the people of Central America, we are undergoing a deeper conversion. Yvonne Dilling is a pioneer in that movement.

Through her life, and now her testimony in this book, she is leading many others to a deeper level of faith.

I have found it a privilege to work with Yvonne on the Witness for Peace, a grassroots effort to maintain a continuous, nonviolent, and prayerful United States presence at the Nicaragua-Honduras border, where U.S.-backed counterrevolutionary forces are carrying out a terrorist war against the Nicaraguan people. Yvonne brings the same commitment and compassion to this effort that she did to her work with the refugees.

Yvonne Dilling has done more than simply identify with suffering people. She is helping to lead the way toward a new North American church, one that begins to see the world through the eyes of the poor— which is to say, through the eyes of God.

—Jim Wallis, *Sojourners* editor
and chair of the Witness for Peace
advisory committee

Author's Preface

It was a sultry, quiet afternoon in Santa Marta, a village in El Salvador. Suddenly heavy trucks and jeeps rumbled onto the unpaved street, and soldiers poured out of the vehicles. Someone with a bullhorn shouted that all the houses of the tiny hamlet would be searched for rebels and weapons. The soldiers forced open the door of every adobe house. In each home they destroyed furniture, broke dishes, threw bedding and clothing into the street, and set everything afire. As the air filled with dark smoke, the soldiers went about shooting the livestock and tearing up gardens.

Three soldiers pushed open the door to Graciela's house. "Where is your subversive husband?" they demanded.

"My husband is working in the rented fields on the mountainside, and he's not subversive," Graciela replied with fear in her voice.

"He's with the guerrillas in the mountains, isn't he?" one shot back.

A soldier pushed Graciela against a wall, his rifle held at her throat. Another soldier forced the terrified children against the opposite wall. The third soldier began to ransack the house. He found what he was looking for. "Admit this is your Bible," he commanded. "Admit you hide communist literature in it. Admit you discuss communist takeovers in your so-called Bible study group."

With each demand he pressed the rifle still more painfully against her throat so she could hardly speak. But Graciela, a brave and proud Christian woman, did not yield to their violence by meekly answering yes.

The children began to cry as the soldiers threatened to "make her a whore in front of the kids." The soldiers finally left without carrying out their threats. From the doorway they warned, "No more Bible groups, no more housewives' clubs, and tell your husband we're watching him."

Graciela's husband didn't come home after that. A child of a neighboring family ran to the mountain field where he was working and told him what had happened. Each day his children left food for him at different spots along the mountain paths. The family had not wanted to do anything which could be construed as "subversive," but in El Salvador it is difficult to avoid that. So when the troops returned one night, Graciela, Ignacio, and their children fled. They joined hundreds of neighbors in an escape which took them over mountains and through ravines and valleys. They arrived in Honduras three days later, knowing their abandoned village lay in smoldering ashes.

The story shared in these pages is about Graciela, Ignacio, and thousands of others from El Salvador whom I met in Honduras. The people are refugees. They have fled military repression and war; they have witnessed horrendous atrocities. They are a result of the bloody strife which ravages Central America today.

In 1981 I began work as an international volunteer along the Honduras-El Salvador border. Many questions prompted me to travel there. What are the roots of the conflict in Central America? What is life like on the receiving end of United States foreign policy? What do the common people say about their situation, compared to what government leaders tell us? These were some of my questions. I spoke Spanish, had studied Latin American affairs, and felt a deep, sincere concern about issues of peace and war, poverty and social justice. I wanted to live among the people of Central America and learn from them. With no previously arranged plans, I set out by bus to see what I might find in Central America.

I did see. Within eighteen months I experienced and learned more than in all my previous twenty-eight years. I learned about Central America and what it is like to be a refugee.

This book is about the Salvadoran people, their way of life, their hopes and fears, their past and present in the isolated Central American mountains where they live as refugees who need to be sheltered, fed, and clothed. These refugees are usually the poorest sector of the society they have been forced to abandon. They suffer from malnutrition and numerous illnesses. Circumstances force them to flee to remote, hard-to-reach areas, and this makes it doubly difficult to find and assist them. To meet their most basic needs week after week, month after month, can seem at times a miraculous feat. As months turn into years, hope withers into despair. The numbers of refugees swell while the war back home intensifies, and the still larger numbers drown the individual human being in anonymity.

To feed, clothe, and shelter these people is not enough. Protecting the refugees from violence becomes a major concern. To keep one's attention focused on the human being in the midst of such confusion becomes a daily and sometimes hourly challenge. The programs of humanitarian groups get twisted by others who have political goals. Even the work of supposedly neutral agencies like the United Nations is sometimes manipulated. Although this work is desperately needed for what little it can do, the bureaucratic red tape of such a complex organization can ruin the most sincere efforts.

In Search of Refuge is about all of this from the perspective of the Salvadoran people with whom I lived. It is written in diary form although I did not keep a detailed diary throughout my year and a half of service. I did, however, make occasional journal entries and write numerous letters to family and friends. These, along with extensive taped interviews done by Ingrid Rogers, were combined to form the book. All the events did happen as described. Only names have been changed to protect the refugees and volunteer workers.

Illness forced me to return to the United States. During the ensuing months, while my body bore the onslaught of chemotherapy followed by radiation treatments, Ingrid Rogers, writer and peace activist, listened to me. She provided the initial vision that this testimony merited the work to bring it into book form. She eagerly committed her writing and editorial skills, her time and energy. When remembering seemed too painful, she encouraged me to go on. We have both offered our best in order to share the saga lived by the Salvadoran people.

In Search of Refuge is written with the intention that people having no previous introduction to Central America, on hearing the experiences of the Salvadoran refugees interpreted through a North American's eyes, might come to understand and empathize with the plight of the people throughout Central America. Knowledge of the region's history, though helpful, is not necessary to read the book. Therefore a brief historical overview is included only as an appendix. It can be better understood after reading about the people themselves.

—Yvonne Dilling
Fort Wayne, Indiana
and Washington,
District of Columbia

Acknowledgments

Perhaps only those familiar with the labor of testing ideas, writing, rewriting, ·editing, and typing will fully understand our need to acknowledge the assistance and participation of others in the long process. We too find, although it may sound repetitious to those who actually read the acknowledgment pages of books, that there is no other way to say it: this book is not the work of one person.

In Search of Refuge came together because several things happened. The Salvadoran people fled their war-torn homes and villages, taking with them nothing but their testimony and their indomitable human spirit; Yvonne went to live and work with those refugees, witnessing and experiencing a reality which would change her life; Ingrid heard Yvonne's story, envisioned that it could be shared with a wider audience, and provided the energy and writing skill to start the project and see it through to completion.

We are deeply grateful to the many friends who read sections of the rough manuscript and offered invaluable suggestions and criticisms. Others helped with the long and tedious tasks of typing or correcting galleys. Our families listened and were sometimes ignored while we lived and breathed the writing task, and we thank them for understanding. Our circle of Christian community listened even when they had surely tired of our topic, and we thank them also.

In addition we wish to acknowledge the work of international volunteers who journeyed to those isolated Honduran mountains to be a presence with the Salvadoran refugees. The internationals came from Europe, Canada, and the United States. Dozens arrived, served, and were replaced by others during the long, difficult months of late 1981 and early 1982. They are not mentioned by name in this book because to do so might jeopardize the good work they continue to do among the refugees. But we felt them with us in spirit during the entire writing process. A few who had returned home learned of this writing project and offered steadfast encouragement and support. Diane Kuntz, Bobbie Johnston, and Rob Boudewijn carefully read the manuscript, corrected it for factual accuracy, and offered timely suggestions. Our thanks to them for this contribution.

The story shared in the following pages is distressingly up-to-date, yet it is incomplete. It continues to be lived out on the borders surrounding El Salvador where the suffering goes on unabated. It is our sincere hope that each reader will be moved to keep informed about the Salvadoran conflict and to take action to alleviate the human suffering there.

—Yvonne Dilling
Ingrid Rogers

IN SEARCH OF REFUGE

I crossed the border into Honduras late this afternoon. It hardly seems possible that I am here after so many months of thinking, dreaming, and praying about this pilgrimage. It wasn't a hard decision to arrive at—to leave the U.S. and travel alone to Central America. I have wanted for so long to place myself in a situation where I could learn to know the Central Americans— especially the Salvadoran people—on their own turf. What better way than to set out alone rather than with an English-speaking traveling companion, and to ride the public buses as the common people do.

It is the first week of February 1981. The events of the past three years have left their impressions deeply imbedded in my mind and heart. I spent so many months following the struggle of the Nicaraguan people, gathering the daily accounts of atrocities committed by Somoza's National Guard. It seemed we had hardly caught our breath after the overthrow of Nicaragua's dictatorship when the suffering in El Salvador took over newspaper headlines.

When the newscasts switched to El Salvador, something inside of me rebelled: "Not another two years of reading reports of genocide and inconceivable brutality while trying to go on about life!" As I thought through my resistance to plunge into the coming task, it became clear that I needed to humanize those cold, impersonal, and objective statistics on torture and death. I wanted to see the faces and learn to know the people who are on the receiving end of U.S. foreign policy. I wanted to learn to know the Christians who shaped a man like slain Archbishop Romero. I wanted to take all I learned about nonviolent conflict resolution in

college and my church community, and put it in a situation where
the hard decisions are called for.

So ... here I am, trusting the old Quaker belief that the
"way will open." The pilgrimage is begun.

February 10, 1981

Three days ago in Santa Rosa the coordinator of Caritas
invited me to observe the refugee work at the border zone
between Honduras and El Salvador. This morning I joined three
other Caritas workers in a dilipidated pickup truck, and we left.
Beautifully paved roads carried us the first two hours through luscious green country; but as we crossed the mountain ridge, we
entered a different climatic zone and left the highway to go deep
into dry, barren mountains. Beyond the town of San Marcos, the
roads became rockier, steeper, and more winding, until they were
no better than cow paths or dry riverbeds. The trip seemed endless. We bounced until our teeth rattled. Dust swept in through
the open windows and settled like a dirty film on our sweating
skin. At each bend I desperately wished for them to announce
that we had arrived. When we finally did stop four hours later, I
was disappointed to learn we were only as far as the car would go
and we would have to continue the trip in a four-wheel drive vehicle.

Fortunately, Valladolid was at a high enough altitude to give
us some respite from the heat. We rested under pine trees and
looked out at the beautiful blue sky. Ramon said that from this
spot at night one can see the lights of San Salvador.

As we waited most of the afternoon for another vehicle, I
found myself getting impatient and suggested we begin walking.
My traveling companions only laughed, saying if I was anxious to
walk, I'd have plenty of opportunity in the next couple of weeks.

Finally, a bus arrived to take us the rest of the way to the
border town of La Virtud. It was a rickety old school bus; I feared
its brakes would give out as we headed down the mountain side to
begin what became the worst part of the trip. Even though the
bus crawled at a snail's pace, I thought several times we would

slide off the side of the mountain. We endured another hour of bouncing before we finally reached the border town.

La Virtud is not pretty. All my visions of a picturesque mountain village have vanished. The starkness of the dry mountains is equaled only by the starkness of the people's living conditions. Homes are built of mud bricks dried in the hot sun and cemented together with more mud. The roofs are of dull orange clay tile. It seems as though dust covers everything, including the people. I have never known such heat. We sweat during the day whether we rest in the shade or walk in the sun; we sweat when we go to bed; we wake up in the night sweating, and we wake up in the morning sweating still. It never ends. Apparently the people just get used to it.

It looks like La Virtud has as many chickens and pigs as it does people. They are allowed to go anywhere, roaming the streets and the plaza, walking in and out of homes at will; they even sit under the table as we eat.

February 12

My invitation to visit the border zone came from Ramon, a priest who oversees the Caritas work here. Caritas is a Catholic organization, one of several agencies operating here under the United Nations High Commission on Refugees (UNHCR). There are several points along the lengthy border between Honduras and El Salvador where refugees have crossed. The UNHCR is in charge of the administration of the work and has assigned each geographic region to a different agency. Here at La Virtud, Caritas is responsible for all of the refugee work except health care. A French agency, "Doctors Without Borders" (Médecins Sans Frontières), has that task.

Every day I learn more about life in the border zone. I hike to the villages—which are called *aldeas*—along with the Caritas workers who visit the refugees and the Hondurans who house them. As I accompany the workers I am getting to know the refugees and understand what refugee work consists of.

Today I accompanied Juanita, a fifty-five-year-old lay catechist who has been with Caritas for years. She was the one who initiated the refugee work sixteen months ago. At that time Caritas had already been working with poor Hondurans in the mountains for about five years. When Salvadorans first sought refuge, they came in small groups and hid in the mountains. They led an almost nomadic existence, avoiding the towns and trying to fend for themselves in the ravines and hillsides. But they were in such desperate need that a few Hondurans befriended and helped them.

Perhaps a Honduran family would invite them into their home, not because of what was happening militarily in the whole region, but simply because they saw desperate people, hungry and in need of clothing and shelter, and responded to their need. Bit by bit so many refugees had settled in the mountain villages that Caritas became aware of it.

One day one of the *padres* suggested to Juanita that she go out and try to assess the needs of these people and proceed with giving them basic food supplies. So Juanita hiked all those hills, got to know the Hondurans who were offering refuge, and asked the families about their needs. At first, the people were frightened. She therefore initially worked only with Hondurans, bringing them food from the Caritas warehouse so that they in turn could help the Salvadorans.

This is how the program started. A few Honduran volunteers said, "We could use a fifty-pound bag of powdered milk every week." Caritas supplied it, and the Hondurans prepared it and fed it to all the children. Soon Juanita sent out more beans, corn, and rice to supplement the Hondurans' provisions because the people, in their unending hospitality, were using up a whole year's supply of their own to feed the refugees. Interestingly, the poorest of the poor always helped the most.

Refugees kept coming. Every week, Juanita heard of new people in a different valley, ravine, village, or Honduran home. Finally, Caritas began discussing the problem on a regional level. They agreed to get more volunteers and a full-time coordinator of the food distribution program. When they set out to find how many they had been feeding, they realized it was over 5,000 people.

Juanita tells me that by now this number has more than doubled. Caritas looks for families who are willing to share their homes or, when this is not possible, let refugees build a little grass hut next to their homes and allow them to share their latrine, water source, and household items like a machete and corn grinder.

Many Salvadorans who cross the border seek refuge in anticipation of violence. They sense the military repression getting closer to their homes. I asked Juanita about this military repression. Often, it starts with simple harassment for no apparent reason. Suddenly soldiers knock on people's doors and ask for husbands or sons, accusing them of being subversives or of being "organized." Perhaps they have been involved in a union.

More often, the individual or family has participated in Catholic church-related activities. Small groups for worship and Bible study have been an integral part of Christian expression in El Salvador—especially in the rural areas. The problem is that the authorities fear any and all signs that the peasantry does not accept its domineering rule. So simply to meet together in a group of more than four is enough to foster suspicion. When Bible study is applied to daily life, and attempts are made to solve community problems, new community leaders begin to emerge from among the rural folk. This signals "change" to the landowners and authorities and threatens their absolute dominance.

Many refugees tell stories of soldiers having come to their home saying, "Do you listen to Archbishop Romero's sermons on the radio? Do you attend the Bible study at the church?" Those are their sins. "Do you have a Bible in the house? Do you hide communist literature in your Bible?" Behind all the accusations lies the general and nebulous suspicion that they are "subversives." People soon realize how dangerous this inflammatory talk can become. To avoid further confrontation, they get out of the way. Others stay until there is actual fighting and they are forced to flee.

February 13

I am beginning to know the Caritas team a little better. There are eleven full-time workers. Some live in town or in nearby villages; the others are seminary students for whom this work serves as practical training. The one-room house where most of the Caritas workers live is full to overflowing right now, so I am staying with two other workers in the house of the coordinator, Eduardo, and his family.

La Virtud is Eduardo's hometown. He lives with his mother and father, three younger brothers, and two younger sisters. As one of the lay catechists, he leads worship here in town because La Virtud has no priest. From what I understand he has worked with Caritas for many years, although he is only about twenty-eight years old. Since we share the house with his family, his mother, Doña Maria, often fixes meals for us. I am learning a lot about the town and the culture just by living with this family.

Another person who stays in this house with us is Alejandro, a volunteer also in his late twenties. He told me he joined the team when Caritas was just beginning, back at the time the first groups of refugees had crossed the border and were hiding in the hills or seeking refuge in the homes of Hondurans. The work then was not well-structured, since only a few hundred refugees had come into the area.

Alejandro has fascinating stories to tell about how he and Juanita first learned to know the region, met people through the churches, and found out bit by bit how many refugees there were. They then reported back to the regional Caritas office in Santa Rosa. When Caritas decided to begin a more formal and structured program, Alejandro stayed on to help. Before that time he had not known any Salvadorans because he was not from the border area.

Diego is the seminary student who accompanied us in the truck the day I arrived. He has been here for several months and will be able to stay only a few more weeks because his school term begins again. Alejandro and Diego together cover a cluster of five villages about an hour's walk away from La Virtud. It is a heavy assignment. Having accompanied them several times, I now understand why we seldom see them around—they are always out walking. It is fascinating to go along on their mountain hikes and ask them about the experiences they have had working there.

I don't know the other workers well yet. Nemecio, Miguel, Julia, and Juanita all have families either in town or in the villages. The others—Rafael, Teresa, Paolo, and Mario—are from other parts of the country. They worked with Caritas in their hometowns for many years before coming to La Virtud to help. Almost all are lay catechists, trained by their diocese to work in areas without a priest. Thus they have had ample experience in leadership and coordination and can work well with the people here. Like the *campesinos,* they too have rural roots, so they understand the people and identify with them.

February 16

Now I see why Ramon assured me there would be ample opportunity to walk once I got to the border zone! We have been hiking several hours every day this week in order to meet with the Hondurans and refugees in the fifteen different villages served by Caritas. Each village has a committee formed of Honduran Caritas volunteers and elected refugee representatives. The Caritas promoters work directly with these committees in their distribution of food and clothing, and in other special projects.

There are often problems such as the drunk who has come in and caused trouble, or there has been an argument about how much sugar to give out, or some of the children have become ill. The "promotion" work, as it is called, includes dealing with these problems, and also offering encouragement for the Honduran host families. We also take time for scriptural reflection, prayer, and singing.

Two of the current Caritas projects directly address the needs of children. Most of the people here are under sixteen. Everywhere I look, noisy groups of kids compete with the noise of chickens and roosters. Out in the villages the Caritas workers have encouraged me to visit with the children, sing songs, and play

with them. Surprisingly, the children overcome their shyness after
I have made only one visit to their aldeas. Everyone is excited
about the two new programs: a milk project and a head lice
project. We go out to the villages to see that these two are being
run well.

I had fun helping to bathe children last week. Diego suggested that while he worked on another project, I should go with
the children to the stream and help them use the lice shampoo,
making sure they rinsed their hair thoroughly. So I found myself
hiking up a dusty trail in the company of about sixty small kids
and three teenage girls. Around the bend we arrived at a beautiful, fast-flowing stream only about knee-deep.

For one hour we washed away the lice and enjoyed the water
before beginning the long, hard process of combing the dead lice
out with a fine-tooth comb. I felt such satisfaction in seeing all
those clean, wet, bronzed bodies of the children. But my pleasure
was short-lived as we stirred up the dust running back down the
hill. By the time we reached the village, the children were
practically as dust-covered as they had been before we set out. I
began to understand the sense of futility that some of the mothers
must feel at wanting to keep their children clean but finding it virtually impossible given the living conditions.

When we got back to the village, the mothers had finished
cooking the milk. This project for the refugees and Honduran
families was initiated only about a month ago. Diego told me that
the mothers cook milk with sugar and a special soy flour to give to
the children along with a high-protein cracker. At first the flavor
seemed so strange that the children did not like it, but within a
few weeks they had all become used to it and eagerly lined up,
each with a cup in hand, to receive their daily glass of hot milk.

Diego asked me to watch the children closely, because
Caritas is hoping to chart increased levels of energy in the
children within a short time. The health team is concerned
about the children's growth rate because the protein intake has
been far below their actual need. I asked Diego about the age of
this particular group and was shocked to hear that most of them

were eight to fourteen years old. Their size had made me think we were working with six- to eight-year-olds.

February 20

Diego and I went to another village yesterday. Since he is a lay catechist, the people insisted on having a worship service. When no priest is present to administer the mass in these isolated aldeas, they have a service called "Celebration of the Word." The news spread through the hills so that in a matter of half an hour over seventy-five men, women, and children had crowded into the back of a small Honduran house. We sat on anything available, crowded so tightly that no handholding was necessary to make the circle of fellowship.

The Scripture lesson was on John the Baptist saying, "I baptize you with water, but the one who comes will baptize you with the Spirit and fire." A long discussion ensued about what it means to have the Spirit. The catechist asked, "What kind of people were the disciples of Jesus? Were they examples of persons with the Holy Spirit?" And the people responded, "Those with the Holy Spirit loved the poor. They shared everything. They wanted to free people from sickness, oppression, and poverty." And so they drew their conclusion: You will know those who have the Spirit ("not by tongues," someone in the back mentions) by their courage and steadfastness in following the mandates of the gospel.

"Be specific!" encouraged Diego. The people mentioned the Honduran farmers who are sharing their homes with the refugees. They pointed out people who do not have the Spirit, such as some "missionaries" who supply emergency food provisions but are more concerned with catching the refugees listening to the guerrilla radio station than with relieving the pain of their empty stomachs. They mentioned soldiers who come through, frightening the children and verbally abusing or raping refugee women. Someone said the President of the United States does not have the Spirit because he sends napalm to be dropped on their towns.

Diego played the guitar, and everyone began to sing the Salvadoran "People's Mass." The affirmation of faith says,

"When the poor believe in one another, then we can begin to talk of freedom; then we are living as the body of Christ." Another song explains, "If the rewards were to be only in heaven, God would not have sent his son to earth, nor resurrected him."

After the worship service as the people began to disperse, Diego and I picked up our small bags and asked for a place to hang our hammocks. One of the families suggested that we go with them, saying their house was not too crowded. So we climbed a nearby hill to get to their home. When I asked the man along the way how many refugees lived with him, he replied, "Four other families."

Upon entering the main room of his house we found it virtually impossible to walk because of all the sleeping bodies, both in and under the beds; but we squeezed through along one wall and walked into a second room. There from the rafters hung another six hammocks; but sure enough, we found room for two more. Quietly we slung our hammocks and climbed in. I had never slept in such crowded conditions before.

Over and over during these past few days I have noticed that the poorer the people, the more generously they treat others. The less they have, the more willing they are to share absolutely everything. This morning they insisted that Diego and I have eggs for breakfast while the children, probably eight altogether, stood by and watched longingly as their mother offered us the special treat.

Talking to the family over breakfast we learned that twenty-five refugees had been living with them for over eight months, sharing the house, the corn grinder, the meager water source, and the small home structure. The Hondurans had expanded the outside corridors of their home with thatching in order to gain extra space for more people. They had totally disrupted their own way of life to accommodate those who had nothing.

For a family to eat a meal together all at once is impossible in these homes. With not nearly enough spoons or dishes to go around, everyone takes turns eating; as one finishes, the bowls and utensils are washed up for the next person. Many children eat with their fingers. As I looked around I could not help but think about the children crawling on the same floor the pigs use.

When we prepared to leave this morning, people begged us to stay a while longer. "Stay with us for lunch," they said. "We'll cook up a chicken and have soup." They are so excited to have visitors, so pleased to be able to share. I am humbled again and again by their hospitality. Since we insisted we had to move on, they ran and filled our canteens with water, helped roll up our hammocks and tuck them into our shoulder bags, and watched us start our long hike back into town.

February 22

In the short time I have spent at the border, it is difficult to assess the role of the military. In La Virtud, I have not noticed any problems with security; the soldiers mostly keep to themselves in the command post or at the immigration offices. And yet I sense from all the Caritas workers a strong animosity toward the military. There must be a cause I am not aware of yet.

Yesterday as Diego and I returned from Guarita I gained a first impression of the fear that must lie in people's hearts here. We had hiked from village to village to get back to the main road, sweating as usual, stopping for rest, going on, and feeling as though we would never get out of these mountains. At one point we were resting at an adobe brick warehouse when in came a Honduran worker for World Vision, a U.S. based Protestant aid organization that I have heard people complaining about.

Diego warned me to be cautious when talking to him, and not to let him know I was with the Catholics. He also stated he would not talk to the person for the sake of his own safety. I was puzzled by his apprehensiveness.

Soon afterwards as we rested in our hammocks the worker came over and struck up a conversation, asking me where I was from and what I was doing. I told him I was a Protestant interested in visiting the refugee zone because my church back home had been aiding the refugees. I wanted to leave it at that, but he suddenly became persistent and brusque, demanding to see my passport. When I explained I had left it in town because I thought I would not need it up here, he insisted that I write my name on a piece of paper for him. I asked him in all innocence why he wanted that. He just smiled and said, "Because!"

By then Diego had overheard part of the conversation; he stuck his head into the room and announced we had to leave. I got up right away, sensing that somehow through this worker I had had a brush with the military.

Late that same afternoon came our second experience. We had hiked all day long until we finally reached the main town of Guarita. There we rested for an hour before packing our bags and heading on. The last stretch promised to be much easier since it led right along the main road to the intersection where the bus passes. A small yellow pickup truck came by as we were walking along. Diego waved, and when the driver stopped we asked if we could have a ride in the back. He agreed, so we climbed in.

It never occurred to me that we might be in some kind of danger. When we reached the turn-off where Diego and I needed to separate (he was going to another village while I was returning to La Virtud), Diego signaled the driver to stop. He reminded me to be cautious, said good-bye, and jumped off. He was about to leave when one of the men leaned out of the car, asked for his name, and demanded to see his papers. I watched the scene from the back of the truck, puzzled that Diego complied without objection; to me the person next to the driver had looked like another civilian. After Diego had put his papers away he came over to me, hugged me, and whispered in my ear, "Be very careful with these men." Then he left. I became frightened.

We continued down the road but had not gone more than two miles of our six-mile journey, passing two homes and coming to an isolated place, when the truck suddenly stopped. My heart stopped also. The two men climbed out and asked to see my papers. Although they were dressed as civilians, they asked with such authority that I knew better than to challenge their right to do so. I told them that since I was just visiting the area, it had not occurred to me to carry my passport with me to the villages and that I had left it at the main refugee center with the Protestant church organization, CEDEN. I knew enough not to mention Caritas since CEDEN has a much better working relationship with the authorities in the region.

They immediately launched into a lecture about the importance of carrying my papers with me at all times, and about the danger of being in this area where all kinds of subversive activities are going on. They began interrogating me: "Why are you here? What is your name? With whom are you staying?" The questioning continued for several minutes. Finally I convinced them that I was just passing through and was on my way back to the Protestant church group where I had left my passport. They accepted my explanations but ordered that as soon as I got my papers I should go back to Santa Rosa and present them to immigration to make sure they were in order.

When the men got ready to climb back in the truck, I said politely, "Excuse me, but who are you?" One of them replied, "I am the director of DNI." (DNI is the national investigation body connected with the army.) These men—not just secret service employees, but the director—were driving around this isolated area questioning people. Why were they in plain clothes? What are the subversive activities they're looking for? Why are the refugees suspect? I was terrified. What was their purpose in questioning me at an isolated place in the road?

February 23

I am not sure what exactly I envisioned as a "border" between Honduras and El Salvador, but it certainly wasn't this. No customs signs or border crossings indicate where one country ends; the people just seem to know it. In some places the border is a river, in others, the very top edge of the mountain, in yet others I am uncertain what it is. The border makes a strange turn right here around this town, so that one can look out toward El Salvador in opposite directions. My concept of north, south, east, and west has become totally confused. The border itself seems to matter neither to the Hondurans who live here nor to the

Salvadorans who have taken refuge with them. Many of them are related to one another, and apparently the concept of a border has been imposed upon them by outside forces while they would just as soon pretend it did not exist.

February 24

Diego and I walked three hours down to the river Sumpul, which is the border line at this particular point. Last May (1980) Honduran soldiers lined up here on one side to push back into the river more than 600 children and women who were fleeing as the Salvadoran National Guard did a "clean-up operation" on the other mountain slope. The Honduran government denies to this day that it ever took place.

I listened half the evening to stories of the Salvadorans and the Honduran families with whom they have found refuge. The next morning, two young boys took me over to the Salvadoran side, where the mountain slope is still scattered with bones of all sizes. There are no whole skeletons. The people say the *Guardia* chopped up the bodies after shooting them. Every single skull I saw had been smashed in the face, probably so as to render it beyond recognition.

I wondered how the people had been able to continue using the river for drinking and bathing; six hundred bodies is a lot of blood and bones! They told me the vultures and dogs devoured the bodies within a week or so. There was no decent burial. They pointed to the fast-flowing water over the rocks: no problem here, but the people downstream can tell you; they vouch for the flow of Salvadoran blood.

Beside the river Sumpul grows a beautiful tree, brilliant green, with large thick thorns. I thought of Christ's crown of thorns, pushed down on the heads of these people, mocking their faith that their oppression will come to an end.

March 1

Today I witnessed one of the biweekly visits of the Organization of American States (OAS). Their helicopter landed in the yard behind the military command post at about 9:30 this morning. Out came an officer from El Salvador, an officer from the Honduran army, and an OAS representative who, as someone later told me, was Argentine. Also along with them was Jack Binns, U.S. ambassador to Honduras. I am not surprised that the U.S. ambassador comes to the border zone, because the U.S. obviously has vested interests in the Salvadoran conflict, given all the military and economic aid they keep pouring into that country. But I am shocked to see a Salvadoran officer openly visiting the refugee area in Honduras, thereby proving that some kind of collaboration exists between the armies.

The representatives first spent some time in the command post. Then, accompanied by Honduran soldiers, they went over to our warehouse in which Caritas stores provisions for the refugees such as grain, other food, and clothing. It happened to be distribution day; so in the midst of all the confusion of calling out names and filling bags with rice, beans, and corn, in walked these people dressed in uniform. Of course the refugees were frightened. Fortunately the representatives merely looked around the warehouse and opened a few grain sacks; when they were satisfied, they left.

My Honduran Caritas co-workers reacted more negatively to the presence of the U.S. ambassador than to the foreign military personnel. They are very sensitive to signs which show that Honduras is not in control of its own future—that its destiny is in the hands of the U.S. government. They commented that no one sees Spanish, French, German, Costa Rican, or Mexican ambassadors in the border zone—only the U.S. ambassador. Yet most of the aid for refugees is not coming from the U.S. but from European countries.

March 7

Caritas has offered me a job as coordinator of an education program for elementary-age refugee children. The Honduran schools began two months ago, but a decree from the government forbids Salvadoran children to attend. About 60 percent of the refugees in our area are under the age of twelve, so the need for an education program is great; understandably, the parents are eager to see it begin. There will be a push to organize schools as quickly as possible.

I am excited, but insecure. The excitement comes from the opportunity to stay for six months or maybe even a year. This is what I want more than anything: to be with the people, know their lives more intimately, learn from them, and completely immerse myself in their struggle. Yet I am insecure because I don't know enough of their culture. How can I organize a school program without thoroughly knowing life in these mountains? I don't want to set up a program that is foreign to their experiences.

At this moment, the challenge feels overwhelming. I wish I could have a month just to visit with the people, learn about their lives, and feel more comfortable in their culture, particularly with their language. The accent of these mountain folk is different from the varieties of Spanish I have heard before. To understand and be understood, I need practice; but it looks like there will be no time for that, apart from the project.

The children are enthusiastic, and the parents just as much so, although they act a bit more reserved because I am still a stranger in their midst. The people have a long history of experience with foreigners; they tell me about Peace Corps workers who came to their town to perform a service and offer material betterment for them, but did not seek to know them. I don't want to be that kind of person. I want to earn their trust and be their friend.

Every time I have gone out this past week with one of my co-workers they have introduced me as "the person who is going to organize school for the children." Expectations are high. They are waiting to see what kind of work I will do. I have trouble knowing exactly where to begin. The children and their parents obviously want a formal education which would involve the first six grades, but the Caritas team is talking merely about organized educational and recreational activities, more along the line of a summer camp program.

My first tasks are to learn to know all the villages where refugees live, to take a census of the children, to have the adult refugees choose the most capable among themselves to be trained as teachers, and to solve the problem of where to hold classes. For the latter maybe we can borrow some benches and find an extra room or a corridor of a house.

Even the task of getting to know the paths to twelve different villages, each a different direction from town, feels overwhelming to me right now. I asked Diego if he could draw me a map. He laughed, saying that I better just learn the paths by walking them.

March 11

Today I got back together with the people of La Majada whom I had met on my first visit to an aldea. The village had just started the new *lactarios* program: milk mixed with soy flour for all the children every morning. Already they are much more energetic and lively; their arms and legs have more flesh on them, and their stomachs are less protruding.

I again took the small children to the water hole to bathe. On the long way up and back they talked continuously about how much they like the milk now, and how they obediently stand in line to wait their turn. They want to know whether they will still get their milk after school starts. I assured them we would work that into the program. This is just one example of something I would not have thought of when organizing elementary schools. We have to make sure the children still receive their daily glass of hot milk and soy flour, because it obviously helps to meet their nutritional need.

March 15

This morning I accompanied Paolo, Reina, and Julia to a village called La Haciendita, located near the Salvadoran border. We gathered at about 8:30 in the morning for worship. Some fifty people came to join us. Paolo, the lay catechist in charge of the service, encouraged the other lay catechists to lead us in singing while people gathered. Then he came over and sat down quietly beside me. He told me not to turn around, but that three men had come up to the back of the group and were setting up a recorder to tape everything he would say. He suspected they were people from ORDEN, the Salvadoran paramilitary death squad, who would try to catch him saying something that could be construed as "subversive" or "political."

We sang for about five minutes while people gathered around the worship center under the shade of a big mango tree. Most of those who came lived within a ten-minute walking distance; those nearby brought benches from their homes. Just as we began the opening song, we heard helicopters flying and bombs falling in the distance. I looked at my watch: it was 9:00 a.m. During the hour-long worship the sound of explosions continued, muffled and threatening like distant thunder. I could not concentrate on what Paolo was saying. The refugees also were clearly uneasy and distracted, but no one referred to the noise at all.

On the way back to town after worship we took a detour to one of the small Honduran rivers and swam for about two hours. Back in La Virtud we relaxed for the rest of the afternoon. We kept hearing the distant bombing until about five this evening. Several of my co-workers are talking about the event in low voices, too low for me to understand it all. They mention names of towns in El Salvador. I feel edgy, as if anticipating a thunderstorm.

March 17

Amidst the peace that comes these days with participating in the works of mercy, I experience anguished moments of feeling that I do not totally belong. Why do I want to be part of the in-group? Why my continual need to see others affirm my worth? It is such a strong desire, yet I tell myself it is irrational. I have been here such a short time. I am a foreigner, outside the Catholic circle, and even further outside the circle of lay catechists, delegates, and priests. This is not only a Latino world; it is also a man's world, even exclusively a church man's world. I feel alienated.

This morning when several of us planned the day's activities, I felt included. I knew that yesterday's census had been carried out well, and my sense of accomplishment gave me enough self-confidence that I convinced myself I did not need the praise and recognition of others. Yet in the afternoon, I was excluded from a meeting, and now I am hurt and angry.

I suddenly want to be alone. I cannot bear the public room we share with seven others, nor the ham radio and all the meetings that go on here. It is too much, too public. I feel rejected because I have been excluded from a meeting to which I could have contributed. After the good work I have done these past days, I deserve to participate. I try to console myself by thinking that any other group would show even less trust in a person who had joined them only a few weeks earlier.

In any small town or rural community where people have lived together all their lives, someone relatively new is seen as an outsider, lacking the history everyone else shares, and therefore less deserving of confidence than the others are. But all that rationalizing does not help the feelings.

Where do the others go when they need quiet time? They must need it too! I miss not having an intimate friend. I want this close friendship to develop with my co-workers, especially the women on the team.

March 19

How drastically feelings can change! Was it only two days ago that I felt left out from my group of co-workers and strongly sensed I did not belong here? That was Tuesday. Then came Wednesday, a time of giving totally to others, with no thought for myself, with no self-centered preoccupations.

We were in La Virtud yesterday, about five kilometers from the border, when at 5:30 a.m. we got word that refugees were pouring into a small village on the Honduran side and that they needed medical help and food supplies. Eduardo immediately woke the French doctors and told them that he and I were leaving to check out the situation, but would send someone back to let

them know about the medical needs. The reports had been confusing; some talked of hundreds, some of thousands, but their
guess was unreliable since I doubted they had ever seen a thousand people together.

It took us forty-five minutes to reach Los Hernandez. As we
came over the last hill, we could hear the noise of children, much
louder than I was accustomed to, and I realized that indeed many
people must be there, even at this hour in the morning.

About a hundred refugees had gathered in the home of a
Caritas worker. They were men, women, and children—complete
families in about half the cases. We learned that they had been
without food for three days while hiding in caves on the
Salvadoran side. Eduardo and I opened the small warehouse
where we store grain; it contained a week's supply of food for the
refugees who already live in Los Hernandez. Then I proceeded to
help organize groups to husk corn, grind and cook it, and make
tortillas.

Eduardo returned to La Virtud to ask the French doctors to
send out medical teams with packs of medicine. The wounds I
had seen so far were mainly surface wounds, mostly on children,
caused by flying pieces of metal which had gotten beneath their
skin. Other injuries had come from running barefoot and half-
naked through rocks and mountains; some had fallen and hurt
themselves; others had cuts in the feet which had become
infected after three days of walking on open wounds.

Refugees kept arriving in a slow but steady stream. By 10:00
a.m. the yard was packed with women and children, about 150 in
all. At first I thought those were all that had come to Los
Hernandez, but when I walked around to another house I saw
that the yard there was completely filled also, with perhaps
another 500 people.

I began to get an awesome sense of the emergency situation.
Most of the refugees had not eaten for days, and the food supplies
in Los Hernandez would be used up by evening. There were no
latrines, no sanitary facilities, and very little water. And the
refugees were now saying that more wounded were being

brought across and that they had seen wounded on the other side of the border.

As soon as the medical team arrived from La Virtud, we decided that Francesca, Marie-Lou, and I would go nearer to the border to help those wounded who needed immediate medical attention. A Honduran peasant volunteered to take us, since we did not know the way.

During our hike we could hear bombing and gunfire exchange on the other side of the mountain ridge. Mortars exploded twice, though not on our hill. Even though this was Honduran territory, we came across craters caused by mortars which were fired from El Salvador but had exploded clear over here. Three times we rounded a bend to be greeted by shots. We threw ourselves on the ground, retreated on hands and knees, and tried another route. I thought with bitterness of the demonic nature of military weaponry: no human faces in sight, only the sounds of bullets and explosions which wound or kill.

We finally stopped under a large tree with a spring flowing next to it, about 400 meters above the border. Here we waited for refugees to climb up the steep wooded hill, ready to treat the wounded. It seemed like a whole society was migrating. From the way they talked to each other I sensed that they were a cohesive community, having come from the same towns or villages.

Surprisingly few needed medical treatment; apparently most of the wounded had already been brought over earlier. One young boy arrived with both legs full of little pieces of metal. At first it looked like dirt had gotten imbedded in the skin, but when we started pulling small pieces out, we realized it was shrapnel from a rocket explosion. His muscles were tense and hard as stone. We pulled bits of metal from his feet on up to his waist.

A mother arrived carrying a two-year-old whose foot had been slit open by flying debris from an exploding mortar. The entire sole was one gaping wound, slit from heel to toes. The injury had happened just this morning as they were coming down to the border, but the child had already lost a lot of blood, since the mother had nothing but a slip to wrap around the foot. We poured antibiotics into the wound and sutured it; then they had to go on.

Most other injuries were minor, such as cuts requiring two or three stitches. Only twice did we treat bullet wounds to the arms and legs. The people were definitely shell-shocked. Those who were injured usually just said, "A bomb exploded." Even the healthy refugees found it difficult to talk; they simply said, "It's the Salvadoran army," or, "La Guardia," the National Guard.

One time Francesca and I noticed a woman coming up with a tiny catlike creature in her arms. It turned out to be a baby, born that very morning. The woman had walked for miles during the last hours of her pregnancy before giving birth to the baby at dawn; she then had lowered herself into the Lempa river to cross over into Honduras, soaked herself to the skin, and emerged with enough strength to climb the hill until she reached us under the tree. With horror and admiration I tried to comprehend the trauma her body had experienced today. Francesca checked the baby. Its respiration and color were fine, but the mother's milk had not let down yet, and the baby needed food. So I found another woman who nursed it under the tree before moving on.

Every now and then helicopters flew overhead looking for people. We were close enough to the border that at times they flew right above us. During those moments we huddled as closely as possible near the trunk of the tree, the leaves and branches of-fering cover. The refugees always rested until a fairly large group had gathered, but once the place became too crowded to offer protection from the helicopters, they moved on as a group.

One man stayed to coordinate the coming and going. He seemed to know many of the people; I later found out that he was well known and respected in the town from which most of the refugees came. Whenever a group had rested for twenty minutes, he encouraged them to keep moving and make room for others, and showed them the path toward Los Hernandez.

We kept bandaging minor wounds until 3:00 p.m., when all of a sudden the flow of refugees stopped. I asked those who were still resting under the tree whether more people would be coming, and they answered, "Oh, there are hundreds! Hundreds and hundreds!" But they weren't arriving. I could not figure out what was keeping them. Finally I asked, "If you say there are hundreds, what is taking them so long to get up here?" A man responded, "Well, they need to cross a deep river, and the few swimmers who can carry them across are exhausted. They, too, have been without food for three days and have been bringing people across on their backs or on makeshift rafts since the early dawn hours. Now they must be resting or going more slowly."

Only then did I fully realize that their flight to Honduras had involved swimming the Lempa river. I questioned further and was shocked to learn that only five men down there knew how to swim. Immediately I decided to go down. We were just sitting here waiting, watching helicopters fly around, and listening to bombs fall. I could not bear the frustration of knowing the imminent danger for all these people while we were doing nothing.

Francesca said she could not go since she did not want to jeopardize the organization for which she worked. I felt glad not to have a commitment to anybody which would keep me from going. Quickly I scratched a message for the Caritas team on a little sheet of paper: "If something happens to me, know that I made the decision I *had* to make," and stuck it in the bottom of Francesca's backpack.

I was fully aware of the danger of walking into a war, but I knew I had no choice. So I informed the Salvadoran who had put himself in charge of keeping the refugees moving that I would help swim people across if someone could guide me down to the river. He burst into tears. "Please," he said, "my three children have not come over, and I have been waiting all day long. Could you please bring them?" He gave me their names, begging me to help. We both cried. I tried to reassure him, "Yes, we'll bring all the children. We'll make sure they all get across."

My guide and I climbed down the hill in a dry creekbed, straight down a rocky path which was so steep that it seemed like a dry waterfall. We barely arrived at the shore full of crying babies and half-naked adults when down that same hill came Ramon,

Alejandro, and Paolo from the Caritas team. We smiled at each other and headed into the water. They had brought a thick rope which we proceeded to tie across the river in order to help those crossing fight the strong current.

The river at that spot is about 150 feet wide. On the Salvadoran side, the bank drops straight down and the water was way over my head. I tried to touch bottom, but couldn't. The smooth lava rock along the bank seemed as if it were completely vertical. On the Honduran side, the ground dropped immediately to about shoulder depth, where it extended like an underwater plateau for about a third of the distance across. When I swam over to the Salvadoran shore the first time, I was amazed how far the current had carried me downstream. I realized I could not cross with someone on my back unless I was able to hang on to the rope.

I have no idea how many children I carried across on my back. Some were so small that we tied them onto me. Others were old enough to hang on, but most of them were terrified, crying, gripping like steel. I tried carrying a girl about twelve years old, and I barely made it across; I couldn't even hold my own head up, swimming under water the last part of the way because she weighed too much. I knew then that it would be impossible for me to bring adults over. But there were all these women, holding out their babies to me in anguish, saying, "What should I do? If you swim my baby across and put him down, what will happen? What if I don't get my turn next?"

The parents agonized over the decision to send the children over first, not knowing whether they would make it, or to go on their own without being sure the children would be able to follow. It was so difficult to coordinate the crossing.

A bit further upstream people had inner tubes which they used to take a woman and her child over together. They also had tied together two floating logs on which two or three older people could sit while two swimmers pushed the logs across. Alejandro and I ended up carrying mainly babies and young children, leaving the logs and inner tubes for grandparents who didn't have the arm strength to hang on.

No matter how long we swam, the Salvadoran side remained packed. There were probably a thousand still in that small area, trying to hide in the foliage, frantic that they would be killed. Whenever I came over, people went hysterical, grabbing me, shouting, "Me next! Me next!" They were pushing, shoving, crying, and screaming. "Mommy, don't leave me!" A mother asked me to take her five children across, but her older ones were scared, saying "No, Mom, you go first," and the little ones wouldn't let her go. I tried to reassure them, "Don't worry! We'll get you all!" But it never worked.

The people were terrified and inconsolable. How could I make the decision which one to take when there were so many? Often I ended up just grabbing a child's hand out of the many that were stretched out to me, and heading across. Occasionally the two seminary students, who were stronger swimmers than I, took a woman across while I carried her child; they had her hang on to the rope, with them on both sides of her trying to block the current. Crossing the river was far more traumatic for grown-ups who didn't know how to swim than for children who could trust their adult carriers. The women said their Ave Marias as they lowered themselves in the water.

Whenever I took very small children, the mother laid the baby flat on my back and tied a piece of clothing around us. I tried to get into a floating position to keep my back entirely out of the water. The babies gave deafening, bloodcurdling screams, so loud that I thought my ears could not take it. The older ones did not scream, but hung on to my throat so tightly that I was afraid I would be choked. In their terror they grabbed anything to hang onto, no matter how often I tried to tell them to hold on to my bra straps. Padre Juan, who was swimming near me, had children pull so hard on his beard that it brought tears to his eyes. With me they grabbed handfuls of hair or my ears, but mostly my neck. Choking was a more real danger than drowning!

Two thirds of the way across the river refugees awaited us to take the children and carry them through shoulder-deep water to shore. Once in Honduras they felt safer. Many people rested, too exhausted to climb up the steep hill right away.

But we were about to find out that their safety was equally threatened on either side. We had been swimming for not more than thirty minutes when we suddenly heard helicopter noise. I was on the Honduran side of the border, getting ready to head back into the river, when everybody started running for shelter under the gigantic rocks which are strewn on the bank.

Alejandro and I rushed to help the children hide, pushing them under the boulders and urging them to lie still and quiet, as close to the rock as they possibly could. We managed to get them all hidden before the helicopter arrived. But when we ourselves started looking for cover, there was no room left. There we were, like two moving targets, circling a huge boulder in a desperate attempt to keep out of sight.

The helicopter first swooped down low on the Salvadoran side and started machine-gunning the shoreline. Then it went off down the river, gained height, turned around, swooped down, and fired at the Honduran side. It kept turning, up one side and down the other. Those ten minutes spent running around that rock seemed endless. I had never been that close to gunfire before. I could not comprehend it; it seemed unreal that there was some connection between this mechanical bum, bum, bum sound and people getting hurt. I thought: "I am going to be killed— right here, any minute now. I will hear that noise and then see blood on my own body."

But all of a sudden, miraculously, the helicopter flew off. Not a single person had been directly hit. Alejandro and I looked at each other, saying, "Let's go." And we headed back to the river, dove in, and swam across. As soon as they saw us, people on the other side came running down. "Me next! Me next!" They were more frantic than ever.

I had made maybe ten trips across when we heard the helicopter return. This time I was caught on the Salvadoran side. At the sound of the dadadada, we all started running again. But this side didn't have nearly as many places in which to hide. The only cover available were trees and bushes. So Padre Ramon and I rushed under a tree, like the hundreds of others seeking cover under any bush they could find. I thought, "This is crazy. We are not protected whatsoever."

Just then two little boys crawled in my lap. I held them tightly in my arms, very close to the tree. Ramon sat right beside me, and we held hands. He too was soothing children whose parents had already crossed to the other side.

The helicopter made swoop after swoop. This time, several people had remained in the river. Instead of running up the bank they had jumped into the water and were hanging on to the ledge of lava rock. Each time the helicopter made a swoop, they ducked under water. The soldier in the helicopter was incredibly intent on killing people. Over and over again he lay a path of machine gun fire only a foot away from the people in the water. Once he swooped so low that he almost touched the tree tops above us. One little boy was killed. I saw him jump into the water with an arc of bullet holes in his back. He was flailing his arms, still trying to swim while blood was streaming all across his back. Then the water carried him downstream.

Suddenly a bomb exploded within six yards of us. No one was hit but the air blast covered us with dirt, flying debris, leaves, twigs, and stones. Ramon next to me said, "She is bleeding. I think she must have been killed." He was referring to an older woman on the other side of him who was holding a baby— probably her grandchild. A few minutes later he reached over to take the baby. The woman was dead.

The assault probably lasted twenty minutes, although it seemed like we spent hours under that tree. We could see the soldier leaning out the open helicopter door during a swoop, straining to see where the people were. Then the helicopter rose, made a big turn, gained height and speed, and came back down to fire over the same ground.

Just to watch that cold-blooded maneuvering sickened me. He came so close that the propeller shook the treetop and made the dust fly. Certainly the soldier must have seen that he was firing at women and babies. Some children panicked and ran, but as soon as they did, the helicopter spotted them and turned for another round. I felt like live bait, especially with the children darting from one bush to another.

When the helicopter finally left, I felt numb. I had seen only two people killed. How, oh Lord, so few? We could have all been dead. Now, as the terror of the bombardment subsided, I felt the exhaustion from the previous hour of swimming. Padre Ramon said, "We need to go. We'd better get out of here." I was so glad he said it; I could not have taken it any longer, I was so scared.

We carried children one last time, barely making it across. On the Honduran side we pulled on our clothes and began to scramble up the dry creekbed which offered more tree coverage than the path. Halfway up a few mortars exploded, but we managed to reach the tree, our makeshift first-aid station. With relief I saw that some others had arrived to begin swimming. There were still hundreds left on the other side.

I did not get much time to recuperate from shell shock. Some people said they had seen Honduran soldiers out in the hills. The large group under the tree dared not go, afraid to walk into unknown territory. Only two men decided to head toward Los Hernandez. The rest of us waited until dusk to make sure the helicopters had stopped flying; but even then we continued to hear mortar fire and gunshot exchange. On our way to the village we found the bodies of the two men who had left. They had been killed by Honduran soldiers, shot in the back.

Los Hernandez was incredibly crowded with almost 3,000 people. The Honduran military had arrived around four o'clock in the afternoon and surrounded the village, saying that it was a guerrilla camp and that all the people had to be shot. By then, other Caritas workers had arrived. They talked to the captain, urging him to call his men off, but he refused: "We won't leave. We have orders to protect Honduran territory."

When we got to the village it was night. Since I had not eaten the whole day, I gratefully accepted a couple of tortillas and drank some water. All the refugees lay down in the dirt, exhausted. They had no blankets. The doctors worked all night long. A new medical team arrived from La Virtud to attend to the sick: people with dysentery, chest colds, terrible diarrhea, and—most frequently—shock.

Since more Caritas workers had come to help take care of the refugees, we decided we might as well head back to La Virtud; but when we got to the edge of the village, the captain refused to give us permission to leave. He asked for our identification. It was pure harassment—he knew all the international workers from the meetings we had held together. Finally, after much argument, he let the internationals go; but the Honduran Caritas workers who had not brought their papers had to stay and sleep on the ground with the refugees.

March 21

The morning after the river crossing, Charles, a UNHCR representative, arrived from the capital city. The refugees are now under the UNHCR protection, but the situation is still volatile. Never before has such a large number of refugees come over all at once. The Honduran soldiers, convinced that they are guarding a guerrilla camp, don't want anybody to move. The anxiety level remains high.

Two nights ago the military came in and woke up people to search for guns. In order to protect the refugees, we decided that Caritas workers would sleep in the paths leading to the village, thereby preventing soldiers from entering without our knowledge. Twice now I have slept on the pathway in the dust, without a blanket, having wrapped a piece of rock in my sweater for a pillow.

Half of Miguel's two-room house has been turned into an emergency clinic. The French medical staff are working around the clock, assisted by refugees who know first aid. I volunteered to help all day yesterday. We worked together cleansing wounds, rebandaging, and giving shots. The people have come over in such worn-down health! Many children have terrible infections in their feet after walking for days on open wounds. Some have toes matted together which need to be separated with a razor blade in order to clean out larvae which have infested these wounds.

One little girl's face was covered with boils. Francesca told me to give her penicillin, cleanse her face with alcohol, and try to open the boils with a needle. The mother and father both tried to hold the child down while she screamed and thrashed about, terrified of the needle in my hand. Just the tension in her face from crying broke many of the boils.

Then they told me to give a shot to a baby who suffered from severe malnutrition. I could not do it. The baby's bottom had no flesh; the skin was just hanging there. I was afraid the needle would hit a nerve or a bone.

A young boy had a hole in his head, the size of a quarter. Worms had gotten into the abscess, right against the lining of his skull. I have never heard a child scream like he did when they dug in against his skull with tweezers and pulled out an inch-long worm.

A large number of babies are dehydrated. Their bodies have so little liquid left that when we pinch the skin, it remains pinched rather than resuming its original form. If help does not come soon, we will lose many of these children.

At night I find myself listening to the horrendous, desperate sound of whooping cough. The doctors are expecting an epidemic of this highly contagious disease by the end of the week. People cough and cough until they have no breath left and I think they have died—until I hear them breathing again.

March 22

The UNHCR has decided to construct a tent city since the new community of refugees is far too large to be absorbed by the surrounding Honduran villages. The military has agreed to the relocation, but the place they are proposing has no road access. The UNHCR found an equally unacceptable spot without a water source. I hope they will soon find a proper area, because the conditions in Los Hernandez are becoming truly unbearable.

In addition to the continuing battle against infection and disease, the food shortage has turned into a drastic problem. The doctors can easily carry their medical supplies in from La Virtud, but the transport of dry corn, beans, rice, salt, sugar, and oil to feed 3,000 people is nearly impossible. To make matters worse, the soldiers want to check every single package, purse, or backpack which leaves or enters the village. When our fifty-pound sacks of corn and beans arrive, they dump out the grain to check the content, convinced that we are trying to sneak guns into or out of the area. It is pathetic.

We proposed that male refugees carry the fifty-pound sacks from La Virtud to Los Hernandez, but they wanted only women to go. Of course that meant repacking the grain, since the women could carry at most twenty-five pounds for a one-hour hike through the mountains; it also meant using twice as many people, so the military objected again. We tried asking refugees from other villages to help out, but they were harassed so terribly that they did not volunteer a second time.

The food problem is further aggravated by the lack of utensils and other resources. The Honduran campesinos have been marvelous, offering all they have: their homes, stones to grind corn from dawn to dusk, every pot and pan they own. Their stoves keep cooking all day. Yet it is still barely enough to get everyone fed. Now we have decided to send the grain out to all the other villages where the other refugees can prepare the food; the women from there will then bring in thousands of fried tortillas and cooked rice and beans, carried in baskets on their heads. We will need to work out distribution methods....

We still have no good drinking water. The breast milk of many nursing mothers has dried up because of last week's trauma and the present living conditions; now their babies suddenly have nothing to eat.

March 23

After six days with hundreds of people suffering from diarrhea, all of Los Hernandez smells like an open latrine. Without tools, cement, or wood, it is difficult to build outhouses. We borrowed a few tools from Honduran homes, dug into the hard, rocky soil, and managed to assemble a primitive thatched hut around two pits covered with boards except for a hole in the middle—two latrines for 3,000 people. It isn't nearly enough, especially during the night when those with diarrhea have to stumble all over sleeping bodies to make it to the edge of the path in time. So they just squat on the ground. The stench is insufferable. Pigs roam everywhere, digging around in the human waste.

Fortunately, the worst will soon be over. The UNHCR and the military have agreed on a piece of land for a camp. It's a former cornfield along the Gualguis river, right below La Virtud.

I am beginning to know the names of some in this new group of refugees. The man I met under the tree the day we crossed Lempa is called Chema. He had begged me to bring his children across, but when I arrived at the riverbank and saw hundreds clamoring for help, I knew it was impossible to search for them. Today I learned that they made it across safely. It is wonderful to see Chema and his children together. The mother, though, is presently in a hospital in El Salvador. How long will the family have to remain separated?

March 24

A year ago today Archbishop Romero was shot while giving mass in San Salvador. Our activities continued as usual, but we mentioned the anniversary of his death to one another. There was little time for reflection. Perhaps our working as if it were any other day is the most important tribute we can give to the beloved pastor of these people.

I remember on March 24, 1980, coming home to the news that Romero had been killed. Who would have thought that I would be with the Salvadoran people a year later! And the killing continues. While we slept peacefully during the dawn hours, another innocent refugee was murdered this morning. The soldier claimed he had "bad papers," so he shot him in the neck. Willy, one of the French doctors, went to examine the body; when he asked what had happened to the papers, the soldier responded, "They were bad, so I threw them away."

This whole week's experience is hard to believe. Only the sight of 3,000 people crowded into Los Hernandez tells me the events actually happened. I would like to go back to the river to see the place where the bombs fell, and the trees we huddled under, trying to hide from helicopters made in the U.S. But we cannot go back. The military has cordoned off the river, claiming that paramilitary men from El Salvador are patrolling the area and that they keep us out for our own protection. During the night, when all is quiet, we can hear children crying who are lost out there somewhere. It is the most agonizing sound I have ever heard; yet we cannot go find them.

As I walk through Los Hernandez, children come up to me, smile, touch my hand, and tell others, "She carried me across." I don't remember any particular child; but they are all dear to me because we shared that experience. Among the Caritas workers we often joke and laugh with the priests about their swimming in their underwear, despite the strict moral attitudes of these people. When we meet each other, hot and sweaty from hiking the hills, someone is certain to remark, "How about a swim?" We all laugh and then go about our work.

I do feel a special closeness to Manuel, Paulo, Alejandro, and Juan who also went down to the river a week ago. They understand what it is like to come near death with other people. I recall the second time the helicopter came, when we were huddling under the tree with no protection from the machine-gun fire other than the foliage which kept us out of sight.

I was certain I would die. Yet it was not a deeply spiritual experience. I remember that I did not pray in the traditional sense; but now I understand what it means to make my whole life a prayer. I have prayed with my hands and feet every day since then. I prayed with my whole being as I held the children under that tree and as I swam people across the water.

When I saw the boy fall wounded into the river, I knew I had no right to pray that God save me. My life is no more precious to God than the lives of all those children and anguished parents. Yet I did not die. I gave up my life in those moments, and it was given back. There is release and freedom in that knowledge. I want to make every minute count now.

March 27

Yesterday I accompanied the first group of one hundred men and fourteen women to prepare the new location below La Virtud. The material for the tents—bright green and orange canvas—had arrived a day earlier, along with a UNHCR person who taught the refugees to build a simple, two-sided A-frame structure.

As soon as we got to the new place, the men began cleaning off the cornfield with machetes. The women divided into two groups; one half began building mud stoves and putting rocks on the ground for fireplaces, the other half cooked tortillas, beans, and rice in Honduran homes and carried the meals back to feed everyone. By the end of the day the first two tents stood erected and the land was cleared of boulders. The people felt exhausted and frightened.

The military had insisted this first group remain at the construction site; accordingly they now found themselves in this strange place, separated from their families, unable yet to envision the settlement for 3,000 people they had set out to build. Even the word *campamento* was new to them. And their future looked completely insecure.

As we settled down to sleep in the tents and the group grew quiet, one of the men began reciting the rosary. In the darkness of the night, all the tired voices joined in. At the end someone said, "I feel better. Now I can sleep." Faith had removed their fear.

Early this morning the work continued. Some of the men built a sunshade out of four poles with tree branches tied over the top, to keep the women out of the hot sun. The women constructed worktables by lashing small branches together. We brought in a corn grinder and cooked our first meal down here. Slowly, we are getting it all together. The plan is to bring refugees in from Los Hernandez as quickly as the men can erect the tents. This afternoon the first fifteen families arrived.

April 1

I awoke this morning in the Caritas house. What an ever-changing dormitory. Grand Central Station! During the night, some Salvadorans had returned from the Santa Rosa hospital. With sleep-filled eyes we greeted one another. Among them I recognized the boy whose legs had been filled with bits of mortar from a blast. Marie-Lou and I had cleaned him up under the tree and poured soap and sterile water into his wounds while he moaned with pain. This morning we smiled at one another but didn't speak. I was overwhelmed with the realization that we were both here, alive.

Every night, different people stay with us in the Caritas house. No one ever asks who they are; we are simply together. The beds fill up, then the hammocks, and finally the floor; sometimes people lie wall to wall by morning. Occasionally, I am the only woman. Often children join us, or a mother with children. The crowdedness does not bother me, since we are rarely in that room other than to sleep our seven or eight hours before we dress and leave.

April 4

The work for Caritas is now divided into two areas: continuing the promotion in the fifteen aldeas and caring for the tent city which will soon hold 3,000 people. We have split the camp into three sections for organization purposes. Two run along one bank of the river, a very long and narrow strip; the other one is further down on the other bank. All the Caritas promotion efforts will apply to the camp as well. A thousand additional children are now eligible for the different programs. The needs of the new group are much greater than those of the former refugees.

Out in the villages, resourceful people find ways to cope and survive; it is not so difficult, for example, to find ways to use a discarded tin can as a cooking utensil. But with 3,000 people in one small area, it is a different story. La Virtud's town dump has emptied out over night. The refugees are going from home to home begging for anything: discarded cans, pieces of string, pots in any condition, pieces of cardboard they might lay on the floor for a bed, broken glass to use as a stirring spoon or to cut their food. They are ingenious with the things they receive! All the leftover trash is creatively transformed into something useful.

April 6

Yesterday's meeting with my co-workers was a good experience. The discussion in Spanish flowed well; I understood virtually all of it without difficulty and was able to contribute without stumbling over words. I am glad about my language improvement, especially in the idioms of the local area. It helps take away the insecurity of being new.

How interesting that we can feel so close yet know very little about each other's personal lives! The intensity of our work and the threats we live with—malnutrition, disease, and military surveillance—unite us as brothers and sisters.

Yesterday one of the French doctors heard soldiers explain, "If someone runs, he must be shot because he is guilty; otherwise, he would not run in the first place." The more I understand how the military thinks here, the more frightened I become. The captain and the sergeant of the local command post met today with representatives from each of the agencies. The captain mentioned he had attended a border meeting with Salvadoran soldiers and paramilitaries from ORDEN. They will pay any price to be allowed five minutes in the refugee camp. The captain says he knows that guerrillas are among the refugees, but since they are unarmed he is forced to let them stay in Honduras.

April 7

I am getting more used to this lifestyle: the perpetual layer of grit on everything, the dust on our hands and faces and on the straw mats that cover the bed at night, and the total lack of privacy. What a luxury privacy is! Here it is hard to find a place to change clothes. My quiet time comes once the candle is blown out, at night or before dawn. I sense that others take that time too. People wake up an hour or so before dawn but stay quietly in the hammock just to be able to think and be alone.

Yesterday two extra hammocks appeared late at night as some journalists arrived from Europe. The night before the UNHCR representative Charles knocked on the door at 10:00 p.m. because he could not find a place to sleep; so again an extra hammock was hung from the rafters.

Amazingly, the physical surroundings seem of little importance. All this is part of life here: the dirt floor, the mud walls, the pigs, chickens, and dogs meandering in and out of the house. Last night, someone forgot to bolt the door to the house after coming back from the latrine. At five o'clock this morning the pigs pushed the door open and came in squealing, waking up everyone as they dug around for something to eat.

April 10

With the March 18 baptism into emergency work, the school program was temporarily forgotten. But now the people start asking once again, and my co-workers have agreed that I must take leave of the emergency work as well as the construction of the new camp in order to return my attention to the education project. The day after tomorrow I am to begin an intensive teacher training course for twenty-six refugees who have agreed to teach the children in the villages.

I feel somewhat disappointed, not only because it has been so exciting to watch the camp grow and organize itself and help in the people's struggle to survive, but also because the Caritas people there work as a team whereas I am on my own. The school project is to have four coordinators eventually, but for now the organization is left up to me, and I feel alone. On the other hand, I am grateful for the push back to my original assignment; without the push I doubt I would tackle it.

Several weeks ago it was decided that each agency working in the border zone would send two or three of its workers to represent the agency at joint meetings held every week. Although my co-workers are complying, they are apprehensive about this development because soldiers attend the meetings. The staff is worried about being seen and known by the Honduran military. I have difficulty understanding their sensitivity, but perhaps this is because I am North American and have not grown up feeling threatened by soldiers.

In all the meetings I have attended so far, no one from Caritas spoke except the coordinator. When I mentioned this to Alejandro on our way home, he smiled and said, "The coordinator has the protection of the United Nations, and we don't." I have a premonition that in the months to come, I will learn to understand the implications of that statement.

April 14

The construction and organization of the new camp is coming along beautifully. It now gives the impression of a bustling city, full of activity and purpose. Yet outward signs of what people have suffered remain visible in the children—they're thin with extended bellies. An increasingly frequent topic at our weekly meetings is the poor health of the refugees. The crowded conditions allow disease to spread, and the water for cooking, bathing, and drinking is insufficient and dirty. The pigs from town now go to the camp to scavenge among the tents for their food, increasing the risk of contamination for children who run around barefoot or naked.

The French health team is working frantically to prevent sudden dehydration which has already claimed so many children's lives. The mothers feel helpless. Francesca said yesterday, "Unless the people get more food and cleaner water, we can do nothing, because all our medicine cannot cure the problems caused by malnutrition and the water shortage."

Day after day, babies are brought into the clinic with their swollen feet. We have set up a special tent just for rehydrating children. In the tent, a nurse and other health workers help the mothers get fluids back into the child's body by feeding sterilized water every fifteen minutes and by giving the mothers plenty of liquids to increase their own breast milk supply. The most endangered children are rehydrated intravenously. The doctors are saving many lives, but the feeling remains that we are fighting a lost cause unless we can improve the physical conditions.

The adults show more resistance to sickness. Although many have been very sick, most of them are now recovering. We have lost a number of the elderly however, invalids 85-90 years old who were carried across the border in hammocks. Since they had no utensils to boil their drinking water, they drank from the dirty river, contracting worms and parasites which cause diarrhea. Their bodies could not withstand the dehydration, and so they died.

Caritas is now working at constructing a water system. The refugees have tapped a mountain spring and built a cement holding tank. Unfortunately it always takes several weeks to get supplies, like tubing for the water system, all the way from the city into these isolated mountains.

April 16

I often walk among the tents and visit with the families to get to know them better. I am touched by the anguish mothers go through as they watch their children get thin and gaunt, with their bellies more and more extended each day. A feeling of powerlessness encompasses them. They have no financial resources, and they are barraged by foreigners who tell them to boil water, even though they have neither pots in which to boil it nor a container in which to keep boiled water protected from the dust and dirt.

The teaching I absorbed as I was growing up, either through direct words or just by listening to conversations around me, was that the poor are poor because they are lazy or don't care. The poor in Central America are teaching me that is a lie. These mothers do care! They care as much as my own mother, as much as any woman cares about her children. But they are paralyzed by the lack of resources and knowledge.

Daily we see carpenters building a small coffin for a child that has died during the night. When I ask Francesca what the baby died of, she says, "Dehydration and diarrhea." The mothers stand by and watch the small procession of family and friends as they carry the little coffin to the cemetery on the other side of town. I know each one is wondering, "Will my child be next?"

These people are not lazy. Even though all the material and supplies are freely distributed among them, they are not looking for handouts. On the contrary, I am amazed by the creativity, initiative, energy, and industriousness of these people. The Honduran population is poor, but from the garbage and trash that Hondurans have thrown out, the refugees have salvaged things they can use to help ease their daily burden. Lately, the Salvadorans have begun making kitchenware. We receive soybean oil from the United Nations in one gallon tin cans, and the refugees have learned to take those cans apart and reshape them into breadpans, skillets, and dishpans. They are so well made that Hondurans prefer them over those they can purchase in stores because they withstand the heat better and do not warp or leak.

April 17

It is getting increasingly difficult to work with the UNHCR. The red tape involved in starting a new program is not just a nuisance—it is costing lives. We desperately need better food for the refugees. All the children should have fruits and vegetables in addition to the beans and rice they receive. For weeks we have been trying to start a child nutrition program, but help from the UNHCR gets bogged down in bureaucracy. Infants are dying daily, and the UNHCR is insisting on written project proposals to spell out the need. Without formal requests, they cannot manage to bring in a truckload of vegetables.

Last week we got together and drafted a proposal asking for several thousand dollars to launch a nutrition program. The UNHCR insisted the request had to be typed. It was crazy. We said, exasperatedly, "The people are dying! And you want us to *type* this report?" Now where in these mountains were we going to find a typewriter? Fortunately, we managed to locate one in the mayor's office. Once we had typed up the letter, they informed us they wanted two copies of it. Finally the funds came through today. Since our first verbal request at least two dozen children have died.

The Honduran National Commission on Refugees and the UNHCR have announced that the new camp we are building can only be temporary since the refugees need to be relocated farther away from the border. The UNHCR would like to move them fifty kilometers inland, but the Honduran government does not want Salvadorans that far into their country. They have settled the conflict for the time being by agreeing to look for a place about ten kilometers from the border.

All this hard work to build the camp, only to be told that it will have to be redone! Fortunately, my Caritas co-workers assure me that the bureaucracy here is likely to delay the relocation for at least a year, even though the commissions are talking about three months.

The agency coordinators who come into the refugee zone from the capital city have no idea what is going on here. They rush in, get a one- or two-hour overview of the situation, and then fly back to Tegucigalpa to do their political analysis from a distance. While they are making grandiose plans for a tightly controlled and well-constructed camp at a new site, we are living here day to day trying to keep the children alive, to get a water system installed, and to return people's lives to some semblance of normality. The agency representatives in the capital city make the decisions, and we here as field staff need to carry them out. No one consults us, yet we are the ones who have the closest contact with the refugees, know what they want and feel, and can see the changes that are already taking place.

I have not been here long enough to see through the politics behind the different interactions of the aid agencies, and I don't understand the full implications of this relocation issue. But it is clear to me that the Caritas staff interpret the relocation as a further attempt by the Honduran government, and particularly the army, to maintain complete control over all the movement in this border area, no matter how much the militarization disrupts the lives of Hondurans in these villages. It seems that the soldiers are spending more and more time walking the hillsides, reminding the people they are constantly under surveillance.

April 20

Holy Week was a powerful experience for me, a Protestant amidst Catholics. I followed in spirit my own church's schedule: Palm Sunday, Love Feast, Tenebrae, Easter sunrise. Here, the week's emphasis is mainly on the suffering which Jesus endured. It is so important to these people whose lives are filled with suffering also. How they empathize with the desperate woman who wanted to touch Jesus' cloak, or with the Mary who wiped Jesus' brow as he carried the cross, or the disciples who were frantic in the garden and reached for the sword. . . .

The countless processions through the streets were depressing and alien for me; we had four on Friday alone. Meanwhile, all the work continued as usual. We found a little girl who got lost March 18 when 3,000 crossed the river to flee to this side. We think she wandered alone in the hills for over two weeks, afraid to let anyone find her because she did not know whether she was on the other side of the border. She apparently was wounded in the foot, which had become infected as she wandered the hills. Worms have eaten a third of it away; two little toes are gone. One of us held her while they cleaned up that foot. She would not talk; we do not know how much else she has endured.

Then I returned to the afternoon service in the church, where people reenacted the shoving on of the crown of thorns, the taunts, the offer of a sponge with vinegar, the stab in the side. Dear Lord, such depression in what has always been the most joyful week of the year.

Then came Saturday, the traditional day of silence in this town. We went about our work for only part of the day. In the afternoon I helped the village women make bread from some donated wheat flour. What a treat! Saturday night I went down to the camp to sleep with the refugees. They are a special group, those that arrived on the eighteenth. Some of them I had helped across the river.

We talked until late, just visiting. I slept in my clothes, wrapped in a blanket, on the dry earth under a mango tree. At 3:30 a.m. all arose to go to the dry river bed "to wait with the three Marys and disciples in the hardest hours," the hours of despair, before the revelation of the empty tomb. Songs of mourning, pain, and suffering filled the air.

At about 4:30 a liturgy began. First they elaborated on their own suffering: three children a day have died of diarrhea and dehydration this past week. Many are sick with parasites, cough, headaches. "We are strangers expelled from our land by foreign forces," they said. Suddenly I felt transported to another time, standing among the teeming masses on the shores of the Sea of Galilee.

But for these people suffering and resurrection are not a matter of the past. "How is Jesus resurrected in us?" the catechist persists. Finally an old voice calls out, "Only if we carry on with his work of building a better world where justice dwells and suffering is ended."

Then follows the liturgy of light. It is almost dawn now, yet the trees shade us. From a central candle—the light of Jesus which is for all the world—candles are lit and passed one to another. With the passing, one says the name of a loved one "who has gone before us, following Jesus' example." For fifteen minutes the valley is filled with voices recalling the names of children, mothers, fathers, priests, nuns. . . .

Monsignor Romero is mentioned over and over. "He is a light for us." Then the candles return slowly to the center and are extinguished. The catechist says, "But look, the dawn has come!" Light surrounds us. We had not noticed it for the candles. But it is dawn, the stone is rolled away, the tomb cannot hold him. The power of death, so strong over these people, is broken. In struggle we shall overcome, we shall return home.

April 27

We have finished the teacher training course for twenty-six refugee adults who are now ready to begin classes in ten of our villages plus the town of La Virtud. The course was a good experience, but I am exhausted. I feel as if I have taxed my creativity to its limits. It is exciting to work with the twenty-six instructors, but the tasks ahead seem immense.

Most of the teachers have completed only a fourth-grade education. We have neither textbooks nor teachers' guides nor any other motivating materials such as pictures or toys. The parents desperately want a formal education with six grade levels for their children; but I don't see how we can do it since we haven't the funds and the UNHCR hesitates to appropriate money because it wants us to engage in a larger program three months from now.

I had taught the instructors how to do a census during the teacher training. Their completed census shows that in the villages we have 1,000 children between the ages of seven and twelve ready for classes. Since most are illiterate, or at best have completed only first or second grade, we will simply divide the children into two groups, beginning and intermediate level, and teach them accordingly. We will start out with just the alphabet, basic writing, and numbers.

Throughout our course I took care to involve the instructors in as much decision-making as possible, partly because they know life in their villages better than I, and partly because they need to "own" the program for it to work well. Seldom has anyone asked them or valued their opinion before; so we are spending much time hearing each other's viewpoints and affirming one another's ideas.

One basic decision-making process concerned the purchase of necessary supplies. We all came to an agreement that we needed to buy a pencil and a notebook for each child; that notebooks were preferable to loose paper; and that the teachers would need a larger notebook, a pen, chalk, a chalkboard, and erasers. For the chalkboards we bought plywood, sanded it, and painted it black. After a carpenter had shown us how to build a simple A-frame, all the teachers participated in making their own chalkboards. We agreed that they would also make their own erasers out of scraps of cloth stuffed with old rags, provided I could find needles and thread to sew them up like puffy little pillows.

Next, they dealt with the question of where to locate the school in each village. Several teachers were able to raise the issue at the refugees' weekly meeting. In many cases it was agreed that the men would either construct a sunshade out of tree limbs, or that the classes would start out meeting under a tree until something else could be constructed. They determined that the most economical and the fastest way of getting benches for the children would be to use bamboo, which is available in many of the villages, and to find other adults to help make the benches.

All these were not my decisions, but ours. Their participation in this has made them feel more secure about their responsibilities in the villages and their own sense of worth. I am thrilled to see those changes.

We spent a good part of our time in the teacher training course just learning to know one another, because we needed to establish trust before anything else could get done. These weeks have not been without problems. For example, we had a hard time agreeing that songs and games are educational tools. The teaching method used in these mountains is old-fashioned rote memorization, with the teacher standing at the chalkboard and tapping it with a ruler. I tried to convince them that they could teach differently.

We discussed educational values, learned songs, and at my insistence even played games together, although they never quite overcame their shyness at being seen playing games. I thought this was just a particular attitude of the instructors who had been chosen, but after a few days of listening to other refugees talk in the villages, I realize that it is a cultural problem and that it is my fault for not recognizing it. Now I regret that I pushed them so much, because the refugee adults are saying all they see in the schools is games and songs, and to them that is not education.

Another culturally related problem has to do with class distinction. Teachers here are considered "educated" persons, rev-

erently addressed as "professor." Their education sets them apart
from others; seldom are their opinions challenged and seldom are
they questioned. They rationalize that they use their brain so they
deserve to eat better. Some of the refugee instructors even said
that to me! To counteract this deeply rooted stereotype, as we
were distributing some clothes we discussed the possibility that
maybe the men who are working in the fields deserve a better pair
of shoes than the men who will only sit in the classroom with the
children. "In fact," I suggested, "you could go to classes barefoot
and it wouldn't matter."

"Oh, but they won't respect us," they objected. "We have to
dress nicely. And isn't it *true* that we ought to eat better because
we are using our brains?"

"No," I said, "physical labor uses more calories than the
brain does." We also talked about the importance of being clean
and teaching the children cleanliness, but stressed that they did
not need finer shirts to do so. It was difficult for them to accept.

On the whole, in spite of some difficulties, I am feeling more
at ease with the school program. I look forward to what lies ahead,
although I am still anxiously waiting for the Caritas director to
find the three other promised coordinators. There is no way I can
do this all by myself.

April 30

Each day I go out to a different village to observe schools and
visit with teachers to help them with difficulties and to praise
them for doing well. Their task is incredibly demanding. Since we
don't have enough instructors, many teach both the beginning
and intermediate levels, one in the morning and the other in the
afternoon. It means that some children have only half a day of
classes, and those not in school tend to hang around and bother
those who are trying to learn.

Having an open-air school is awkward and unpleasant for the
teachers, because in addition to the unoccupied children, the
parents and other adults walk around and watch or even make
comments and put them under pressure.

We still have too few benches and nothing for the children to write on. The students sit on rocks and stack up other rocks in front of them as support for their notebooks. We will never be able to teach good handwriting this way.

Nonetheless, the children are learning the ABCs and writing their letters. I can hardly read the letters in their notebooks, yet it is delightful to see their pleasure with what they have achieved. Often they will come to me and ask for additional work. "Can you give me another problem? I want to see if I remember how to add." "Can you write my name? I want to see what it looks like." Or they bring me little scraps of paper and say, "Could you write the letter L on this for me?" I am touched by their eagerness to learn.

Sometimes I feel overwhelmed by seemingly petty problems. What does one do in our situation to get pencils sharpened? When I asked the instructors what they use in their own home, they replied, "A machete." But we cannot buy a machete for each school; nor does anyone in the village have a machete that is not being used in the fields. Also, the little ones cannot use a machete by themselves, and the teachers can't spend all their time sharpening pencils. Shall we go to the expense of buying regular pencil sharpeners? Where could we even install them in an open-air schoolroom?

Another problem is where to store the teaching supplies. The refugees in the villages live in grass huts. The children are in cramped quarters with small brothers and sisters able to reach into every box. So how do students and teachers take care of their pencils, notebooks, chalk, erasers, even their chalkboard? There is very little sense of communal property, so even in a village where everyone knows the chalkboard belongs to the refugee school, leaving it out overnight would be inviting someone to steal it. This has already happened once.

Perhaps I should be grateful for these little problems, since they give the instructors a sense of community as they try to decide together what to do. They are becoming increasingly aware that in the past no one asked their opinions because they were considered ignorant peasants. I value their ideas and help them regard the education program as their own.

The parents living in the new camp as well as in Los Hernandez are clamoring to have schools start in their areas too, but I lack the energy and time to take on this additional responsibility. Since I didn't want to repeat the training course without assistance from other teachers, I came up with the idea of asking some Honduran teachers to help me. But I made the mistake of consulting them without checking with my Caritas co-workers.

Many Hondurans are not sympathetic to the refugees being here, for political reasons. They agreed to help me, but Eduardo believes they did so simply because I am a foreigner. Some might even plan to work as spies for the military. So today I discussed the matter with the Caritas staff. When I mentioned starting a school, they told me that is three months down the road yet. Of the 3,000 in the camp, 30 percent are school-age children, which would mean another 900 children for the program. I can't prepare another twenty teachers to take care of those 900, nor can they spare people right now while they are still building the bare necessities such as kitchens and the water system. School in the camp will have to wait, even though many idle children are a problem and parents fear they are forgetting what they already know.

May 2

We have a continuous flow of journalists and other international visitors. It takes time and energy to talk with them, orient them, and show them around. My Honduran co-workers are distrustful of international visitors and don't want to take them to the villages. Since many of the journalists don't speak enough Spanish to do interviews on their own, I end up assisting them. Fortunately our doctors are willing to help also, especially Willy who speaks English in addition to French. But the doctors can't do much when they are confined to their clinics all day long.

The Caritas workers argue that assisting the journalists is not my responsibility and not part of my job description, and that it is not helping the refugees. On the other hand, no one wants them to go off by themselves asking everybody questions, particularly since they may talk to some Hondurans in town and gain an entirely different impression of the work than they would if they talked to people who are sympathetic to the plight of the refugees.

Because I am an "international" myself, I feel responsible to share the conditions here with the rest of the world. So I assist the visitors in addition to working my regular hours. Having built up enough confidence with certain refugee families to learn about their history before they came to Honduras, I can now take journalists to them to hear their stories.

Aside from journalists come representatives of charitable organizations such as the World Council of Churches, the National Council of Churches, and different Catholic programs from all over the world. A few other U.S. organizations are also investigating possibilities of work and funding. Perhaps it is because I am from the outside that I see the importance of that. Those who have never left this small country, like my Honduran co-workers, don't realize the aid these people might be able to offer once they learn of our program, or the importance of the media in drawing international attention to the situation in El Salvador.

The people from CEDEN often call me over the radio to ask if I would meet a certain international person and give an overview of the refugee work we are involved in. Unfortunately there is much mistrust between the Catholics and the Protestants as they try to work here together. The conflict pains me, partly because I believe in ecumenical efforts and partly because I am a Protestant working with a Catholic group.

I enjoy being with the Catholics; in fact, of all the groups here, I feel most in tune and sympathetic with the working philosophy and the staff of Caritas. I may not get much out of memorizing rosaries and the Ave Maria, but worship with them is nonetheless very meaningful.

One area where I had hoped I might be of special help as a Protestant was in improving the contact between CEDEN and Caritas; but having developed good working relationships with the people of CEDEN, my Caritas co-workers now look on me with suspicion. They don't say it, but I feel it in their jokes and their attitudes. I know the Caritas coordinator, Eduardo, frowns upon my getting calls from the CEDEN representative in Tegucigalpa asking me to take time out of my work to help them with international visitors.

May 5

Not very many days here are "typical" or "normal." But when they are, this is how I spend them. I wake up between 4:30 and 5:00, as soon as dawn breaks. For one precious hour of quiet time, I lie in my hammock reflecting on the previous day and thinking about the day ahead. The others are awake too, but no one speaks.

By six o'clock, the radio is turned on. We listen to the news, first from a Salvadoran government station and then from the rebels' clandestine station. The official broadcast announces how many guerrillas have been killed in the most recent effort to wipe out "communism." Most of it is sheer propaganda, but we listen because the reports indicate where the military is presently involved in groundsweeps; if they are fighting near our border, we can expect more refugees.

The government forces inevitably say they have suffered no casualties whatsoever, but then the rebel station broadcasts, "Well, they may say they had no losses, but somehow we captured twelve pairs of boots, twelve uniforms, and twelve M-16 rifles." Usually the truth lies somewhere between the two extremes. We are interested in learning where they are fighting because refugees from that area or town will be upset and worried about the news and should be visited that day.

As we talk about the news we get up, dress, tie the hammocks up out of our way, straighten the room, and have coffee. Then we either help fix breakfast or do odd jobs in the house or around town. Breakfast is around 7:00. Usually, we eat beans and tortillas, occasionally eggs, and very rarely some fruit; once in a while we have hot powdered milk and sweet bread. Half an hour later we are on our way to the villages. The hike takes about an hour. We walk quickly, since it is somewhat cooler in the early morning hours.

Instruction in the schools starts at 8:00 a.m., and I observe all morning until 11:30; then I meet with the teacher to talk things over, check notebooks, or discuss discipline problems. We talk about questions or the need for new ideas to teach a certain concept. The teachers show less and less hesitation to share their lack of knowledge with me because we have affirmed from the beginning that none of us is an expert and that we will all be learning together along the way.

This takes me through noon. For the lunch break I usually join the family of a Caritas worker from that village; sometimes I eat with the refugee teacher. In the aldeas, the people are even poorer than in town, so lunch is just bean soup and tortillas. Then we all take a siesta because the day has become terribly hot. How nice it is to swing in a hammock in the shade of the corridor outside the house! Midday is very quiet—the cows stretch out, the pigs lie down, even the insects quit flying.

At 2:00 p.m. classes start again. I usually get up early from the siesta to walk to another village for the afternoon classes. Of course I always choose the closest village, since it is the hottest time of day to walk. Without fail I arrive wet and sweating from the hike. The refugees have grown used to seeing me walk to the well and pour a dipper of water over my head before classes start. The children seem to view my visit as a special treat, perhaps because we serve so many villages that I don't get around all that often. Inevitably at recess they ask me to teach a new game. We have a lot of fun as I try to describe in Spanish the games I learned in elementary school.

After classes dismiss at 4:00 p.m., I spend time with the teacher again before returning home. These opportunities to talk on a one-to-one basis are important for both of us. From my observations I get an idea of what to include in the teacher training classes.

At around 5:00 I begin looking for my co-worker to hike back to La Virtud. If he or she has already left, a couple of refugees will walk at least partway back with me. It simply is not acceptable here for a woman to be out walking alone at night.

We arrive home sweaty and dusty, so a bath is in order. That does not mean I hop into the bathtub! The very first night I arrived, Padre Ramon took me outside in the courtyard behind Eduardo's house, showed me the water tank, and asked me if I knew how to bathe. He laughed at my startled look, then said when he first came to Honduras from Spain 20 years ago he certainly had not known how to proceed. Here in the rural areas most women bathe in a bra and half slip. The Caritas men bathe in jogging shorts. The other men apparently bathe before dawn or after nightfall because I never see them. We just dip a bowl in the water tank and pour the water over us. It's quite refreshing in this heat; I don't miss warm water at all.

The supper hour and time afterwards are for sharing the news of the day from the various villages. Perhaps there are journalists or other visitors who would like to talk, and often it seems the day is just beginning instead of ending. When I left the U.S. I thought I was done with long meetings and long agendas; but here I am, deep in the mountains, and still in meetings. Once a week the Caritas team gathers; on Wednesday nights there is a joint meeting of Caritas, CEDEN, the French, and someone from the command post to discuss new developments related to our work and to try to find solutions to various problems. On nights without scheduled meetings, we can do other work, but often we are so tired that we just take a stroll through the streets of the town or buy a Coke at the local *cantina*.

It seems unfair that my job involves more paperwork than that of the other volunteers. I resent this, because it fills many of my evenings. Part of the problem is that it means working by kerosene oil lamp or flashlight. Flashlight batteries don't last long, and the quality of the kerosene is so poor that it burns a thick, black smoke. I tried using candles, which are almost as cheap as the kerosene oil; but they draw attention to my office because candles here are used only for a wake, very rarely for general lighting. When people see candlelight in my room, they step in and ask me who died.

At night when I try to work at my desk I am often interrupted. I have a little office room all to myself which we call the "education center." It holds several desks and the school supplies for all the villages. Since there are no windows, the only way to have light during the day is to leave the doors open, and in the evening the air is too stuffy to close the doors. As a result, everyone who walks by can see what I am doing. Inevitably they stop to say hello, make a few comments, and talk a bit. The endless interruptions become frustrating. But the other day Willy, our French doctor, explained why they do it: Hondurans assume that no one could possibly want to be all alone, and so they think it very rude to leave me by myself. Therefore the last one to talk to me tends to stay and stay and stay.

I struggle with the use of my evening hours. Keeping informed about daily events has become as important as the paperwork for the school program. As confrontations with the military increase, refugees move in and out, and policies change, I feel I am missing out on something unless I spend time with the French doctors or my Caritas co-workers. Discussing and analyzing the day's news often fills the entire evening.

I am still staying at Eduardo's house with several other volunteers. Sometimes I think I ought to move in with the rest of the team to have more opportunities to talk with them. But then again, at the end of a long, hard day it is nice to relax in this family setting and not be barraged with more work. I am trying to maintain a discipline of writing letters and journal entries. Of course this also has its difficulties. Eduardo's brothers and sisters want to lean over my shoulder to see what English looks like. Spanish sounds surround me and interrupt my flow of thought. I feel tempted to give up writing.

May 10

Today is Sunday, a day of rest, although it is rarely restful. I decided to spend the afternoon visiting friends in the refugee camp below town. But my visit was short-lived. Soon a boy came up to me, pulled at my sleeve, and whispered in my ear that two drunken soldiers were in his tent scaring his family. I followed him to the tent at the far end of the camp, and sure enough, there, drowsily swinging in a hammock, lay a soldier with his shirt half-unbuttoned.

I went over, shook his shoulder, and asked him what he was doing. He said he was visiting friends. I pointed out that soldiers aren't allowed to come into tents, but he insisted he had been invited. When I asked him to leave, he flatly refused. Finally I suggested that we go talk to his captain together. He sobered up a bit and agreed to leave. I said I would go with him. It was obvious that he didn't want me along, but that he was willing to get going.

First he took a while to find his gun which he had thrown over to one side of the tent; then he walked out and immediately started climbing the hillside rather than taking the road. Afraid that he would go only part of the way, I followed him. I realized at the time that it was probably risky, considering I had no idea where I was going; but knowing that the people below had seen me follow him, I trusted nothing would happen.

We walked all the way up the hillside, through the underbrush, and to the edge of town. I appreciated learning just how close the command post is to the refugee camp if one takes this shortcut through the underbrush! The soldier was so drunk that he could hardly climb the mountain. When we got to the command post and I asked for the captain, the guard immediately wanted the soldier to go inside; but I waited, wanting to make sure the captain knew that one of his soldiers had been at the camp drunk.

The guard said the captain was in the dining hall eating supper, so we went to the dining room next door. I informed the captain that I had found the soldier drunk in the refugee camp where he had intruded in some people's tent, upsetting them. All the captain did was sternly send the soldier off to his barracks. Then he turned to me, smiled, and asked what I was doing later tonight. He left me speechless with outrage.

May 12

The paradoxes in our daily life give rich food for thought. On the one hand, I daily observe the Salvadorans' exuberance, determination, and joy in simple things. In the midst of their need, they find reasons to be happy and tell jokes. Despite great suffering, they retain hope for a better future, trusting that this situation, too, will pass. Joy, hope, and courage are all intricately woven into the fabric of their Christian faith. It is a powerful witness to us who accompany them here.

At the same time I am confronted with the secretiveness, paranoia, pain, anger, and vengeance which characterizes life so close to a war zone. The atmosphere of suspicion and distrust weaves its tentacles into the life of every person in the country; no one can escape it. The people have grown accustomed to living in a state of war; and although they have taken refuge, they know that the war continues.

Hardly a family exists who hasn't suffered pain and anguish at the hands of the military and who doesn't truly despise the Salvadoran government. Yet in spite of all the evil they have been exposed to, they have retained a marvelous purity of thought. When we talk about long-term hopes and dreams, I am touched by the simplicity of their visions for the future and the things they say they are willing to sacrifice or even die for.

The refugees are uncomplicated farming folk with a clear sense of what it means to be fully human. They know that to give birth to ten children and bury five of them in infancy is not in keeping with God's purpose. They want shelter for their families, meaningful employment, land to cultivate, health care, and education. Like parents anywhere else in the world, they want a better life for their children. That is no different from what my parents have wanted for me.

May 15

Yesterday I went with a U.S. journalist to interview refugees. We found a woman with three children who had just arrived Thursday. She had lost sixteen members of her family. The soldiers castrated all the men, shoved the genitals into their mouths, and left them behind the house to be found by the family. Neighbors witnessed it all.

I am not surprised that some people come to a point of supporting the guerrillas. Unlike the military, the guerrillas seem to respect the opinions of the peasantry, and tend to try to persuade the people to their cause rather than coerce them. Some people keep disagreeing with the rebels or remain indifferent, but given the brutal nature of the Salvadoran armed forces, the guerrillas find it relatively easy to win civilians to their perspective simply by treating them with human decency and compassion. "The guerrillas would *never* torture anyone," the people tell me, "not even those they fight against. It would contradict the very principles they are fighting for."

May 18

Today a group of refugees came to us with the idea of giving the camp a name. They had decided to call it "Archbishop Romero Camp." We watched them make a crude sign out of wood and nail it to a tree. Of course, within two hours the military came and insisted they take down the sign.

Archbishop Romero has been very influential in these refugees' lives. Many of the lay catechists among the refugees were personally trained by the archbishop. The people love him because he spent time with the campesinos in the mountains rather than stay in the capital city. He took off his fine, expensive robes and accompanied the poor. The people love recounting the times the archbishop came to visit them, when he sat in their hammocks, when he baptized their babies. They sing a song about their pastor who stayed with his sheep rather than leaving them alone on the hillside.

A week ago the lay delegates asked some of us teachers to help them learn to read aloud in order to be better able to present the Scriptures. Before we began the instruction, we met to share expectations. I told them I hoped to learn to know Archbishop Romero better through them. This opened the floodgates. The meeting took a completely new direction as everyone wanted to share some personal experience with the archbishop.

"Oh, if only you could have been there when . . . ."

"Remember when he taught us the course on . . . and the National Guard came?"

"I had decided to become a lay delegate and the archbishop came to my house and talked to me . . . ."

"I'll never forget the time we decided to build the new church . . . ."

They went on and on with unending enthusiasm. They talked about listening to the archbishop's homilies, broadcast every Sunday over national radio. He had the nerve to say exactly what was happening! He dared call things by their name, criticizing the government and telling them to stop repressing the people.

Our meeting, which had originally been scheduled to last for thirty minutes, went on for over two hours. It showed how deeply they love the archbishop and how inseparably the people's remembrances are connected with the struggle in their country. Because of church leaders like Romero, the Christian faith for them has again become the great affirmation of truth and justice it was meant to be. They say that the archbishop will have died in vain if they lose his vision of a kingdom of love and justice. They remind themselves over and over again, "If we don't want him to have died in vain, we need to live on with the vision. That's what resurrection is all about."

May 20

The Salvadoran people here are deeply religious and faithful. One of the earliest things they requested when we built the camp was a tent they could turn into a chapel by putting in a simple cross and some benches. Although far too small to hold all the people, it would be a sacred place where they could go on their own to pray and recite their rosaries.

Since then, we have had many open-air "Celebrations of the Word" with the refugees. The lay catechist links biblical reflection with their daily lives. Since so much of the Bible is the record of an oppressed people seeking freedom from bondage, the refugees always find rich biblical material to which they can relate.

During one of the first worship services in the camp the lay delegate compared their crossing of the Lempa river to the Hebrews' crossing of the Red Sea. "Yahweh opened the water so that the people of Israel could cross safely out of Pharaoh's land and escape Pharaoh's army. Similarly, Yahweh guided the bullets of those helicopters so that of 3,000 people, very few were killed." Another time a delegate explained, "Moses wasn't able to lead the people immediately into the Promised Land; they spent forty years in the wilderness first. Even afterwards they were recaptured many times. We know what they felt when they said, 'We hung up our harps and wept because we could no longer sing our songs in a foreign land!' "

The people's vision of the kingdom is one of the here and now, realizable on earth as it is in heaven. They are also overcoming the notion that the institutional church has to be recognized as the only church. They find it important to meet regularly for worship, even in the absence of a priest. Lay catechists have started Bible circles and catechism classes for the children. When a priest comes, it is a holiday; virtually all 3,000 people gather to worship, receive communion, and celebrate.

May 22

The military continues to be present at the meetings of the aid agencies. Since the topics are mundane, like how to get a glass of milk to each child, they accuse us of holding secret meetings where more sensitive information is discussed. Every time we take the jeep to attend to a medical emergency, we must stop at the command post for clearance both going and returning. Medicine boxes are checked and sacks of grain are pierced to see if a weapon is concealed within. Even the clinic has become suspect.

The military comes through almost daily, looking for evidence that doctors are treating wounded guerrillas. We can do nothing to change the soldiers' minds about the refugees. Right before the March invasion the Salvadoran army had informed the Honduran military that they would clean out a guerrilla stronghold, and no one should be allowed to cross the border because no civilians were left in the area. It was a lie, but they believed it; to this day they have remained convinced that the refugees in our camp are guerrillas. Today a soldier walked in on the treatment of a little girl, a diabetic with an internal abscess on her abdomen. The abscess had broken open to the surface; she was near death. The soldier muttered "guerrilla," making sure all of us heard him.

May 25

The generosity of the Honduran host families is overwhelming. They would never even consider giving less than their very best. Yesterday on my visit to one of the aldeas I stayed with the Serrano family who have one laying hen; in the morning, the egg is divided among the four smallest children. When I arrived, they said, "Let's celebrate! We'll kill the chicken and have a big meal together." Of course I objected, knowing that I couldn't possibly eat that chicken. Yet I also realized their deep desire to show how much they welcomed me.

Later that day, a father, mother, and three children came walking up the path. It was obvious they had just crossed the border. The children had underpants on; the man wore only a pair of trousers, and the woman an old slip. They asked whether they could take refuge here. My hostess took her son into the house where I overheard her say, "We need to give them some clothes." When I went into the room, I saw her pull out a cardboard box which contained her family's clothing. She pulled out a dress, a shirt for the man, pants for the boys, and a dress for the little girl and gave them to the refugees. It must have been the Serranos' only change of clothes.

I thought of Christ's blessing for the poor. These were the works of mercy that Christ calls us to do: to feed the hungry, clothe the naked, take care of the sick, share one's home with the homeless. These people are vibrant with joy. They never complain about their poverty or feel like martyrs when they give.

They do not share in order to receive riches in heaven, but simply because it is right to share. It is what Christ would have done.

May 29

I am impressed with the refugees' industriousness and their amazing creativity. To me the Honduran countryside looks dry, infertile, rocky, eroded, and mountainous; but a Salvadoran man I once talked to said, "This is not even hilly. Where I farm at home, I tie myself to a tree to keep from falling off the mountainside while I sow my seeds and harvest my crops. This is nothing! We'll be able to farm it."

Three weeks ago when I was observing schools I heard a new family had come into the village. I went over to meet them, since part of my job as a Caritas worker is to make sure that the Honduran host family gets registered to be eligible for food provisions, and that the Salvadorans are able to build a grass hut nearby and to share items like the latrine, the corn grinder, and a griddle to cook tortillas.

As we sat around talking, the Salvadoran man said, "You know, we could grow vegetables here!"

The Honduran replied, "I have lived on this plot all my life, and my father lived on it before me. We have never been able to grow vegetables. The soil lacks minerals and is dry and infertile. When the rains come, they wash all the top soil away. We can't grow anything here, except out in the corn and bean field." The refugee said nothing more.

When I came back to the village today, I couldn't believe my eyes. The Salvadoran had managed to build an irrigation system up the mountainside in a partially shaded area under a tree, had received some tomato seeds from another landowner, and had planted a little tomato garden. Already the plants were coming up where the Honduran had said nothing ever grew in the thirty years he had been farming the land. For the coming three months, the Salvadoran will be able to keep both families supplied with tomatoes.

I have become particularly close to one refugee couple and

their extended family. Whenever I am in the camp, they insist that I stop to rest and enjoy a cup of hot, sweet coffee. In Ignacio's family too, the industriousness, creativity, and generosity are noteworthy. Ignacio asked me one day if he could borrow ten *lempiras,* which is about five dollars. I agreed to loan him the money for a month, expecting I would never see it again. This morning he came to return the ten lempiras. I could tell he felt very proud. When I asked him what he had done with the money, he led me to his tent and showed me the hammock he had made. He had bought fishnet rope in town, woven the hammock, sold it to a Honduran family for 20 lempiras, returned what he owed to me, and kept the rest for his family to live on.

His wife, Graciela, told me yesterday, "Yvonne, the hardest thing about being a refugee is not to have anything to give to people when they come to visit. At home we used to be able to make sweetbreads or cakes to give our visitors along with a cup of coffee. I want so much to be able to do that again! I feel terrible when you come out here, having hiked the mountains, with your body not used to our way of eating, and all I can offer you is beans and rice. In El Salvador we could have given you so much more!"

I said, "Did you own the land?"

"No, we rented," she answered.

"Could you farm it?"

"No, we didn't have enough to farm," she said.

"Then what did you have?"

"Well, we went out in the woods, dug up a tiny orange tree that had started growing, and planted it right next to our house. We also had a mango tree. So even though we didn't own the land or the house, we had fresh fruit for the children—enough to give food away to other people who were poorer than we."

May 30

Tomorrow I leave for a four-to-six-week vacation. I am not ready to leave, and I don't really want to go back to the U.S.; but I feel I have to keep the commitment I made to my church. It is a difficult time to be leaving, not only because I have come to a point where I feel settled in, but also because we seem to be entering a time of transition. The military harasses the refugees more and more each day, and their hostility toward the Caritas workers is increasing also. The military makes disturbing comments in our meetings as well as around people in town who tell the Caritas workers afterwards. Their accusations suggest that we have contacts with the guerrillas or that we preach subversion— nothing more specific than that. The soldiers show a growing animosity each day toward my co-workers as well as the French doctors.

Medical teams of two or three have gone out to a number of villages for consultations, and now the military questions why the people can't come into town. The doctors reply that because of the long walk, Hondurans and Salvadorans tend not to bring patients in until they are very sick; therefore the doctors believe they can do more good by going out to the villages. The soldiers seem to be convinced that the medical team goes into the mountains to treat guerrillas. They have not accused the doctors directly, but have dropped comments in town. Day after day more incidents tell us that the hostility may soon escalate into open repression.

So I don't feel like leaving, and yet it is a good time to take a break. I am emotionally exhausted from the constant tension of the work—and I must say it would be nice to sleep in a bed with sheets again.

July 15

It certainly feels good to be back in Honduras after my six-week break of visiting family and friends. I enjoy speaking Spanish again. Even the sweltering heat feels good. So much has happened here that it seems like far more than six weeks have passed. I spent yesterday with friends in San Pedro Sula, visiting and catching up on the events of the last month.

Already in July the newspapers are filled with predictions about the upcoming November elections. There are reports on all the party politicking and on the different parties' perspectives on the domestic problems here. What frightens me most is the amount of negative news coverage on the conflict in El Salvador. More and more articles criticize the refugees, alluding to the threat they present to the employment situation here, spreading rumors that they are to be relocated to the interior of the country where they will be given land which should be given to Honduran farmers, and accusing the refugees along with the Caritas staff of channeling food and armaments to the guerrillas. All these comments are filling the Honduran population with anxiety about the Salvadorans' being given refuge in this country.

An increasing number of articles are about the search for weapons channeled into El Salvador across Honduran territory, either by Hondurans or Nicaraguans. Interestingly enough, people who have relatives in the armed forces and in high government positions say the soldiers themselves are making money by selling weapons to Salvadoran guerrillas. I am amazed by the extent to which economics takes precedence over politics; although the soldiers and high army officials might totally disagree with the rebels in El Salvador, this does not stop them from making money by selling the arms they have received through U.S. military aid. The newspapers claim that trucks full of arms have been captured heading toward the Salvadoran border, and that these weapons have come from Nicaragua.

The local people tell me another story. They say the black market of arms, spearheaded by Honduran military officials, functions inside the fruit and vegetable markets. Many feel that the search for arms going to El Salvador is an excuse to tighten the surveillance on the civilian population in this country. There are rumors of a military coup to take place before the elections; the unemployment is worsening; people who disagree with the government are disappearing; soldiers have set up military checkpoints along most of the major routes in and out of the cities. I heard that the short three-hour bus trip between San Pedro Sula and Santa Rosa now has a checkpoint where everyone is required to leave the bus while soldiers search suitcases and bags and review people's identification papers.

The priests and nuns talk of escalating repression against anyone identified with Caritas. Three young men from our team who live near the border were called in to the command post at La Virtud last month. Soldiers told them they were being followed and watched closely because the military wants evidence that they are preaching subversion among the refugees and the Honduran population. Their identification papers were confiscated, copied, and scrutinized, and the men's pictures were taken from the front and both sides. One was even fingerprinted.

Two seminary students who had come to work for a few months of their vacation time, Mario and Paco, left the border zone a week ago. They were taken off the bus at a military checkpoint before they reached their destination. Mario was interrogated by the National Department of Investigations, the DNI, about his relationship with Caritas, about his work in the border zone, and about several priests and the type of work they do. Then he was released. But Paco was held overnight, also interrogated, and accused in general ways of being "subversive" and preaching "subversion." Both men felt rather shaken by the experience and were glad it was time to resume studies at the seminary in Costa Rica.

July 16

This afternoon Padre Ramon told me what happened to one of our volunteers from La Majada. While I was gone, Luis Alonso was picked up by several soldiers and taken out into the countryside where they interrogated him and tried to make him confess that he was sending Caritas food to Salvadoran guerrillas.

"We have observed you for several months and know of all your activities," they claimed. "If you confess, we will let you off."

Of course Luis denied their accusations, saying he would be willing to show them the records the committee keeps on the amount of food for the refugees in his village—data which is turned in weekly to the UNHCR.

Luis was pushed around, harassed, called names, and

eventually released late in the evening with parting threats that he shouldn't be surprised if he didn't make it home without a bullet in his back. They also said if he talked to anyone about the interrogations, he would be risking his life.

Luis had the good sense to tell his family as well as the Caritas team about the incident, so that they would be aware should something else happen. About a week later, soldiers arrived at Luis' door again, this time to take him to the command post in La Virtud. Immediately after they disappeared over the hill, Luis' wife, Juanita, sent one of the children down the main road to town to tell the Caritas coordinator that soldiers had picked up her husband. Luis never arrived at La Virtud. Instead, the soldiers took him in the opposite direction and walked through the countryside over a mountain ridge to another town; there they climbed into a vehicle from the command post and drove him to the capital city, nine hours away. When Luis did not show up at the command post in La Virtud, Eduardo radioed a UNHCR official in Santa Rosa de Copan who in turn contacted the national leaders of Caritas.

It was only through the persistent efforts of several priests from our diocese that Luis was found. The priests were talking with an official at the jail in Tegucigalpa, listening to denials that Luis Alonzo was in that jail, when suddenly a door opened and closed and the priests saw Luis inside the jail. They insisted on being allowed to see him. Luis had been held for over a week and continually interrogated about guerrilla support activities. When the Caritas priests insisted he could not be held any longer without a formal charge, they charged him with illegally concealing a weapon. Apparently, when soldiers had searched his house in La Majada, they had found two small pistols. The Caritas priests succeeded in getting that charge dropped after proving that the weapons belonged to the owner of the land Luis was farming and had been entrusted to Luis as part of his job as caretaker for the landowner's property.

Next came the very unsubstantiated but more serious charge of collaborating with Salvadoran guerrillas, a charge which could have taken months and months to disprove. Luckily, the prison officials changed the charge to Luis' being a Salvadoran citizen illegally working in Honduras. They demanded his birth certificates from La Virtud, an absurd request considering that Luis was born in the early 1940s and of course those small mountain towns do not have accurate records dating back that far. Furthermore, the inadequate records available from those early days were all burned or otherwise demolished during the 1969 soccer war when La Virtud was taken over by Salvadoran soldiers. The prison officials refused to accept testimony of old people from La Virtud who had known Luis since he was a small boy. Testimony from Luis' mother that she and her children were born in Honduras was equally unacceptable.

The priests feel there has been a cover-up, because the national record-keeping center in Tegucigalpa, which holds copies of all birth certificates from the entire country, was missing the 1940 volume for the county of Lempira, which includes La Virtud. On the other hand, the prison officials quickly found proof that Luis Alonzo was baptized in Sensuntepeque, El Salvador, when he was a baby. Of course Luis was baptized in Sensuntepeque! About 80 percent of the entire population around La Virtud has been baptized in El Salvador. Not until 1969 was a road even cut to link La Virtud to any major city in Honduras! Travel to El Salvador has always been closer and much easier for those who live in the border area.

The charge was ridiculous, but sadly it sufficed to initiate deportation proceedings. The UNHCR representatives feel their hands are tied at this point. All they managed to obtain was an agreement from the Honduran government to deport Luis to Costa Rica rather than to El Salvador. So a few days ago Luis was put on a plane for Costa Rica where he has been placed in a Salvadoran refugee camp, alone and away from his family.

Luis told the UNHCR that before he was released from jail he was forced to place an X beside his typed name on a blank piece of paper; so he does not know what confession they will say he gave. To feel more protected against the kind of treatment

Luis received, the other Caritas workers have requested identification cards stating that we are employed by Caritas which is working with the United Nations. Caritas at the national level has apparently agreed; but an action on seemingly effortless requests can take months and months in Honduras, so I don't expect to see the ID cards for quite a while.

July 17

Diego, Padre Ramon, and I are spending the night in Valladolid, although we had expected to be in La Virtud by now. So much has happened today! I wonder what repercussions it will have on our work in La Virtud.

We arrived here about noon, to be greeted with the shocking news of a military invasion. It began early this morning at about 5:00 a.m. when several helicopters landed on the soccer field outside Valladolid in a neighborhood area called "Los Patios." Helicopter after helicopter unloaded Salvadoran soldiers with weapons and flew off again to bring back more soldiers.

On hearing the helicopters, many Honduran children ran out to see them land. One child told me the soldiers who had jumped from the helicopter had asked him what the name of this town was and whether it was in El Salvador or Honduras. Apparently, their strategy was to come into Honduras and then return by land to El Salvador to attack through the "back door" those same towns that were to be bombed from the air. Now we understand the reason behind a special meeting the government called with all the agencies just one month ago. On June 19, Colonel Mejias who heads the government's commission on refugees, told everyone that all refugees living in aldeas within four kilometers of the border must be moved out of the area immediately. When the agency representatives protested that such an immediate move would be impossible, Mejias gave them fifteen days in which to complete the task. The military clearly did not want refugee trouble in the area they were going to allow the Salvadoran military to use in its "back-door" invasion.

I climbed a hill with several Honduran children, sat down at the edge of a cliff, and witnessed the helicopters bombing villages only a few miles away. The children knew the names of all the towns we were looking at. We watched the helicopters fly over, saw the flash of light, and seconds later heard the accompanying boom and saw the smoke rise from the trees and clusters of adobe houses.

We met a CEDEN jeep with people headed back to San Marcos to contact the local newspapers to get some journalists up here. On their way to La Virtud, the CEDEN staff had encountered hundreds of Salvadoran soldiers. They managed to take pictures before the soldiers turned them back. I wonder what the repercussions of those photographs will be!

Since the road is controlled by Salvadoran soldiers from here down to La Virtud, we obviously are not going on tonight. I keep thinking about the refugees and Hondurans who live in the villages closest to the border and who certainly will not be able to sleep tonight. Those bombs are falling very close to them. From our distant perch on the mountain one does not really grasp the destruction that comes from those flashes of light and those thunderlike sounds. There are wounded and dead out in those mountains, probably mostly civilians.

It is evening now, and the bombing has stopped.

July 19

I am finally back in La Virtud. Whatever welcome I expected, it certainly was not the level of excitement the last two days have brought. Nor was I expecting to be plunged emotionally and physically into the work quite so abruptly. I am reeling from shock and can imagine how much greater still the shock must be for the refugees.

I must backtrack and try to record the last leg of our journey when we finally were able to get past Valladolid and continue on to La Virtud. On our way we stopped at La Majada to see Juanita and her family. Tears sprang to Juanita's eyes as she saw us pull up to the courtyard gate of her house. It was an emotional greeting for us all; Ramon, Diego, and I were in tears and could hardly speak. Juanita asked for news of Luis, and only at that moment did I realize she was not yet aware of his deportation. Padre Ramon informed her of what he knew. The last Juanita had heard was when a lawyer had come to ask for a birth certificate which would prove Luis was Honduran. Unfortunately all she could produce was a baptismal record—the fated document from El Salvador.

"I should have known better than to give them anything with El Salvador printed on it," she wept.

Ramon tried to reassure her that Caritas in Costa Rica will make every effort to keep in touch with her and look after Luis, even though he was sent to a refugee camp run by the UNHCR. She seemed most consoled by the information that seminary students who had been working with us were not far from Luis and had promised to visit him.

We shared a cup of coffee, all finding some comfort in silently sipping the hot, sweet drink. Then Ramon sent one of the children to bring Luis' mother over. She laboriously made her way to Juanita's house, leaning heavily on her grandson for support on the rough, rocky path. After exchanging greetings and briefly sharing the news, Ramon pulled a letter from his pocket which Luis had dictated to a Caritas worker in Costa Rica; addressed to his mother, it was a moving and eloquent expression of his love for his family.

Luis placed his wife and children under his mother's care. He spoke of the responsibilities he hoped his oldest sons would take off Juanita's shoulders, even though they are already married and have children of their own. He hoped his youngest sons, ages twelve, ten, and five, would help with household chores and take care of the cows. He joked a bit with his younger sons, saying that although they had never liked to collect firewood and kindling, this now was their job and they should do it in love for their mother. Everyone, he said, should give an extra measure of love to Juanita for him while he was gone. He talked a bit about the different climate and culture he had found in Costa Rica, mentioning he was glad that at least the language is the same and expressing hope that his sojourn in a foreign land would not be long.

Throughout the entire reading of Luis' words, tears streamed down Juanita's face. Yet she maintained an aura of dignity and strength which I find difficult to put into words. We all wept as we listened to Luis' letter and sought ways to comfort Juanita. We could imagine the pain she must feel, and her insecurity about the future.

She mused, "We used to dream about going to another country, but we always thought we would go together, and not under these circumstances." After awhile, she regained her composure, thanked us for delivering the message, and asked in a beseeching way if we would stop by regularly to visit or spend the night whenever possible. We reassured her we would. Then we continued on our way to La Virtud.

Ramon and Diego explained to me why Luis' letter had been addressed to his mother rather than his wife. In these mountains, the cultural norms dictate that a man's first responsibility is to his parents, even after he is married. However, we left the letter with Juanita, understanding that Luis had followed the rules of his society but that the letter was indeed meant for his wife.

Back to the military invasion. When we reached La Virtud we learned that during the evening of July 16 all soldiers in this entire border area had been told by their captain to go into the command post and not come out for any reason. So there they stayed during the entire invasion by the Salvadoran military. The cooperation between the two armies is evident.

Journalists who arrived in time to cover the historic event splashed the news all over the front pages of the major Honduran papers, decrying it as a violation of sovereign Honduran territory. The problem is that denouncing the event does not undo what has already happened. Now the Honduran government simply has to denounce the event too, and the Salvadoran government will say, "Okay, we won't do it again," and that will take care of it on the international level. But the fact remains that the two governments collaborated in allowing this to happen.

The repercussions for the refugee work are grave. Four of

our villages will have to be relocated immediately because they are within a stone's throw of the border where suddenly, overnight, military command posts are being constructed and the Salvadoran army is too close for comfort. We had schools all set up in the four villages. It seems trivial, but I am upset about all the reorganization this will mean as we try to get the affected children into other schools and decide what to do with the teachers.

I know this is the beginning of a difficult time for all of us; the Salvadoran army has never been this close to the border before. The people here tell me that for the last ten years this whole mountain area had been controlled by the rebels, and the army had not been able to get in. This is why it was so important for the military to invade Honduran territory and attack from behind to retake the area.

Late this afternoon Teresa and Rafael, two of our Caritas workers, came in with a very shy, skinny, little boy. They say he has come over the border all alone. Refugees from his village do not remember his name but recall that his mother and baby brother were with him when they fled. Since he was somehow separated from his family, Teresa and Rafael decided to bring him here and keep him with us, hoping the mother will come across the border later.

We cannot tell if this little one is in shock or what exactly is wrong. We ask him what his name is, and he gives a name no one has ever heard before. He also does not know for sure how old he is, but thinks he is ten. How can a ten-year-old not be sure of his age or name? Maybe he has lived in conditions we cannot even imagine. We are hoping that as he gains confidence in us, we will find out more of his story. For now Teresa has decided we should call him Manuel. He accepts it. Perhaps he is fearful, not knowing who we are and what side of the conflict we are on. I am sure this war has confused many, many children.

July 21

Yesterday I went to find Prudencia to see how the recent weeks' events have affected her and her family. When I told

Eduardo I was going to walk to her village, Mescalar, he laughed
and said I wouldn't find anyone there. I looked at him rather puzzled and he explained they had all been so afraid when the
Salvadoran soldiers came through on the seventeenth that they
packed up and moved to the area around La Majada. So I walked
to La Majada and began asking around.

Luis' wife, Juanita, told me that all the people from Mescalar
had moved to El Campo.

"El Campo?" I asked. "Where is that?"

She smiled and explained, "It's a new *caserio* which has
come into existence because of the forced relocation of the people
from across the valley." A caserio is essentially a diminutive
village or aldea. Each village like La Majada is surrounded by
quite a few caserios, in essence nothing more than a cluster of
maybe six to ten houses relatively close to the village but far
enough away to warrant having their own name.

Prudencia, Carlos, and the children were delighted to see me
when I finally located them. The name "El Campo" is very apt,
for the location is nothing but open countryside. Only one Honduran home is in close proximity. As I looked around from the
grass hut that Prudencia and Carlos are constructing, I could see
twenty-five to thirty other huts being built and recognized the
smiling faces of people from Mescalar. Prudencia, Carlos, and the
children were glad for a break; so we sat down to a lunch of bean
soup and toasted tortillas while they told me what had happened
in the last several days.

La Cañada and Los Filos, the border villages the Salvadoran
military were most interested in taking over on July 17, are right
at the very top of the mountain ridge. From there one has an open
view of the caserios Peñas Blancas and Mescalar. Before all the
warfare started along the border area, the town Prudencia's family
lived in was very close to those villages, particularly to La Cañada.
On the seventeenth the first noise they heard was the drumming
sound of the helicopters bringing Salvadoran soldiers into Honduras. Anyone who has ever experienced bombardment is struck
by fear at the sound of those war machines.

Most people in Mescalar and Peñas Blancas left their *ranchitos* that morning, knowing that a grass hut would offer little protection from gunfire. They left and hid in gullies behind big boulders strewn along the creek bed. Carlos said that, more than anything else, they suffered simply from the insecurity of not knowing whether soldiers were near them or what was happening to friends in other villages.

Later on that afternoon they decided to go to the home of Elpidio Cruz, the Caritas worker from Mescalar who has an adobe house with a tile roof which offers more protection. Upon arrival they noticed others had had the same idea; the inside courtyard was packed with people. To be in such a large group somehow gave them a sense of security. They barricaded the doors, closed all the windows, and tried their best to keep the children quiet during the long afternoon hours.

Late that night soldiers arrived and pounded on the door. When Elpidio opened, the soldiers demanded water and told him they were on their way to La Cañada to clean it of those "communist subversives." Starting tomorrow things would be very different all along the border area. The soldiers made no attempt to hide the fact that they were Salvadorans in Honduran territory.

I asked Carlos and Prudencia about the importance of La Cañada and Los Filos. They explained that for many years Salvadoran soldiers had been unable to get into those areas. Since the Salvadoran government offered no social services to the towns and villages along the border, friendship and appreciation developed between the guerrillas who fought against the Salvadoran government and the general civilian population.

There has always been a sense of respect and cooperation between the guerrillas and the civilians. They were able to supply and coordinate their own social services, without help from the Salvadoran government. I asked Prudencia what she meant by "social services." She said, "Oh, you know, starting schools, getting tubing in to supply water to the villages, or training first-aid workers and nurses to take care of the health needs." Prudencia sarcastically spoke of the so-called government that is supposed to take care of its people in El Salvador but in fact has not offered anything to those who have lived along the border for over ten years.

She also had heard from people in La Cañada that the guerrillas up there would not fight against Salvadoran military should they try to take the area. It would be a waste of their ammunition, particularly since the Salvadoran army would not be capable of holding it very long anyway; the army would briefly take control, but would lose it again when the troops were called elsewhere to fight. Then the guerrillas would simply come back in. As the conversation progressed there was no question but that Carlos and Prudencia feel friendship and support for the guerrillas, yet fear and disdain for the Salvadoran military.

Here the children took over, excitedly telling me what happened after the *muchachos* were forced out of the villages along the border. They said that the very next day they found soldiers in their villages stealing chickens and pigs, taking whatever they wanted, calling the children names, and upsetting the school classes. At night shots were fired randomly through the air, several times penetrating the grass huts and terrifying the population. After a sleepless night the people began talking about needing to move farther from the border to get away from the Salvadoran soldiers.

Yesterday, the twentieth, Carlos along with several other men started looking for a place to relocate their families. They found the open countryside up the hill from La Majada would probably be as good a place as any; at least it was another mile away from the border. So that day they disassembled their ranchitos stick by stick, post by post, and carried them along with their few belongings to the new location.

The water situation here will be desperate when the dry season starts. Luckily we are in the rainy season, so there is plenty of water for those who moved to El Campo. Carlos expressed concern for Elpidio and Victoria, the courageous volunteers who have now been left alone in Mescalar. They can't as easily uproot themselves and move to a new location since they have a more permanent adobe home; but they feel frightened and insecure about what the future may bring them.

After lunch Prudencia and her oldest daughter, Elsa, walked to the stream with me to wash the lunch dishes. Elsa commented sadly, "I wonder how many more times we will have to pack up our things and move before we can go back to El Salvador." The longing in her voice brought tears to my eyes, and I brushed them away quickly.

On the way back from El Campo I stopped to visit friends in the camp below town. It was exciting to see how much they have achieved in the six weeks I was gone! Much work has been done on the new water system and the holding tanks for chlorinated water. Also, a nutrition tent has been set up to take care of malnourished children. The nutrition program is going so well that the people are celebrating their first week since March without any deaths of children. We are all hopeful. It feels good to return to our refugee friends; I value their friendship deeply.

July 22

Earlier this month while I was still gone, Caritas rented a new house to use as a dining room. How good it is for the entire staff to eat together! The fellowship around the meal table is precious to us all. It will become more and more important now that we want to talk several times a day about what is going on, where movements of soldiers are, and what is happening to each one of us. The soldiers have the Caritas volunteers under close surveillance, so we need to keep track of one another.

While I was gone another North American arrived—a nutritionist from an international development program, CONCERN. Carole stopped over last night to introduce herself. After she left I asked my co-workers what they think of her. As I expected they showed an initial resistance, like they do to any foreigner, because they are suspicious of newcomers. Given the environment it is difficult not to become absorbed with looking for a spy behind every bush.

The Hondurans are particularly wary of North Americans,

always wondering whether someone might be with the CIA. They
are suspicious of U.S. journalists too, and are much more willing
to talk upon discovering that a blond stranger is European. They
always refer to the North Americans as "gringos."

The refugees are more pragmatic, perhaps because they
have such great need. This morning down in the camp I asked
folks what they think of the new "gringa" and realized, after talking with mothers from one end of the camp to the other, that
Carole has won their hearts. The mothers point to the temporary
nutrition tent, soon to be replaced by a permanent building, and
say, "She is saving the lives of our children."

Carole has been training a young crippled refugee man to
coordinate the new nutrition center. Chalo fairly bursts with pride
as he displays the tables and graphs where he is learning to record
the weight gains of each undernourished child. The refugee
women who have volunteered to cook for the program also speak
proudly of the new things they are learning. The rest of the
Caritas team will soon be praising her too, once they realize she
shares their work philosophy to help the people help themselves
rather than offer handouts. It is a philosophy the Salvadorans
quickly recognize and appreciate.

July 25

The school project expanded by leaps and bounds while I
was gone, thanks to the good work of Ana Celia and Paco, two
seminary students who were able to come and coordinate the
project for those six weeks. Ana Celia is still here, but Paco had to
leave. Two weeks ago Barbara, a Spanish schoolteacher, arrived to
work with us for four months. It feels good to know that Barbara,
Ana Celia, and I will be working as a team for a while. I had
dreaded coming back and taking on all this work by myself.

Apparently Paco managed to get schools built in all the
villages. While I spent months trying to get lumber, Paco seems to
have accomplished it in about three weeks. I mentioned it to
Miguel who smilingly pointed out that Eduardo generally gets
more work done when he is dealing with men rather than women.

This attitude angers me, but I am grateful the schools are built. I didn't want to be a carpenter anyway.

While I was gone Ana Celia and Barbara, with the good help of Paco, were able to finish the teacher training course I had started for those who are going to teach in the camps; so about four days before I came back, schools were initiated in the camps with some thirty-five teachers and over a thousand students. They had a big festival to celebrate the inauguration of the schools, to which they invited all the children from the villages.

It must have been quite a day! Graciela's oldest daughters, Ana Luisa and Marlene, excitedly told me about the songs they wrote for the festival and about how much fun it was to have the Caritas workers help them plan games and small theater acts. The women prepared food for all the kids from the villages. During the festival, after the new teachers had been introduced, the children and their instructors were recognized school by school. As they came to the platform, each group recited a poem they had learned and sang a song they had written for the occasion.

Full of enthusiasm, Marlene and Ana Luisa told me about their new teachers and what they were learning in school. Pride shone on their faces as they each showed me their own pencil and notebook and the words they were writing in their books. Their hunger and excitement for education is gratifying to see.

August 1

We just received word that three international workers with CEDEN have been deported from Honduras: Minor, a Salvadoran; Nestor, a Guatemalan; and Maria, a Colombian. All three were in leadership positions, and CEDEN is scrambling frantically to try to cover their work areas.

Apparently Minor, Nestor, and Maria have been in the same situation as the French doctors and I regarding our permits to stay in Honduras. Each month we have to go to Santa Rosa to renew our visas. When Minor, Nestor, and Maria went the last time, they were told they could not have them renewed. They were not given any reason; the immigration officer merely said he had orders from higher up and they had twenty-four hours to get out of the country before they would be forcibly deported. Imagine— twenty-four hours to explain all of your duties, put papers in order, gather up your belongings, make plane reservations, and get out of the country!

The UNHCR tried to help them as much as they could, arranging flights for them to Costa Rica where they would be close enough to stay in contact with CEDEN workers and finish up the work they had pending, even if from a distance. The UNHCR is trying to negotiate their readmission to the country. When we discussed the deportation in last night's Caritas meeting, my co-workers saw it as another sign of increasing repression and felt all international workers are in vulnerable positions, perhaps because they often communicate with journalists.

Significantly, Nestor had been one of the first people to come upon Salvadoran soldiers on July 17 as they landed near Valladolid, and had managed to take pictures which he immediately turned over to journalists. So on July 18 and 19 his photographs covered the front page of the major Honduran newspapers, making it impossible for the Honduran government to ignore the accusations that Honduran territory had been violated by Salvadoran soldiers.

The Caritas team decided that for our own safety no more international workers should come; moreover, Hondurans should assume the leadership positions presently covered by international workers. They specifically referred to my own work in the education project, but also to programs the foreign priests are leading. We don't want the work with the refugees to be hurt because of our being forced to leave the country quickly. The French doctors are as upset as we by the deportation of Minor, Nestor, and Maria, feeling it may be their turn any moment. We must all be very cautious in what we say to journalists about the Honduran army.

August 3

The flow of visitors in and out of this little town never ceases. Six months ago we could have been in the isolation of the

Himalayan mountains but today this feels like the international hub of Latin America. In addition to journalists we receive representatives of the many different agencies who are funding our projects. Every afternoon as I return from the villages or the camp, someone new is waiting in the hope that Willy or I will help them meet the right people for interviews or an overview of our work here. Quite a few journalists need help with translation, so I continue to do that. Sometimes I take journalists with me as I go visit the schools. I like taking them to La Majada because the world needs to hear about the horror the people there have experienced.

On the hillside above La Majada, in a different direction from El Campo, several families have built their grass huts against or between huge lava rocks. They feel safer next to the rocks, knowing their grass huts alone offer no protection during bombardment. I often take journalists to the Gonzales family which has a particularly poignant story to tell. The family consists of an elderly couple about sixty-five years of age, a few young grandchildren, one forty-year-old son and a smattering of aunts, uncles, and cousins who have built their ranchitos nearby also. Señora Gonzales can tell the journalists in an articulate and emotional way what she suffered personally at the hands of the Salvadoran army after some of her children opted to join the guerrillas.

The first time the soldiers came into her town, they were looking for all the men, wanting to take them away. Luckily—or, as Señora Gonzales puts it, "by the grace of God"—someone had seen the soldiers approach and alerted the men in time to flee to the hillside and hide. The soldiers said they knew the men were guerrilla supporters, threatening the women with torture and other physical abuse if they did not get their husbands to stop their subversive activities.

Several weeks later soldiers came again and took one family who happened to be cousins of Señora Gonzales. The entire village stood in horrified silence as they forced the family into a house and set it on fire, burning the people alive. The soldiers announced this had been done as an example for the rest of the town. That very night many families fled, not knowing where they were going but heading in the general direction of Honduras. Señora Gonzales' family decided to stay because it was close to harvesttime.

Less than two weeks later, the soldiers came back. They interpreted the Gonzales' not fleeing as insolence and lack of respect for what the soldiers had told them. As punishment they raped Señora Gonzales while forcing her family to watch and holding her husband at gunpoint. They also undressed the children and threatened to rape both the boys and the girls, although they did not carry out the rape.

Then the soldiers took the point of their bayonet and ripped open the belly of Señora Gonzales' daughter, who was in her eighth month of pregnancy. They slit her all the way down the front, beginning at her throat, tore out the fetus, and threw it to the dogs outside who hungrily tore it apart and devoured it. Her daughter's husband went insane over this incident. Although he is here now, he spends most of his days staring off into space, not speaking, not working, unable to function or get on with life.

Señora Gonzales weeps uncontrollably whenever she gets to this part of the story; but she says her life had to go on because she needed to take care of her other grandchildren. Overcome with grief, she will say, "Even though I am crying, I must tell you because the world needs to know the horrible atrocities the Salvadoran army commits." She feels more determined than ever to do everything she can to help overthrow the Salvadoran government, so that one day these grandchildren will have a better life and their mother will not have died in vain.

It amazes me that I am able to translate that story for the journalists and not break down. The first couple of times I did, and I had difficulty sleeping the nights following the interview. Now I find I can translate those stories with dry eyes, whereas the journalists often shed tears as they listen. I wish the Gonzales case were exceptional, but I could take the journalists to at least half of the families here in La Majada and let them hear a similar story about atrocities they were forced to witness or endure.

I have yet to hear anyone tell of torture they suffered at the hands of the guerrillas. Instead, they speak of them as "los muchachos," an affectionate way of saying "the boys"—as those who are protecting the civilian population against the wrath of the armed forces and who are liberating their country.

All members of the Gonzales family, particularly Señora Gonzales, have a delightful sense of humor. They are able to laugh at themselves and they joke about the circumstances under which they currently live. The other day Señora Gonzales was trying to convince a translator who had come with a group of Congressional representatives that they should visit her house way up the hillside. La Majada can be reached by car, and most visitors prefer to stay right there to talk to people; but the refugees who live further up on the hill want to show how they have built their ranchitos and how they are secluded between the big boulders for protection.

When this particular group was invited to climb up, the translator objected she did not have good enough shoes, and already she was getting blisters on her feet. Señora Gonzales pointed to her own calloused, wide, dusty bare feet and grinned, "You ought to try my shoes on. They never have given me any trouble," and then cackled her charming little laugh in which all the visitors joined once the translator had explained the joke. This ability to find humor in the midst of their difficult situation is one reason why it is so delightful to be here among the people.

Señora Gonzales urges us to stop at her house whenever she sees us out visiting the schools. Time and again she is so insistent that we finally agree. Then she starts joking about the special meal she has prepared for us. The word she uses for the typical noonday hot soup is "sopa de mentira," which literally translates as soup of fibs or lies. She calls it that because "real soup," for her, has to be cooked with meat, not just a few chicken feet and lots of vegetables. She serves it with the herbs and spices that grow wild in the countryside. Her "sopa de mentira" is absolutely delicious, even though she thinks it is not quite the quality it would be if she had some meat to put in it.

Señora Gonzales argues that her house is the best place to
relax for the afternoon *siesta* because it is "air-conditioned." She
laughs until she doubles over as she points to her air condition-
ing—places in the walls where the grass thatching has fallen away
and the breeze comes right through.

All of these jokes endear Señora Gonzales to us because it is
such a relief to be with someone who can help us see the brighter
side of life up in these hills. The determined spirits of so many of
these people give us the courage and strength to keep working
hard also.

Recently I had another moving experience while I accompanied a British photographer out into some villages to take pictures. He spoke no Spanish but was able to approach the people,
having them sit in certain positions, encouraging them to go on
about their work, and doing it in such a way that the people
responded with all the dignity they possess. The faces he captured
on his film, particularly those of the older men and women, were
very expressive and intense. Of course the younger persons came
up to ask if it might be possible to get a copy of that picture some
day, explaining in their shy way, "We don't know how long
Grandpa will be with us, and it would mean so much to have a
picture of him when he is gone."

Part of the dignity in these people is a reverence for life that
comes from understanding their fragile situation; they must live
for the moment because tomorrow is guaranteed for no one.
Something about the way Mike became one with the people as he
photographed them made the people grow quiet, and one could
see their life experiences and suffering shining through their
eyes and their lined, weather-worn faces. I am indeed looking forward to seeing those photographs with the important testimony
they will give about the lives of these people.

Translating for Mike did not require much energy, since he
had only very simple requests: "Go on about your daily work," or
"Please continue and don't be bothered by my presence," or
"Could you sit here in the sun?" Mostly I watched in silence,
looked at the faces, and contemplated what history some of these

old people could share. Mike and I spoke little on our hike back to La Virtud, still absorbed by what we had seen and felt that afternoon.

August 4

How marvelous it is to be hiking the hills again and to see all the work that has been done in the villages! I hear the children's welcoming cries as I arrive at a school early in the morning. Enthusiastically they clamor over each other to show me the writing in their notebooks and eagerly await their turn to read for me what it says on the chalkboard. As I walk through the villages and caserios, I wave to many people—not strangers, but familiar faces and, in many instances, friends.

In every single village a "school" has been built, meaning a zinc roof supported by posts. There are no walls. In most schools two classes are held simultaneously with the children facing opposite directions. The noise under the tin roof in these shelters is quite deafening as the children recite their vowels or their numbers in unison or sing the songs that go with their lessons; nonetheless, everyone seems happy to have that roof overhead.

I had been expecting the teachers to complain about the lack of textbooks and other school supplies, but the physical surroundings preoccupy them much more. They say the cows and pigs have been coming to investigate at night, pushing the benches and rocks over to sleep in the shelter and to get out of the rain. It seems that even the animals would choose a more domesticated life up here if given the option! No one would mind the cows and pigs sleeping in the school shelter at night if it were not for the cow piles left behind that have to be cleaned up every morning before school can start, and the stench that continues to hang over them, especially as the noonday heat beats down on the roofs.

August 5

Since we are not hiking the hills alone any longer, I have recently been paired off with Nemecio who is in charge of the agricultural work for Caritas. These last several days of hiking with him from village to village have provided us with an opportunity to know one another more personally. Nemecio is young, perhaps twenty-one years old. He told me he recently married a fourteen-year-old. When I expressed my shock at her marrying so young, he laughed heartily. "That's the way we do it," he said.

Nemecio has been involved in the church most of his life. During his training as a lay catechist he learned general leadership, a skill that is sorely lacking here in the outlying areas of the country. When Nemecio chairs a general meeting, he keeps the discussion directed and focused and respects the different opinions expressed. Anyone with those skills is sought out for all kinds of community leadership positions. As coordinator of the agricultural project Caritas has started, Nemecio is trying to get the refugees to work in collectives rather than on individual plots of land. The UNHCR is paying for rentals of land and also providing seeds and fertilizers, but the agreement is that the people will work the land and share the harvest collectively.

Nemecio talks about his dreams for the project as we hike the hills. He is particularly excited about the different groups that are finally expressing interest. A number of women want to plant tomatoes, cabbages, and radishes, and are willing to work together.

Persuading the men to work in collectives has been more difficult. Naturally their main interest is to assure their own children of having food to eat. The idea of dividing the harvest among so many other children does leave them a bit insecure. And of course they point out that some men are willing to work harder than others and put more effort into the project. "How will that even out at distribution time?" everyone asks.

Nemecio feels challenged; and he is a good person to head up the project, since he has lived in these hills, knows the land and the growing season, and knows what the people like to eat. On the other hand, he says it takes more diplomacy than knowledge of agriculture to do the job of helping groups work through questions and differences.

Nemecio was one of those picked up and taken to the command post while I was on vacation last June. We have had chances to talk about that, and Nemecio admits he is frightened. "As a Christian, I am not afraid of dying. But I do fear being tortured. I am also worried about my family and what could happen to them because of my work."

As I listen to Nemecio, I feel guilty because as a North American, with my blue passport with the eagle on the front, I somehow warrant more protection than these Hondurans who are doing exactly the same work as I. I recognize I am not worth more. Yet Christians from a country like the U.S. can come into this war zone and do the works of mercy Christ called us to do— feed the hungry, clothe the naked, visit the sick—without putting their lives in jeopardy the way a Honduran does.

Nemecio says with bitterness, "We are all members of the United Nations and therefore ought to receive equal protection. But some countries that put more money into the United Nations wield more power than others; accordingly, you gringos get United Nations protection, and we don't."

August 6

The rainy season is in full swing now. Back in February when we were in the midst of the dusty, dry season, I had no idea of the changes that would come about. Suddenly the humidity has climbed so high that we don't have to hike to become sweaty; even as we lie or sit still in the shade we continue to perspire. I don't know the temperature, since we have neither thermometers nor television to give us the weather report.

On a typical day, the rain usually stops about six o'clock in the morning, about the time we are getting up. We want to be hiking the hills by at least seven in order to get a full day's work done before the afternoon rains come. The early morning walk feels like hiking through a sauna since the rain that has soaked into the ground begins to evaporate as the hot sun strikes the earth. When we stop to take a breather, we can feel the steam rising from the ground as the hot sun hits it. A straw hat and a cotton handkerchief are an absolute must as we hike—the hat to fan our faces with, the handkerchief to wipe away the perspiration. Before classes start I dip my handkerchief in cool well water and wipe my face and hair.

Most people know me well enough by now that they feel comfortable teasing me about my white skin getting flushed and red from heat and exertion. I am glad merely to sit still and observe classes, fanning myself with my straw hat while I cool down. I no longer mind the midday hike from village to village, because by noon most of the moisture has evaporated from the ground and, although the sun beats hot, the humidity level has dropped.

Rarely do I stay until the end of the afternoon classes because at about four o'clock the skies cloud over. Once it starts raining, buckets and buckets of water come down. It is a lovely time of day because the sun continues to shine and the contrast of the bright rays with the luscious green foliage and the purple-blue rain clouds is an exquisite sight to behold. Usually we try to be back in La Virtud before the rains start. On Saturdays when we have our teachers' meeting, I try to dismiss the instructors by three o'clock so they can get home before the downpour.

For the next few hours, the rain will come down very hard and then let up. Meanwhile the dirt streets, deliberately built six to eight inches lower than the sidewalks, have turned into rivers. We rarely wear our shoes at this time of day; rubber thongs are the only sensible footwear. The rains usually drizzle off by suppertime, early enough to walk around the village, run errands, or visit the camp, although walking to the camp now can often mean sliding down the muddy hillside.

Late in the evening, the rains begin again. Many nights our meetings do not finish in time and those of the Caritas team who have a family in town end up staying with us because they cannot get home without being soaked to the skin. One night last week I tried to walk to the French doctors' house with Barbara. We had umbrellas and rain ponchos, wore our rubber thongs, and held our skirts up well above our knees; but with the current rushing down the streets we had not gone more than a few steps before we were soaked and needed to return to the Caritas house.

With the precipitation has come a gorgeous array of mountain flowers which seem to be able to withstand the onslaught of the downpour. A less pleasant result of the rain is the dampness. We can hardly keep our clothes dry or get them off the clothesline before the next shower. The blankets we now use smell of mildew, and the houses, being made of dried mud brick, have taken on the moisture.

Insects abound. Where during the dry season we had virtually none, mosquitos, fleas, and flies now make our lives miserable. Fortunately it is cool enough at night to have to cover up with a blanket, which helps keep away the mosquitos. On the other hand, the musty blankets provide a nice dark haven for the fleas. My legs are scarred from flea bites which itch every bit as much as a mosquito bite. In these surroundings, with the dirt and all the germs, one can scratch an insect bite in the morning and see it infected by noon. I wonder if my legs will ever be smooth again.

August 7

Ana Celia has had to leave. We are now down to only two coordinators for the education program. I don't feel like writing; I'd rather find a private place for a good cry. Ana Celia worked so well with the refugees! She brought creativity, exuberance, and energy to our team. We will be hard put to replace her. Now that she is gone, I feel safe enough to record the circumstances of her work with us, whereas until now I was afraid to have anything on paper, even in English.

Everyone here thinks Ana Celia is a Honduran seminary student. She had to maintain that disguise in order to work here among the people. In fact Ana Celia is a Salvadoran woman from a wealthy family in the capital city, San Salvador. She joined a Catholic order that sent her to Honduras less than a year ago for the novice stage of her study and commitment. Her novice training includes practical field experience in rural areas; so when I found out through Caritas' priests that she had studied preschool and elementary education, I convinced them to send her to the border zone for her field work.

The few months she spent here have been life-changing for Ana Celia, and I ache with her on having to leave and go back to the city. One afternoon as we hiked back to La Virtud after having visited schools she confessed, "Yvonne, until I came to Honduras I had no idea how the poor of my country live and what they suffer. I never slept in a room with a dirt floor before, and now you tell me the majority of my people live in homes like these. I never had to eat an entire meal of just beans and tortillas, without meat, fruit, or vegetables; and yet that is the main diet of most of my people."

Ana Celia loved working among the poor, learning to know their plight and history, and realizing that the life she had known in San Salvador was not the life most Salvadorans know. In her solidarity she was tempted many times to tell the refugees that she, too, was a Salvadoran, to let the people know she was one of them. I could tell how she secretly delighted in using idioms that only a Salvadoran would know and use so easily. As a result, over the last couple of weeks people started asking me whether she was Salvadoran, and I had to look them straight in the eyes and deny it. Ana Celia lacked enough experience in this militarized zone to recognize she could be deported simply on the grounds of pretending to be Honduran. Moreover, she would have come under suspicion immediately because she was connected with the Catholic Church in El Salvador.

Last week, when Ana Celia was absent from a Caritas meeting, the team decided it would be best for her to leave, considering her naiveté about the dangers to herself and the fact that the other seminary students had been picked up and interrogated by the DNI. Ana Celia lived with a Salvadoran refugee family because of the crowded conditions in the Caritas house. A few days before, a Honduran soldier from the command post had stopped by to ask for her, claiming the captain wanted to see Ana Celia's identification papers. These papers would have proven her a Salvadoran citizen with a Honduran permit to stay in the country for only six months. I can just hear the remarks the captain would have made at our next meeting, accusing Caritas of deceiving them about their staff people. From then on all the staff would have needed to bring their papers in regularly for scrutiny by the immigration officer.

So Ana Celia has left, taking her cheerfulness, her talent in music and discussion leading, and her congeniality. As I think about her I come to realize how much I have counted on her for reassurance that the refugees understand what I am trying to explain in my often-stumbling Spanish. She has always been so good at quietly reminding me, "Say it again in another way," or "Say it again more slowly." I will miss her tactful guidance and her companionship.

August 8

Barbara and I need to write a formal project description to solicit more funds for the schools. I feel cynical as I remember last April's discussions with CEDEN and the UNHCR leaders who told me not to make long-term plans because they would be starting a nationwide project at the end of the year. They advised us merely to organize recreational activities for the children because all the education tasks would be handled by them. Now Charles, the UNHCR leader, announces that their projects will not take shape until the beginning of next year; so he wants to hear what we have already done, what our philosophies are, and what areas of education we are incorporating. I feel both pleased and exasperated when Charles responds. "That's exactly what we had in mind." Did they have anything concrete in mind at all?

The CEDEN coordinators have mentioned wanting me to work on a committee to organize the education project at the national level. The Caritas team regards the proposal with suspicion, and I tend to agree with their viewpoint. First of all, only the local rather than the national CEDEN staff have proposed collaboration. Second and more importantly, the political, economic, and health situations are not likely to improve, so that the refugee work will remain in the emergency stage. Since education does not fall into emergency refugee work, the UNHCR and CEDEN will never get around to taking on the project at the grandiose level they have talked about. Accordingly for the time being Caritas is continuing the school program as before, working month by month but trying to plan ahead at least through the end of the school year.

I feel frustrated with the diocesan team's repeated promises to find more coordinators. Whatever happened to the four-member team I was to be a part of? How many years must the children miss formal and much-needed education while everyone focuses on emergency work? Some effort ought to be put into making sure that these precious years in their young lives are not wasted.

I am so glad that Barbara is here working with me. Since Spanish is her native tongue, she has better ideas of how to write the formal project proposal in that language. We also finally got a typewriter, which will help immensely. Still, the other work continues: training the teachers, visiting the schools, hiking in the mountains, attending meetings.... If we write a project proposal, I want to do it well, but I resent the very idea of sitting at a typewriter in a six-by-six foot space called the "office" where cows, pigs, and chickens walk through at will, while I could be visiting with people out in the villages, accomplishing more important tasks.

August 10

Ray Bonner from the *New York Times* is here. He has a great sense of humor and a lightheartedness which is good for all of us. His investigative reporting methods are fascinating to watch. Yesterday afternoon we were sitting on a bench in the plaza drinking the perennial sign of the 20th century—Coca-Cola—when Ray suddenly sat up straight in response to some activity at the command post. There at the entrance with the local captain was a blond-haired man in camouflage army fatigues, an M-16 rifle slung over his shoulder. They walked into the local *cantina* to get beers, so Ray decided to drop by there also. He came back to report the man was Capt. Sheehan, a Green Beret.

Ray invited Sheehan to join all the other internationals for supper at the house of the French. There were also a group of

German and Austrian journalists, so the supper table was full. The French made sure plenty of beer and rum were passed around the table after dinner, as conversation ebbed and flowed. At one point someone asked Sheehan a direct question about the Green Berets here at the border.

Sheehan launched into a garbled analysis of Honduras in which he said little more than, "Honduras wants peace—peace and bread." Then he shared the surprising news that the Green Berets "are here to help the Honduran people." He said they would be sending in Green Beret doctors and nurses to take care of the Hondurans in the villages all along our border area. Since when are the Green Berets interested in health care?

August 15

We had a visitor from the U.S. embassy today, Antonia, the woman in charge of refugee affairs. She was talking with some of the French team when I walked into their house. She said she had been hoping to meet me, a comment which immediately put me on guard. She was checking out the *New York Times* article that Ray Bonner wrote on the Green Berets. Antonia was not so concerned about the Green Berets' presence here, nor about what Sheehan had said. What concerned her was proof that he had been carrying a gun. Apparently the Green Berets here are to be unarmed. Yes, I told her, he certainly did have a rifle slung over his shoulder.

Antonia told me that the embassy staff had been very interested in a June *New York Times* article which quoted me. She said that when it was released the State Department called the embassy in Honduras for verification of the event, which they gave. They were also interested in me.

Antonia's next words slowed my heartbeat: she said they had analyzed the quotes by me and since I had not said anything against the Honduran army, but only spoke against the Salvadoran army, they decided not to come out to talk to me. She was very casual, but made sure that I heard her concern: "If you want to continue working here at the border, don't let your name come out in the U.S. press again." That's a frightening kind of message to receive from one's own embassy.

August 22

I am worried that the French doctors are working far too hard. Although there are now seven or eight of them, the workload has increased so much that they can hardly cope. At the beginning of the rainy season they initiated a new program of visiting a different village each day. Since they can drive partway in their jeeps and then hike, it is easier for them to undertake the journey than it is for parents with sick children to come clear into town and risk getting caught in the rain on the way home. The result has been that we can accompany each other to the various villages, thus gaining time to develop deeper friendships, to coordinate our work better, and to talk over the events that shape our lives.

The French team usually divides up in such a way that four stay in the clinic in town, two go down to the camp, and two hike to the aldeas. I think the village visits are harder on the doctors and nurses than on me. I spend a good portion of my time in the schools sitting quietly, observing, taking notes, and then talking with the teachers. In contrast, the doctors and nurses are constantly on their feet, struggling with crying babies and frustrated mothers and fathers, and dealing with the inevitable problem of having not enough or the wrong kind of medicines available.

The health condition of the children out in the villages is mixed. On the one hand, the parents have more resources to supplement their children's diet. They can, for instance, increase the vitamin content of the meal by adding wild plants and roots to the soup and beans. Also the village people have access to fruit trees which grow wild in the countryside. On the other hand, it is difficult to carry a sick child the long distance into town. In most cases the parents wait until the child is very ill before they bring her to the clinic; they seek help too late. Thus the major reason for the doctors' decision to visit the villages was the hope to treat these children before they become too ill.

There are countless varieties of malaria here. When I ask a doctor or nurse what is wrong with a particularly sick child, they respond, "Some kind of malaria is all we know." Malaria seems as common these days as flu is during the winters back home. I feel more concerned about the health of the French team than I do about the refugees right now. The people have built up more resistance over the years, and the international staff is working such hard, intense hours that their own resistance falls even lower.

Recently we were terribly worried about Dr. Vicente, one of our best and hardest-working doctors. His illness was first diagnosed as hepatitis, so he simply stayed here to rest. As the days passed and he did not improve, the doctors took him to Tegucigalpa, where he was diagnosed as having mononucleosis and malaria in addition to hepatitis. With a combination of these three diseases his life is indeed in danger. The Honduran doctors at the hospital in the capital city are at a loss to treat Vicente; he certainly would be in even worse condition were it not for the French doctors who attend to him there.

Most of the French health staff stay for only six months because of the harsh working conditions here. The rest of us can at least count on a good night's sleep, whereas the doctors and nurses find most nights interrupted with a medical emergency of one kind or another. The strains on their physical health and the exposure to so many new illnesses are taking their toll on them.

August 24

We have had so much rain in the past two weeks that the food situation is becoming desperate. The roads are washed out at several places between La Virtud and Santa Rosa where the large food warehouse is located. In anticipation of the rains we had ordered an extra week's supply of corn and beans; but in this humid, hot climate the grain quickly deteriorates inside the damp storage rooms. Both the corn and the beans are becoming insect-ridden and require more cleaning. The flavor and quality are going down drastically. Since the germ in the grain of corn is sensitive to moisture, the corn is starting to spoil. We can see the darkened germ when we open the bags and sift our hands through the corn. The flavor of the tortillas reminds me of the musty smell of our damp and mildewed blankets.

The children who are not in the special nutrition program, but have been able to maintain good health until now, are beginning to lose weight because they lack sufficient calories and protein. Graciela shared her concern about her children's gradual weight loss. I too noticed that their ribs, elbows, and wrist bones are protruding, and their cheekbones are much more pronounced. Graciela is filled with anguish and feels completely powerless. She knows very well that a balanced diet must include fruits, vegetables, and protein, but she is unable to provide this food for her children.

Of Graciela's five children only one, her three-year-old, Rosita, has needed to go to the nutrition center for supplementary feeding. Often she returns with the piece of cheese or hard-boiled egg and vegetable soup and promptly shares it with her brothers and sisters. So the food that is meant to help Rosita regain her strength ends up going to others. The older children, especially eleven-year-old Eva Maria, understand that Rosita needs the food, but no matter how mature a child is, a gnawing belly is difficult to live with; so the children eagerly eat when Rosita volunteers to share her food with them.

I know it is probably not a good idea because it shows partiality, but I have taken to buying fruits and vegetables in town and bringing them down to Graciela's tent almost every day. I must walk by seventy-five or eighty children when I carry my backpack to Graciela's tent, forcing myself to look straight ahead and telling myself that if I can at least help Graciela's five children it is better than nothing.

I try to be as inconspicuous as possible as I go into Graciela's tent, hang my small backpack on one of the hooks inside, and make a comment to Graciela, Marcelina, or one of the other two sisters that there are a few things for the family. Then I leave and go about my day's work in the camp. Of course the family, especially Graciela's mom, Marcelina, wants me to come back and partake of the good lunch she has fixed. How can I explain to her that as much as I enjoy her family's hospitality, I would rather eat in the Caritas house in order to leave all this food for her children?

One morning last week a group of four visitors and journalists had stayed overnight down in the camp. Later, coming out of the camp and ready to head on their way back to the capital city, they mentioned to me the wonderful breakfast they had at the tent of my friend Graciela. Graciela often fixes extra coffee for visitors because her tent is close to the entrance of the camp—but breakfast? When I showed my surprise, they proceeded to tell me they had been served eggs and fried bananas, the very food I had left the evening before for the children.

I was furious. I could have grabbed Graciela's shoulders and shaken her, it upset me so much. Tears came as I thought of those chubby, white North Americans who could have gone into town to drink and eat to their heart's content and yet had eaten that food in front of those skinny children. I understand the visitors' dilemma also; to reject the hospitality of these people would have been rude. But all I could think of was those skinny children who had watched the visitors eat the breakfast meant for them.

Luckily I ran into Ignacio, Graciela's husband, before I arrived at their tent. He was working with the carpenters under a mango tree. I asked Ignacio point blank, since we are good friends, why Graciela had fixed that breakfast for the visitors.

He answered very honestly: "I tried to tell my wife that I thought the food was for the children, but she insisted you had brought it down to give to the journalists."

I couldn't hold back the tears and began to cry.

Ignacio, uncomfortable with my tears, tried to explain: "You have to understand, Yvonne, that we are used to being generous and it is very hard for Graciela not to be able to offer anything to people who come by her tent. She wants to give what she could have offered them had they come to her home."

I exclaimed, "But the children are getting skinnier and skinnier!"

Ignacio became very serious. "I know," he said, "but it's just

something we have to work through. Please don't be too hard on
Graciela when you talk to her. It's all part of our coming to understand what we have to do for ourselves if our lives are going to get
any better." He smiled and added, "You wouldn't want her to become selfish either, would you?"

I realized then the tension between self-preservation and the
desire for hospitality so deeply ingrained in their hearts.

Having come to know these qualities in people, I seethe with
outrage when I have to listen to the UNHCR representatives or
Hondurans from the capital city who try to convince us that these
poor peasants wouldn't know what to do if they had fruits, vegetables, and more vitamins in their diet because they have lived for
so many years with just rice and beans and tortillas that their
bodies are completely used to it and don't need anything else.
The arrogance of that attitude among the wealthier Hondurans!

The nerve of a UNHCR official who tells us to write up a
project proposal to get more fruits and vegetables in here and supply him with all the necessary data to request more funds from
Geneva! Why can't they write up that program themselves once
we tell them of the dire situation here? What do they think they
do to justify their high salaries? With my superiors here I find my
human compassion sorely lacking.

August 25

We hear more each day about threats to the French doctors
from the local military authorities. If these accusations were
brought up at the weekly meeting, we could deal with them
directly; but as it is we hear the slander second- or thirdhand from
other soldiers, their girlfriends, or from people who work for the
military such as the women who wash the uniforms and run their
dining hall.

The captain is saying that last July when the Salvadoran
army took over those areas controlled by the guerrillas, they found
a guerrilla hospital with thirty beds in it that was just a stone's
throw across the border into El Salvador. He maintains the hospital was completely stocked with French medicines.

Last night in the refugee camp, as we mentioned the rumor, one of the refugees who has been trained as a nurse smiled and told me he had once worked in that so-called guerrilla hospital, taking care of civilians from the surrounding area. The hospital had only six beds, and all the medicine had been purchased by a Salvadoran doctor living in Germany! Of course this is only his version of the story, and since no one is voicing the suspicions directly, we will not get an opportunity to share his information. What is the correct way to respond to the rumor? All the French team can do is inform their superiors in the capital city about the accusations and hope it can be dealt with at that level.

Word trickles out to our border area that even at the national level pressure is coming down on international workers. Apparently Charles, the head of the UNHCR, made a public statement about the Honduran collaboration with the July military invasion and has come under strained relationships because of that. We international workers have been very cautious since the deportation of the three CEDEN employees.

I feel unafraid for my own safety, never having spoken to a journalist from any of the three Honduran newspapers. Working with the elementary school project seems much less threatening than distributing medicines or food. Still, if the Hondurans ever decided to remove all international staff, I would certainly be included; but we will deal with that if and when it comes.

August 28

Word came this afternoon that a refugee woman on her way into town was raped by a soldier. She is an older woman, forty-five or so, from a little caserio called El Morral. They mentioned her name, but I did not know her. Apparently she made the long trek into town to receive her family's weekly food rations and returned earlier than the other women from her caserio. Therefore she was caught unaware, alone with the burden of her grain sack, when she came upon a soldier. He stole all the grain and her identification papers, then raped her and left her in a ravine by the side of the road.

Rape by a Honduran soldier! My co-workers doubt the incident will be investigated. From experience we know that the captain will just laugh in our faces and say it is the word of a refugee woman against the word of a soldier. Eduardo says that of course the case will be reported to the UNHCR, but we certainly should not expect to see any justice come of it. My anger boils over, not just at Honduran soldiers but at all these men here who take it for granted, who accept it as the way things have to be.

Women in this society are available to be used. I feel such compassion for these women who have been taught their bodies are for any man who wants to take them. My anguish goes even deeper for the Salvadoran women who are caught at the mercy of a foreign and hostile military.

I don't feel the same fear as the other women, because my anger pushes the fear aside. I know if I were caught in a similar situation, my rage, which has been growing for so many weeks, would turn me into a fierce fighter. So often these days I find myself reflecting on the feeling of powerlessness. Once again I am angered by the blatant inequalities in this area. For example, if a French nurse or doctor had been raped, we know the UNHCR would have reacted; but since it was just a simple, ignorant peasant woman, no one cares.

August 29

This has been a most joyful day for us. Many years ago Father Rutilio Grande initiated a harvest festival to offer the season's first ears of corn for the benefit of the whole community and for God. It has been exciting for me to hear the people relate their experiences of past harvest festivals and talk about how those celebrations came about under the encouragement of Father Rutilio. But it was even more exciting to see the refugees organize their own harvest festival in the camp.

Yesterday and today the men, the boys, and the more energetic women climbed the steep rocky mountainside to gather the corn. Then they counted the ears amidst lively discussion about whether people prefer fresh corn on the cob, fresh corn tamales, or fresh cornbread, all of which seem to be delicacies at this time of year before the corn begins to dry.

Early this morning the children were organized into husking groups, and big pans of water were heated to boil the ears of corn—the only item on our menu today. By late morning, representatives from virtually every village had arrived, large groups of people bringing tokens of the harvest from their aldeas. The villagers also brought songs written for the occasion, poetry, theatrical events, and games.

The day indeed became a *fiesta* for us. Oh, the delight on the children's faces as they ate the fresh corn after having suffered so many weeks from the mildewed old grain of last season! The men were also very excited because the UNHCR has agreed to pay them for their harvest and use the food for the refugees rather than to continue to purchase last year's mildewed and insect-ridden corn.

I must really be turning into a Central American! The very idea of a fresh, hot tortilla sounds wonderful to me. If time permits I would like to try my hand at helping the women on the hillside with the *tapiscando*—twisting down the ear of corn so that the rains cannot get inside and the kernals will dry and can later be husked, much the same way we would husk popcorn. Then the grain will be winnowed to clean it from excess bits of dirt, dust, and insects before it is stored in the large 50-to-100-pound bags.

Our harvest day was not quite like the one the bountiful gardeners from my home celebrate, but for these people, given all the odds they had to overcome, it has indeed been a rich and joyful harvest and an exciting day. I cannot close tonight without mentioning how nice it was that the soldiers stayed away and let us celebrate undisturbed.

August 30

Tonight was a special time for the Caritas team as we gathered to worship and share. Nemecio shared how insecure he had felt at first about the idea of working the land collectively; but then the sense of community had grown and the agricultural project had been a success. He spoke of the good experience it had been for him to try to be a leader among and with the people, rather than over the people.

We brought in several ears of fresh corn and roasted them in the coals of our fire after supper, then sat around munching on crunchy kernels and discussing the hard work the agricultural program had taken and all the exciting things that have come of it. Of course my male co-workers laughed when I commented that it thrilled me to see women handling a machete, going up the hillside without being accompanied by the men to cultivate their cucumbers, radishes, tomatoes, carrots, cabbages, beets, and oh, so many other vegetables. I do get excited about all the changes that can come when a group of people like this are given the opportunity.

Inevitably somebody remarks that the schoolteacher ought to be tending to the schoolchildren, and I feel put in my place once again. But I have a rejoinder for them now because we are organizing school gardens for the children. We want to teach the importance of vitamins and minerals, the food value in the various vegetables they are eating every day, the difference between a protein and a vitamin, and other facts about nutrition, so that the children can begin taking responsibility for their own health rather than depend on their parents for it.

The children have finished marking off small plots of land, building twig enclosures to keep the rodents out; on the land they cultivated they now see the first shoots of green come up. It is exciting for a child to participate in that, no matter what age or nationality. There comes the inevitable discussion of how to distribute the food the children raise in their scholastic gardens. Fortunately, this is not a decision I will have to make; in fact, the final arrangement will not be nearly as important as the process by which we make the decision. I want to let the children spend all the time they need to make up their mind.

Meanwhile, I am learning new things about gardening from them. The children of the La Majada school have been telling me that the green leaves from their radishes are delicious in their noonday soup and they want me to try it. I had never thought of eating radish leaves before, but I must admit they do add a tasty, herblike aroma to our meal. The children positively glow when they realize they have taught me something new, and I am thrilled to see the development of an important give-and-take relationship.

The Caritas team grows closer and closer as we share ideas, learn, celebrate, and worship together. During our evenings around the house the atmosphere is becoming much more relaxed. I am delighted that some of the staff, like Nemecio, Ramon, and Miguel, have begun bringing their families to visit us on the weekends.

September 2

Yesterday afternoon Arturo, the driver of our pickup truck, was arrested and had his driver's license taken away. When we saw his truck parked right outside the command post, Eduardo went over to ask why, only to receive the vague reply that Arturo was having a "chat" with the captain.

Several hours later when we needed the jeep, Eduardo again went to the command post, this time taking me along since I also have a driver's license. The captain was irate at seeing me, so I stood off to one side, pretending to talk to some young girls on the street corner; meanwhile, Eduardo, after much discussion, was able to get the keys from the captain. We ran a few errands, collected firewood, and delivered supplies to the camp, returning to the Caritas house around suppertime.

Arturo was still absent. Under normal circumstances, if a man is picked up, it's the right of the wife or daughter to take supper to him at the command post. So I talked to the cooks and several other women, but all seemed too frightened to go near. Finally Teresa and I decided to go ask the captain if Arturo would be much longer and whether or not we could bring his supper.

The anger the captain unleashed toward us took away my breath. First he explained in very crude terms that Arturo had broken the law by pulling the truck into the plaza to turn around and head out of town the other direction; accordingly, his license had been taken away and he would be forced to make the four-hour trip into Santa Rosa to the DNI—the National Department of Investigation—in order to reclaim it.

Of course this was just another case of blatant harassment. The "plaza" is a shabby dust bowl with six benches under trees around the edge. Military and other trucks drive through all the time without causing complaint. When townspeople tried to fix up the plaza in the past by planting trees and flowers and laying stones to make walkways, the captain and soldiers tore everything apart during their next drinking binge. That is why the plaza looks as barren as it does today.

What angered me most was the captain's comment when I asked about bringing supper to Arturo: "You will have to find one of the other men in the Caritas house to keep your bed warm tonight because Arturo will definitely not be coming back before morning." I could have slapped his face.

September 4

Sometimes it seems like I write only about depressing things. This evening I want to describe one of the highlights of my time here: working with Barbara. We call her Barbarita, the Spanish diminutive or affectionate way of pronouncing her name. She has charmed her way into the hearts of everyone on the Caritas team by now with her laughter, her jokes, and her ability to point out uproariously funny incidents in our circumstances.

The other evening she and Paolo came back laughing so hard they could hardly tell us what had happened. On their way back from one of the villages they had come upon two pigs about to begin a fight in the middle of the road. Like the beginning of a boxing match, the two contestants had circled one another, snorting, testing, advancing, retreating, but not really giving any punches yet, as if in anticipation of the actual fight. Finally they jumped in on each other full force, squealing with agony, biting, clawing, pushing, chasing each other, turning head over heels, and chasing in the other direction. Their exuberant efforts and the determined look on their faces indeed made them resemble human boxers.

Barbara laughed so hard in her bubbly way that Paolo had to tell most of the story. We all enjoyed listening to Barbara laugh as much as we enjoyed Paolo relating the incident. At one point the pigs took to biting each other's ears, and another time some nearby children joined in the fun by throwing buckets of water on the pigs, frustrating and surprising them momentarily.

Barbara said even though she knew she might not get back into town until dark, she just had to stay and see how the fight would turn out. Suddenly, as if a referee had blown the whistle, the pigs stopped fighting, touched noses with one another, and walked off in opposite directions, both panting and limping a bit. It was over as quickly as it had begun.

Barbara is such a storyteller! With this incident she will have enough material to keep the children in the schools excited and animated for another week as she visits village after village. Her unique teaching capability enables her to turn her story into a learning experience for the children, teaching them new vocabulary and information about animal life. I myself learn so much by going with her to visit schools. It is delightful to be working as a team. Adding to my contentment today, we received word that a Honduran woman named Delia, an elementary school teacher from a nearby town, will be joining us next week. A team of three! I am feeling better every day.

September 6

Tensions during the past week have been so high that on the spur of the moment some French doctors and nurses decided to hold a party at their house last evening. So they asked one of the local Hondurans to make some sweet cinnamon bread, bought drinks, tied up the hammocks, pushed the benches against the wall, and invited the musicians from the refugee camp to come over and play music. All the local staff were invited to join them. We all needed a relaxing evening with music and a general atmosphere to forget the tension of our daily life.

It was fun to observe the rural Honduran cultural norms clash with the European behavior of the French and German doctors. The local people came dressed in their party best while the French doctors put on their raggedy blue jeans and bright-colored gym shoes and comfortable, faded T-shirts. Such different ideas of what "party dress" means!

When it came to dancing, the French seemed relaxed, willing to enjoy any kind of music be it played by the camp musicians, on the radio, or on cassette recorder with disco music they had brought from home. The Hondurans were much more concerned about dancing correctly, about having partners to dance with, and about the etiquette of not dancing until one is asked.

It is actually more fun to observe these interactions than to participate. Of course in a town like this, with no air movement unless the door and windows are open, news of a celebration spreads fast; also, in a town unaccustomed to private social gatherings, a party like this quickly becomes a town event. It is difficult to be clear about who is invited and who should be allowed to come in; the French doctors themselves are unsure, afraid they might exclude someone who could later cause them problems. Lots of children also want to find out what the excitement is, and once they have come in, the place becomes so crowded that there is no room to have even a party.

In addition, we have the usual discouraging problems with soldiers who either come on the pretense of wanting to know what all the ruckus is about or are themselves out for a relaxing, fun evening. Since the French doctors and nurses have their house on the plaza opposite the command post, the soldiers are aware of any social gathering.

September 9

Brigitte, a German doctor working with the French team, has been keeping vigil over a tiny newborn baby for over a week now. She took the baby in desperation, knowing that the mother was too sick to be able to care or even want to care for the child.

When I first saw Brigitte carrying the baby, I thought she had found a little cat somewhere and was astounded to realize she was holding a live human being.

I have never seen a baby that tiny, even in an incubator; so it is even more surprising that it has survived in this environment for over a week. The mother was severely dehydrated and malnourished when the baby was born prematurely. Her husband is back in El Salvador, and she has five other children to care for, two of whom are sick. She is so lethargic about this newest one that she commented it might be best if God would let both her and the baby die.

Brigitte felt such anguish that she decided to take the baby herself for a while until the mother's strength would return, however long that might take. So Brigitte had to drop her other clinic duties in order to care full time for this tiny creature. She feeds it with a cloth dipped in diluted milk every two hours around the clock. She looks exhausted and desperately wants others to help her, but instead of trusting a young, single Salvadoran woman with the task, she insists on help from international workers.

During a break this afternoon I agreed to spend two hours with the baby. I held it, overwhelmed with the feeling that the child needs love and human touch more than anything else. But how can one give that in our situation? Brigitte and I have to choose either to attend to hundreds or to focus on just one. That does not mean one life is less important, but the international workers need to decide where their priorities lie. Maybe there is a sense of maternal ownership in Brigitte, along with a desperate wish to see this baby survive in the midst of all this death and destruction. She probably needs that psychological boost as much as the rest of us.

After I had spent time with the baby, I asked Brigitte what tent the family lives in and went down to the camp to visit them. Their situation is indeed desperate. It was difficult to hold back my tears as I cuddled the other children and talked to the mother lying listlessly in her hammock in the hot tent. The mother ought to be nursing one of the other children who is under two years of age; instead, I saw a dirty baby bottle on one of the beds with bright red liquid in it. When I asked the woman about it, she said she had taken a few pennies she had and bought some red pop in town to put in the bottle. I could have snatched the baby out of her arms at that moment.

"Why?" I exclaimed. "Why did you do that? You know that your breast milk is good."

Angrily she shot back, "Breast milk! What breast milk?" She pinched her dry, flabby breasts. "There is nothing here for the baby to suckle," she said. "The color of the red pop is so pretty, there must be something good for the baby. It comes from the store, doesn't it?"

My rage and frustration increased even more when I saw a rusty can of Nestle infant formula with its label showing a chubby, blond, blue-eyed baby in the arms of a smiling, well-fed mother, giving the impression that drinking the diluted powder will bring health to any child. Nestle does not reckon with the contaminated water source here, nor recognize that the mothers don't understand the ratio for mixing the powder with the correct amount of water. Nothing is sterile here. Why would someone sterilize a bottle? And where would one keep the sterilized bottle so it stays clean? Oh, what I would give to make the Nestle corporation executives sit in this tent and watch these babies die!

September 12

Now that Delia has joined us to help with the education project, Barbara and I feel some relief from the heavy work schedule. Barbara and Delia are working in town this week while Prudencia and I visit the schools in the five villages closest to La Majada. We are saving time by sleeping in her family's grass hut in El Campo rather than returning to town each night. I am getting a real taste of refugee life—not just a two-hour visit, a lunch in a hut, a siesta in a hammock, or one overnight stay, but an entire week. I must say I love every minute of it. The people I am with make me forget the living conditions.

Prudencia and Carlos' hut is clean but crowded, a one-room, ten-by-fifteen feet A-frame hut in which adults can stand up only in the middle. Carlos has made two beds out of small tree branches lashed together, and Prudencia and the girls have woven grass mats to lay over the top. Prudencia, Carlos, and the two younger children sleep in one bed, with the children's heads at one end and the parents' heads at the other. Prudencia laughingly complains about her smallest one, two and one-half years old, wanting to nurse again when he sleeps with her, although he has been weaned from the breast. So he must sleep either on the other side of his father or with his sister Elsa.

The other two children sleep in the other bed. It is crowded, of course, and they push, jostle, and argue, but in general it seems to be a comfortable place at the end of a long day. I am given the privilege of sleeping in a hammock all by myself. I offered to share it with one of the children, and they might have accepted, but Prudencia adamantly refused to let them.

Everybody sleeps in their day clothes. People wear the same clothes until they are too dirty and it's time to go to the river to bathe. Then they just wash the clothes at the same time they bathe themselves, put on dry ones, and that handles the problem of modesty. I have grown accustomed to sleeping this way; after dark when everyone has crawled into bed, I take off my skirt, drape it over the end of the hammock, and sleep in my slip and blouse. In the early morning I put my skirt back on. Seeing a woman's slip is quite common and accepted here, so my modesty is in keeping with the Salvadoran cultural norms.

Since there is sufficient space between our hut and the next one, and we even have the luxury of a few small bushes and trees nearby, our bathroom facilities are the open countryside. The adults wait until dark and go out one by one. I don't mind squatting on the ground and using leaves for toilet paper, but I do mind the pigs that freely roam about and bother people.

The first night I went out, Prudencia reminded me to take a stick along to beat off the pigs. I was thoroughly bewildered, but not for long. The pigs tried to push me over to dig through what I was leaving behind on the ground. The idea that we eat that pork leaves me nauseated. No wonder everyone is so ill here!

Carlos and his brother-in-law who lives in a nearby hut have been discussing their difficulties with the residence permits. Several of the teachers have come to join us, knowing that I am staying here and we can talk over the problems. These days I spend much time accompanying the teachers to the immigration post because they are afraid to go alone. The immigration chief harasses people when they ask for their one-month extension to their ID permission cards. He asks each person, "When are you going home?" and tells the men they had better clear out of Honduras before the election or they will be turned over to the Salvadoran military.

I don't know how much longer I will be able to write tonight. I forgot to bring a candle with me, so there is just the light of the moon to write by. Besides, I am so interested in the conversations of the adults as they squat by the smoldering fire to talk about their concerns and evaluate the day's events. One of the nicest aspects of staying out here with the refugees at night is to be part of these discussions and to gain a more complete idea of the fears and problems the refugees face. The UNHCR representatives ought to try this sometime; they might learn from it.

September 16

It's a glorious sunny afternoon. The rains will be coming shortly, but I want to stop here on my walk back to La Virtud to record the frightening event of last night. I suddenly understand the fear the refugees have while sleeping in grass huts, unprotected from outside invaders.

Last night we had stayed up until after the children were asleep, talking and visiting as usual; but it must have been rather early, maybe 9:00 p.m. when we all made our way to bed also. Carlos, Prudencia, and I were still quietly talking when all of a sudden we heard gunshots. The first time the noise seemed to come from the other side of the mountain. Carlos recognized the sound of the G-3 rifle carried by the Salvadoran National Guard, with its ricocheting, echoing rhythm "Bum, bum, boom; bum, bum, boom." My heart stood still. I caught myself holding my breath, waiting to see what else would happen. All remained quiet for a while, but suddenly another gunshot rang out, this time very, very close to us.

I don't know what frightened me more, the thought of those bullets racing through our grass hut walls and hitting someone, or the frantic cries of the children which I knew would lead anyone directly to us. Instinctively I grabbed both sides of the hammock, gave them a flip, and landed flat on the floor. The others were already lying on the ground, awaiting what would happen next.

Carlos whispered that the shots this time had been fired by someone from the army, not a National Guardsman. "How do you know?" I asked. He explained this was an M-16 rifle, which makes a "boom-boom, boom-boom" sound instead of the ricocheting noise we had heard before. The children quieted down. I suppose they have grown used to this by now, if one ever does. We stayed flat on the floor, quietly waiting and listening.

After several minutes of silence I asked, "Do you think they are out there looking for someone?"

Carlos replied, "They were just trying to harass and terrorize the people; that's all they mean to do for the evening. Probably the soldiers are aware that a foreigner is sleeping in the village, so they will be more cautious." Little comfort that gave me as I thought about the bullets in their guns!

Some time later I crawled back into my hammock, but I slept fitfully most of the night. In a nightmare as I was chased by soldiers, I finally understood, like the refugees, that to run or not to run would be equally dangerous. No wonder many refugees seem haggard with dark circles under their eyes these days as they come into town for their weekly ration of food. How can they sleep out in those villages knowing that danger is imminent?

September 18

For over a week now Honduran or Salvadoran soldiers have harassed one or another village every night. They make sure they are seen by children or adults at dusk, intending to terrorize the people. Sometimes they don't appear again nor make a sound that night. Other times they search one or two huts, claiming to be looking for weapons and continuing to put pressure on people to go back to El Salvador before the elections at the end of November.

The way they search the huts is cruel and demoralizing. The refugees keep their belongings in cardboard boxes. When the soldiers come, they dump the contents of the boxes onto the floor, even dump grain out, kick things around, and in general try to see how much destruction they can cause in such a small space.

The children are reluctant to go to school now. All the harassment brings back fresh memories of having to flee from their former homes; and if they have to flee again, the most important thing is to stay with their families. So no one wants to be caught unaware down at the schoolhouse, alone at the river, or in town. They want to be together as a family every moment. School attendance ebbs and flows, and even the teachers seem reluctant to continue with classes. The sporadic attendance depends on whether or not soldiers have been seen in their village on recent nights.

I came under heavy criticism from my co-workers because I stayed in Prudencia's village for five days. I guess I had not put that decision through the group process properly. There are rumors around town that the captain claims I went out to meet with the guerrillas. So once again the team is stipulating that no one sleep in the villages for a while. As painful as I find that agreement, we will have to enforce that none of us walks alone or stays out at night.

I am so angry at this limitation of our freedom! "I am just a schoolteacher," I want to scream. And yet the reality is that I am more than that. As I visit village after village, I carry information and help people keep in contact with each other. As long as the people know what is happening in different villages and as long as the movements of soldiers are noted, this disturbs the military. I am sure the captain sincerely believes we are meeting with the guerrillas. In his paranoid way, he has everything worked out in his own mind. He is not open to discussion, listening only to the Salvadoran military. How does one begin to penetrate that mentality? I don't see any way.

September 21

Tonight the local agencies' staff met with the military authorities. The captain blew up once again: he wants to be invited to every single meeting, whether it be with the doctors, the schoolteachers, the Caritas team, or anyone else. He accused us of making fun of him by discussing mainly food and medicine at these regular biweekly meetings. "I know you don't care at all about the Honduran population; all you are interested in are the Salvadorans," he charged. He said he knows we have secret meetings and he will not stand for it. His tirade was followed by silence; there really was nothing to say in this situation. We really are worried about the problems of food, medicine, and education, whether he believes it or not.

September 25

I am depressed and disillusioned as I worry about what to do when Barbara returns to Spain and only Delia and I are left to work on the education project. I like Delia, but she does not have the leadership capability nor the initiative that Barbara does; so I almost feel as if I am training someone rather than sharing the work load. Aside from that, Barbara has become a dear friend.

Why is it so difficult for the rest of my co-workers to understand the need for team leadership on the education program? Is it that they themselves do not have the educational background? No one else on the team has gone beyond the sixth grade; perhaps this explains their lack of empathy for what we are trying to do. Miguel seems to be more understanding than the rest, maybe because as the camp coordinator he has a chance to see the schools in action on a daily basis. The others have so much other work to do in the villages that they have little time to visit the schools and get a sense of what the children are learning.

In our last meeting, the team again questioned the amount of time I spend with journalists. They say it is my own fault if I cannot handle all the educational tasks. They even expressed some anger that CEDEN had called me over the radio to ask me to translate for a representative for the World Council of Churches.

"Who do you work for?" they ask me, unable to see the importance of international public awareness. On this point I don't feel I can give in. The reality we are living with and the farce of the Honduran government's "neutrality" has to be told to the world, and I feel this is just as important as the education project.

I am hurt by the criticism of my Honduran friends. They are right that it claims much of my time. Some days I can spend up to three hours with journalists, recounting our history here, and describing the present repression. Word seems to spread among the professionals and journalists that there is a North American who witnessed both the March 18 crossing of the Lempa River and the July 17 invasion by the Salvadoran military, so they all want to talk to me.

Yesterday a UNHCR representative from Geneva came to visit who does not speak Spanish. As I accompanied him, he casually asked about the invasion and was surprised when I gave him my own testimony. He said in Geneva they still deny that the invasion into Honduras happened. Then he added, "It is so important that a North American witnessed it because this makes the testimony verifiable."

How that infuriates me! The testimonies of dozens of Hondurans who live in the area are worthless because they are nobody, yet my own testimony, just because I am North American, is significant. I am so tired of people treating Hondurans and Salvadoran refugees as nonpersons!

September 28

Every once in a while I stop and force myself to look for something good in the midst of all this negative. Really, it is not hard to find; in fact, I do see much beauty and experience a lot of joy. Last night as I lay in the bed I share with Delia and little Reina, I thought of how good it has been for our team to be eating our meals together. We rarely stay out in the villages for supper anymore, and so we spend our entire evening sharing more intimately, singing to guitar accompaniment, praying together, and analyzing the daily events. As we get to know one another better, our questions become braver and sometimes personal.

The other day, for instance, Miguel mustered the courage to ask me why I sometimes walk out to the latrine with only a shirt and my underwear on. I had thought nothing of it, since it was nighttime and our back courtyard is enclosed by a high brick wall.

"Does it offend you?" I asked.

"Yes, because a Honduran woman would never do that. It implies she is a loose woman."

I was genuinely shocked, saying that in my culture showing one's legs was not such a big deal, as long as I was adequately covered by my shirt.

He laughed and said, "You would hide your breasts from us? They are just for nursing, and everyone has seen that."

He is right, I guess. Here a woman will bare her breasts to nurse her baby in public. She also bathes in the river nude from the waist up, but never without a skirt or at least a half slip on. I bathe in a half slip too, but I cannot feel comfortable bathing without a bra when people are watching. I am glad Miguel brought up the subject. I'll keep my skirt on now even at night when I go out to the latrine. The fact that Miguel was able to raise the issue, even in the presence of other co-workers, tells me that more of a brother-sister relationship is developing, and I am glad.

October 1

Lately I have taken to sitting on our sidewalk steps outside the Caritas house after dark with Alicia, the mother of the refugee family that shares the house with us. By sharing the house I mean that the five of them have a tiny room next to our big one, and we share the courtyard and enclosure behind the house which includes the cooking area, the latrine, and the corridor where people spend most of the daytime hours working in the shade.

Alicia is probably about sixty years old. Whereas men smoke openly in public, I have never seen a younger woman smoke cigarettes; the older women of grandmother-age, however, like to smoke their own rolled cigarettes, but they usually do so after dark. Alicia will sit down on the sidewalk in front of our house in the evening to smoke; so I join her to relax and enjoy the bright stars above this town where no streetlights dim their brilliance. We sit and quietly talk.

Alicia is a very religious woman. Often she recites the rosary. It is calming for me to listen to her steady singsong recital of these words that are becoming very familiar to me in Spanish, although I don't even know them in English. After she has finished her prayers, Alicia says, "Well, it's time to go to bed. We've put everything in God's hands. I feel better and I can sleep now."

Alicia feels the strain more deeply than others, I think, because her husband, two of her sons, and a daughter are fighting with the guerrillas in El Salvador. Before she fled she was living alone in her house with her three youngest children when the Salvadoran army came into their town and began to harass the families where no men were present, suspecting that the men were fighting with the guerrillas. They put Alicia and her children against the wall and held them at gunpoint, asking where her husband was. Eventually they put the points of their rifles against the throats of her and her children.

While they were being held, other soldiers forced another family inside their own house right across the street from Alicia's and set the house on fire, burning the entire family alive. They threatened that this would happen to Alicia if she did not talk. But then by some miracle of God they let her go and they left. That very night she, along with many other villagers, packed up what they could carry in their arms and left their homes to flee to Honduras. She has been here ever since. The events happened over a year ago, and she has no idea whether her husband, daughter, and sons are still alive and well.

I have very mixed feelings about developing close

friendships with the people that they begin to confide in me and share their stories the way Alicia has done. I feel so close to her now, and I can sense from Alicia that it gives her comfort to talk to someone and share all the jumbled emotions inside her—her fear and the constant worry that comes from not knowing how her family is. She needs to talk; if I listen, it will help her psychologically. Yet at the same time, I wish I didn't know, because the repression might escalate to the point that we international workers will be interrogated about what the people have told us.

October 4

Barbara left this week to return home to Spain. I had not expected to feel such a void in my life with her gone. Suddenly loneliness overwhelms me, as if my best friend had left. It was a difficult parting; we both cried, as did many of the other Caritas workers. She has been such a joy with her good nature and her ability to lighten our hearts in the midst of all this tension. Working so closely together on the education project day after day in our politically volatile situation helped us develop a deep friendship in a very short time. It hardly seems possible that she was here for only two and one-half months. Time has a different meaning here. The moments are more powerful, more intense, because of the events going on around us.

So Barbara goes, and not only have I lost one of my best friends here, but I am suddenly alone again with the responsibilities for the schools. The work feels overwhelming. I have not been this depressed for months. Maybe part of my depression comes from this evening's gathering, when the whole Caritas team sat together drinking coffee, reminiscing, and talking about Barbara's leaving. How difficult it is to imagine her back home in Spain, especially for the Hondurans on the team who have never left their country or perhaps not even seen their capital city! We recalled all the good times we had, laughing and singing together or playing the games she taught us, particularly during evenings when we were not able to leave the house because of rain or security problems.

While I miss Barbara deeply, I am grateful for the friendships that have developed with the other co-workers. On the day Barbara left we decided we deserved an outing together to get away and relax. So we packed a picnic lunch, bought a case of soft drinks, loaded it into the back of our pickup truck, and set off in the direction of La Esperanza, a town with natural hot springs about two hours away. Everyone was in an excellent mood, laughing, joking, and competing to tell the most bizarre story about the hot springs—everything from finding the water so hot one could hard-boil eggs to miracles of healing from sitting in the water.

Well, we had driven only for about fifteen minutes, up to the first place where one has to ford the river, when we found that last night's rains had caused a landslide. After moving a few big boulders we were able to continue, only to find a group of people gathered at the river's edge who told us that in the early dawn hours the bus had tried to ford the river and had been carried downstream with several people in it. Standing right in the river we could look around the bend and see the bus, mangled and crushed, hung up in some trees at the river's edge. Apparently they are searching for three bodies of local men who were in the bus at the time of the accident.

We decided to ford the creek despite the swift current and managed to get across, but several people commented that if it rained again that afternoon we would not get back at night. When we got to the next town, Mapulaca, where Delia's family lives, we had to stop and visit for a short while. It was noon by the time we got back in the truck. In the burning midday sun we were all anxious to get to the springs another half hour beyond Mapulaca. Finally Arturo, our driver, stopped and told everyone to pile out and walk from there. We proceeded along the river's edge, most of us dipping into the river, clothes and all, just to cool off.

After walking for about a mile, we arrived at our destination: bubbling hot springs, hot enough in some spots that they would burn you, right in the midst of very cold water. The stream and the smell of sulfur were not much fun, but we spent the afternoon playing in the water, looking around, relaxing for the first time in months. It was marvelous not to talk of anything serious.

At one point Eduardo suggested we might want to have a liturgy together before going home. Everyone talked down the idea, saying it would be too heavy an experience on a day when we just wanted to have fun. Instead, we ate our picnic, drank the pop we had brought along, and sang songs. We were tired and sunburnt, but totally relaxed by the time we headed back to La Virtud.

Yet as we neared the edge of town, after successfully fording the river, and pulled up to the command post to get permission to drive on by, it was as though a dark cloud descended over us once again. The soldiers made us all pile out of the truck, started looking behind the seats, underneath the car, and around the wheels, and asked the usual questions: "Where have you been? Why did you go there? What were you doing?" Obviously the guard did not believe us when we told him we had merely gone to the hot springs to have a picnic together. His suspicion dampened our spirits considerably.

On arriving at the Caritas house we found Crucita, our cook, nervously awaiting us because someone from her family's village, La Majada, had come into town for help from us. During the afternoon five men had been seen walking through the hills close to their village, men whom the refugees identified as paramilitary from ORDEN. They did not bother anyone, but merely walked through the area, apparently to see who lived there. Now the entire village understandably is nervous and frightened. The fear is that the men will return during the night and harm someone. There is nothing we can do; the powerlessness is terrible.

October 5

Alejandro and I spent the afternoon taking photos of children for a group from the U.S. which has been funding Caritas' nutrition work and had asked us specifically for photos which would reflect the health situation of the children and show how the nutrition program is helping them. The pictures will be used for fund-raising in the U.S.

We had a delightful time going from tent to tent, enjoying the opportunity to be with the parents and their children. Of course there were hard moments too. Some children, even after all our work, are still undernourished. We talked to Graciela again, who is worried about how thin her eleven-year-old daughter, Eva Maria, is getting; each of the girl's ribs clearly shows on her little chest. Down another row of tents we come upon a healthy, chubby baby.

We talked to the mother who said, "Don't you remember? This is the baby that was born two days after we crossed the river when we were still in Los Hernandez. It was my first baby." She is pregnant again now. I did remember the birth after she refreshed my memory. It was during one of the nights I slept in Los Hernandez on the ground with six other Caritas workers. Someone came to wake us up at three in the morning saying that a woman was about to give birth.

Alejandro is trained as a nurse and midwife, and I went with him to help the woman. Her contractions were coming irregularly, and Alejandro noted that the baby was high up and did not seem to have dropped into the birth canal at all. So he said it would take several more hours and they should come wake us up at six in the morning.

We gingerly made our way back through all those sleeping bodies and lay down again. The next thing I remember is Alejandro shaking me, saying it was six-thirty and we ought to go check on the woman again. To our surprise, she had already delivered. Her mother had attended her, although she had no training as a midwife.

This baby was the first one born after the Lempa river crossing, and it did my heart good to see the child healthy, with no signs of malnutrition yet. We are concerned that the mother is pregnant already, because this will affect her milk supply, and malnutrition may set in. She will try to nurse both after her new baby is born, because children are nursed here until about age two. So the babies get off to a good start, but when one follows another so quickly, the mother can't keep up with them.

October 7

Today for the first time ever a bishop came to visit La Virtud. Such excitement, exuberance, and celebration among the people! One would have thought the pope himself had arrived, the way they prepared to greet him. For days the refugees and towns-people had been making crepe paper banners, streamers, and all kinds of decorations for both the refugee camp, the town, and church building.

For the Caritas team it was an especially poignant event. These workers, most of whom are lay catechists, were receiving a pastoral visit for the first time since they began their work. So it was a profound religious experience for them. Coming out of a Protestant background, I did not find it as meaningful, but I was moved to see how it affected my co-workers.

The road leading into town goes down a long hill to the riverbed where the refugee camp is, and then climbs the hill again to reach La Virtud. When the bishop's car appeared, the children came running down the hill, and by the time the bishop arrived at the river, virtually the entire town had come down to fill the side of the road. The bishop got out of his car and greeted the refugees in the camp. Then he began walking up the hill on foot, greeted by shouts and slogans and banner-waving. A long procession followed him all the way into town to the plaza and into the church for the celebration of the mass.

The church was packed to overflowing, with people visibly moved to receive communion by the bishop. His homily was powerful, comforting, and uplifting all at once. It felt reassuring to see him stand there, well aware that soldiers were lounging in the doorway entrances, and say that the work Caritas is doing in this town is the work of mercy that Jesus told us to do. "Jesus said that whatever we do to these least of our brothers and sisters, we have done unto him. We cannot see the needs of another and not respond to them. Caritas is the church in action."

As he spoke, I looked around at the faces of my co-workers. Our volunteers from the villages, almost one hundred, were all present, absorbed, soaking up every word he spoke, drinking it in as though their souls were dry sponges. I saw tears on many faces. He said he hoped we feel peace in our hearts which comes from knowing that we are doing the right thing. His homily reminded me of the fourteenth and fifteenth chapters of John, where Jesus prepares his disciples for the disillusionment and discouragement and the persecution which will inevitably come to them if they follow the path Christ chose. I think the people did go away feeling at peace, reassured that the hierarchy of the church is with them and supporting them.

After the mass, the bishop and the priests who had come along with him gathered in the Caritas house, and we had a meal together. It was a joyful time of celebration, the bishop sitting among these simple farming folk, talking as if they were good friends. I sensed spiritual growth and healing of all that the Caritas team has suffered because of its work with the refugees. After the meal we had a chance for more personal sharing. I heard my co-workers express their fears more openly than usual, and I myself talked about my fears regarding our situation. It was one of the few moments we have spent together where we have allowed ourselves to feel anything.

Someone spoke for all of us: "The work becomes so important that we tend to suppress our emotions. It is a subconscious realization that if we allow ourselves to respond emotionally to the events around us, we would be unable to cope. The strain would break us."

Paolo asked the bishop how he interprets the political changes in the country, particularly the repression that has come down on the Caritas workers. The bishop responded, "Most of the political and military leaders are people who understand all the events on a line or plane where one end is communism and the other end is not communism. Every single event is interpreted according to this very simplistic scheme, with everything perceived as communistic labeled 'bad' and everything on the opposite extreme 'good.' This perception gets mixed up with private interests and personal plans and hopes for gain. We have to understand how they are thinking, because it affects us. When they see the work we are doing, they wonder about the implication it will have on their lives, and the changes it will bring to their country. They put those projections of change onto their plane of thinking, and as a result they accuse us of being communist."

The bishop also talked to us about the significance of the upcoming November 29 elections for the national Honduran government. He pointed out that these elections will mark a change from military to civilian rule and to regional importance, as a response to pressure from the United States that Honduras must become an exemplary democracy in Central America.

There is great anxiety about rumors in the country concerning high-level organizing for a military coup before the November elections, because conservative factions in the military do not support the change to civilian rule. And of course leftist political groups are increasing their activity because they fear the elections will not be allowed to take place and do not agree with the parties which are participating in the elections. According to the bishop the military leaders will not let go of their control because of the political unrest in the surrounding countries and the danger that Honduras will be pulled into the conflicts of either Nicaragua or El Salvador.

It is interesting to compare reports from visiting journalists with the statements from the bishop. Most journalists, many of whom are here to cover the elections, say that the U.S. is pressing for civilian rule because it wants to say, "Look at this marvelous democracy in Central America," compared to Nicaragua to the south which is portrayed as a Marxist government.

The bishop said quite a bit more than that, but I have forgotten the details. I just remember being very pleased with his coming and his interaction with the team. Afterwards he asked everyone in our circle to express our greatest fear. I said I feared they would deport me. He assured me that it would not come to that; the church would do everything possible to stand up for Caritas and protect those who are working here and have made the commitment to follow the way of Jesus.

Tonight after supper as we talked about the day's events, I

sensed from everyone, myself included, a deeper feeling of peace because we have heard affirmation that what we are doing is right. Although the persecution may get worse, there is joy in right living, and we will be able to cope with whatever comes.

October 10

Last night brought the heaviest downpour we have had for several months. It started raining before sunset and soon rained so heavily that the noise on our tile roofs was almost deafening. We tried to talk or listen to the radio, but finally gave up and settled down for the night. In several places water leaked through the tile roofing, so we had to get up and rearrange beds. The rain continued for most of the night. We all knew the town would be a muddy mess today, but we had no idea of the extent of the damages.

In midmorning I put on my rubber thongs and walked to the camp. People everywhere were drying out bedding and their plastic ground cloths, clothing, cardboard boxes, and themselves. Of course the tents had afforded little protection for those sleeping inside. Many tents have been up long enough by now that they have started to tear and leak. It had been a miserable night for most people, particularly those who were still sleeping on the ground. The trenches which everyone had dug around their tents to drain the water were of little or no use during last night's rain. The water came down with such force that the river actually cut a new riverbed. Where yesterday we had room to drive the small pickup truck between the tents and the river's edge, today there is just enough space to walk; moreover, the gently sloping land along the river's edge that the men had prepared for gardens has been washed away. The washout now resembles a steep cliff, with barely a five-foot space between some tents and a ten-foot drop-off down to the rushing water.

I needed to visit the schools in the third camp on the other side of the river, and with my lack of experience in flash flooding, it never occurred to me not to try to cross. So I went to a spot where previously we either walked through ankle-deep water with our rubber thongs or crossed over on a big log. The log now was nowhere to be seen; the children told me it had been washed away in last night's storm. So I lifted my skirts up above my knees, intending to walk across. The children suggested that I not go, but I paid them no heed and stepped into the water.

I had not made it halfway across before I gave up lifting my skirt. The water was above my thighs, and the current was too strong even to pick up my foot and take another step. So I simply stood there looking around puzzled, unsure what to do.

Giovanni, one of the refugees who works in the warehouse in the third camp, walked out toward me into the middle of the river and took my hands. Together we struggled against the current and step by step came closer to the other shore. We both arrived safely, but soaked clear up to our waists. The refugee women who had watched us come across from the other side laughed at me, saying I had obviously never been around flash flooding before or I would not have stepped into that river.

Of course in this heat my cotton skirt was dry within an hour, so the discomfort did not last long; but I decided not to chance that river crossing again. After observing the schools and playing with the children at recess, I just stayed most of the day and visited with the people.

October 11

The school teachers are complaining about attendance problems. Children are sick with malaria, typhoid, pink eye, and severe colds, making it very hard to keep up a regular schedule in the schools. I talked with the doctors who said the camp is so crowded that those who are sick cannot be isolated. Moreover, the healthy people are needed to take care of the sick. So for a few more months we will have to put up with the spreading of uncontrollable illnesses.

Aside from diseases, the general health condition of the people is poor. Children are affected most severely. For over a month we have had no powdered milk, their only source of protein and calcium except for beans. In meeting after meeting every

week we discuss the problem with the UNHCR and CEDEN officials, and they continue to say they will do what they can to get
more powdered milk in, but nothing happens. The children need
that glass of milk every morning; it is crucial to their vitality and
general health. We can tell a marked difference after a month
without milk: listlessness, lack of energy to play or pay attention to
their studies.

Instead of working on other aspects of the school program, I
am now trying to find out why the milk supply has stopped and to
press to get it started up again. But this is difficult to pursue from
La Virtud. I get so frustrated I want to jump into the next truck,
drive to the capital city, and buy the milk myself.

Everywhere I turn, I hear another excuse. Either funds have
not come through, or people disagree on whose responsibility it is
to buy the milk. One agency supposedly made a commitment;
another agency had some but used it somewhere else because
they thought our camps had milk already.

It is a confusing and frustrating situation; I want to tear my
hair out at times. It becomes depressing when there seem to be so
many strikes against us. It is ridiculous that as the only education
coordinator I should have to waste my time worrying about the
milk, pink eye, and all these other details, until no time is left to
work on educational tasks.

October 19

I will be sleeping in the camp below town tonight. Right
now I am taking my turn at vigilance because the refugees are
frightened that soldiers will come into the camp during the night.
They feel safer if someone from the staff is down here with them.
It has been a bizarre weekend; my emotions are a jumble of disbelief and numbness.

On Saturday morning we began another teacher training
course with the teachers from the camp, about twenty-five in all.
This course promised to be much better than the last because one
of the seminary students, Roel, came from Santa Rosa to help, and
another Caritas workers, Santos, is helping also. Both are excellent

The Salvadoran madonna and child.

ABOVE: Large families, poverty, hard work, and worry about an insecure future make the women in Central America age before their time.

RIGHT (top): Salvadorans sought refuge in Honduran villages where they built thatched huts for shelter. These were battered by torrents of water during the rainy season and by strong winds during the dry season.

RIGHT (bottom): The La Virtud camp was built in March 1981 for 3,000 refugees who survived the crossing of the Lempa River. The camp was located in a river valley below the town, an easy hike down the hill when it was dry, but a muddy slide when the rains came.

LEFT: Tarpaulins and lumber were provided by the UNHCR to construct A-frame tents. It was left to the people to enclose the two open ends and build a cooking area.

ABOVE: Sometimes families who had been neighbors or friends prior to fleeing El Salvador shared cooking space and the tasks of baking tortillas and boiling beans.

To begin instruction for more than 1,000 Salvadoran children living in Honduran villages near La Virtud, school had to be held outside beneath the trees. Later the refugees erected simple structures, roofed but without walls, as classrooms.

School went on despite insecurity, poor nutrition, intense heat, and lack of modern educational equipment. Teachers and children improvised with rough chalkboards, crowded benches, and short pencil stubs.

Without school desks it was difficult for the children to write legibly in their flimsy notebooks. During my village visits I encouraged them and praised their persistence.

LEFT (top): The tents in the refugee camp were overcrowded. In addition to the women and children pictured here, four men lived in this tent. However, they dared not allow their picture to be taken for fear of persecution.

ABOVE: The continually blowing dust and polluted water made skin infections hard to cure.

LEFT (bottom): The hike into town from the villages was often impossible for the sick, so they had to be carried in hammocks. Frequently they arrived too late for help.

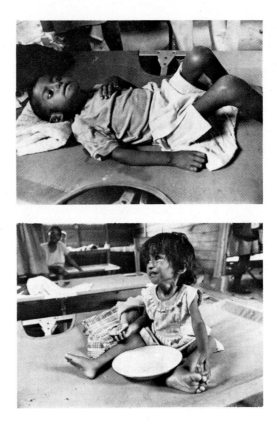

ABOVE: Almost one hundred children died in the three months following the Lempa River crossing. Many suffered from acute malnutrition, diarrhea, and dehydration.

RIGHT: Mothers, powerless to stop hunger and disease, grieved as they watched their children die.

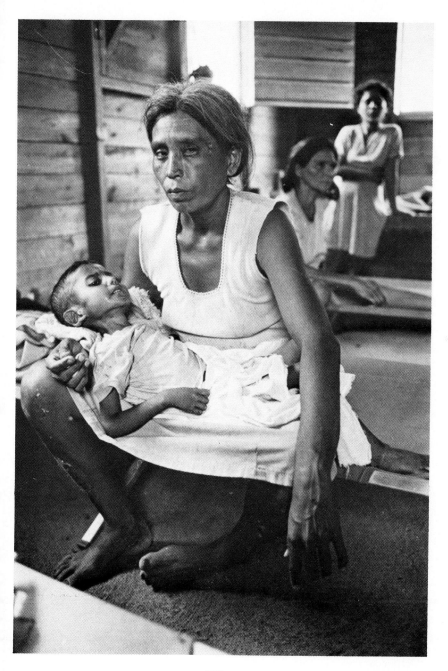

BELOW: The scenario repeated itself hundreds of times over: malnutrition, parasites, diarrhea, dehydration, death.

RIGHT: A cadaver decays quickly in a hot, tropical climate. Cotton closed off the mouth and nose to insects while the little body lay in state and the family prayed.

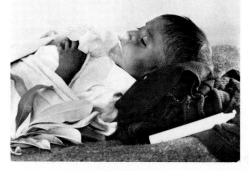

BELOW: The carpenters would have rejoiced to use their skills for building school benches rather than coffins.

The children in the camp were as eager to start school as those in the villages. How could I explain to them that it would take months to prepare enough

teachers and organize an education program for all of them? Their faces revealed incomprehension and disappointment.

ABOVE: Refugees came from the out-lying villages once a week to receive basic food supplies from the Caritas warehouse.

RIGHT (bottom): A foreign land and an uncertain future were not enough to squelch the Salvadorans' simple desire to cultivate the earth.

ABOVE: A deep affinity with God's earth is part of the makeup of the Salvadoran people. Within weeks after their arrival they had begun vegetable gardens.

The men in the refugee camp lived in constant fear of soldiers and death squads. Hondurans regularly accused them of being guerrillas and harassed them for not going home to join the Salvadoran army. In addition to their fear, the men felt guilty for not opposing more actively the Salvadoran government's persecution of the people.

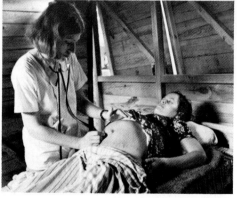

ABOVE: On All Saints' Day (Oct. 31) refugees constructed a simple memorial in the shade of the dry riverbed. Pictures of loved ones—a rare and treasured possession—demonstrated the theme of prayer and reflection.

A French gynecologist from Médecins Sans Frontières examines an expectant mother. What kind of life will await the child?

ABOVE: Thatched ranchitos in the mountain villages were exchanged for a tent city at Mesa Grande atop a high, flat, barren plateau. It was a shock for the majority of the people. Only 3,000 of the total 8,000 had known "camp life" in La Virtud.

RIGHT (top): Our first animal husbandry construction project—a chicken house—stood new but empty after the people were relocated 50 miles over the mountains. It is the only remaining sign in La Virtud today that 15,000 Salvadorans once shared daily life there.

The relocation of 500 people each week meant that work stayed in a perpetual emergency stage. Housing was first priority for each new group, but weeks went by and the initial contingents of refugees were still cooking over open fire and eating without table or chairs.

RIGHT (top): Through folk music the people poured out their hearts about their past and present, their hopes and dreams.

BELOW: Mesa Grande's state of emergency required the construction of communal kitchens. This meant leaving the babies and toddlers back in the tent under the precarious care of the older children.

RIGHT (bottom): Mesa Grande suffered from lack of water throughout its first full year of existence. The shortage complicated daily chores and caused many health and sanitation problems.

The refugees have fled military repression and the bloody strife which ravages Central America. As months turn into years, hope withers into despair.

at developing interpersonal relations and confidence with classroom management, which is very important because many instructors from the camp are overcome with shyness when they stand in front of a group of children. Our total training team consisted of Santos, Roel, Delia, Prudencia, and me. It was a blessing to be working with such a large group for a change.

On Saturday all of us had planned to spend the night together in the new Caritas house on the corner of the plaza, directly across from the command post. Eduardo had rented the house because our old house is overcrowded, particularly now that we spend so many evenings inside. Interestingly enough, no one had wanted to move to the other house—we would rather stay in cramped quarters just to be together. So the house was empty, and we decided we could use the evening to evaluate and plan if we all went over there. During the day we carried over mats, blankets, and a few benches to sit on.

Saturday evening after supper Santos, Delia, Prudencia, and I walked the one block from the Caritas house to the other building, but realized on arriving that Roel had the key to the padlock on the door. It was already dark, and we sat down on the sidewalk steps, waiting for Roel to come, figuring he must have been delayed.

After about twenty minutes of talking and joking around, we began playing one of our word games, a tongue twisting exercise we had been teaching the instructors. Suddenly our game was interrupted by an explosion which looked and sounded as though it came from inside the command post. We froze immediately, thinking we would see soldiers pouring out. But nothing happened.

As we sat in stunned silence, it suddenly occurred to us that we might be blamed for the explosion if we did not get away. So we ran toward the little hospital, a block off the plaza toward the edge of town, only to find the people there huddled together in one of the rooms, terrified. They told us that for about half an hour someone had been throwing rocks over the side of the wall which encloses the hospital, trying to break the lantern. Moments before we had arrived, three men had come into the hospital with guns and masks over their faces and had stolen the lantern from them. Now they were sitting together in the darkness, too scared to move, not knowing what the explosion had meant.

We stayed in the hospital for about ten minutes, but all was silent in the street, so we decided to venture out and try to return to the Caritas house. We found the plaza and all the other streets deserted. As quickly and quietly as we could we rushed back to the Caritas house and knocked on the door. They let us in; all were sitting in the darkness, afraid to have a light on, and wondering about the explosion.

We had not been in the house very long when we heard gunfire, followed again by quiet. The gunfire sounded like it came from one or two streets away. Then all was calm for a while; so we thought the episode was over and decided to go back to the other Caritas house to do our work and sleep. We had barely arrived at the house, unlocked the door, and closed it again from the inside, when shooting began in the plaza right in front of us.

I can't find words to describe my fear at that moment, being in a house that offered so little protection from bullets if someone were to shoot right at us. We all went to the far side of the room, after barricading the thin wooden doors as well as we could, and sat together on one of the mats in the corner, listening to the gunfire which continued for quite some time. Roel told us to put out the candle because they were looking for someone and would suspect any house that had light in it.

The intermittent shooting must have gone on for two hours, until about ten. We all agreed that we needed to get some sleep, so we lay down with our blankets in that far corner of the room and tried to calm ourselves. We whispered for a little while more. I remember one comment Prudencia made to me as we were drifting off to sleep: "There are women up in the mountains firing those guns while we women lie here huddled and frightened out of our wits just at the sound of them."

Once more during the night, at about 3:00 a.m., shooting erupted anew in the street right in front of our house. Of course

we woke up and lay in frozen silence. Then we went back to sleep.
Even now as I write I can hardly comprehend my calm attitude
toward it all.

Sunday morning dawned as if nothing had happened. One
of the Caritas workers warned me not to ask the townspeople
questions about the disturbance unless they volunteered information. Late Sunday afternoon Padre Juan arrived, so the Caritas
team gathered after supper to share the eucharist. We met in our
own house, sang, read the Scriptures, broke the bread, and felt
much better for having spent that time together in worship. But
again, as we were visiting and talking afterwards, shooting began
two blocks away. Soon afterwards someone who had been looking
out the front door announced that soldiers had stationed themselves at both ends of our block. Shooting continued intermittently most of Sunday night; none of us slept very well.

This morning, Monday, rumors are rampant throughout the
town, most of them apparently spread by the soldiers themselves.
One person from town told me she had heard from soldiers that
500 guerrillas had tried to attack the town and that the soldiers
had been successful in repelling them. Another woman had been
told by soldiers that Salvadoran paramilitary men from ORDEN
had attacked the town, wanting to get to the Caritas team, but the
soldiers had "protected" us. They also said in addition to these
contradictory stories that the first explosion we heard on Saturday
night had gone off behind the command post; but one of our
schoolteachers lives on the street behind the command post and
said the explosion definitely happened inside. Some people are
saying the captain deliberately started all this, even exploding the
initial grenade, in order to harass and terrorize the population to
make sure everyone stayed in all night long.

Last night one of the doctors had an emergency case at the
hospital. After a lengthy period with no gunfire she decided she
would risk walking the three blocks to Eduardo's house to radio to
Tegucigalpa that they would need an airplane to transport a sick
patient early the next morning. Frederica had walked two blocks,
past the plaza and on to the street where Eduardo lives, when

gunfire erupted. She dropped to the ground immediately, and then, out of the darkness, a soldier appeared who said he would escort her safely to the house.

Later Frederica said she was sure it had been the same soldier who was shooting. She certainly had not seen any other attackers nor felt that the presence of that soldier beside her meant any protection. Most of the French doctors are rather cynical about the Honduran soldiers, feeling they instigate all this confusion to frighten the people.

Then this afternoon, soldiers arrived at our door saying that the captain wanted to see Paolo. This is the second time Paolo has been called in for questioning. He went to the command post, and two hours later four of us decided to check on him, mainly just to let the captain know we knew Paolo was there, in case he was planning to make him "disappear."

The captain was furious. We could see Paolo sitting on a bench inside the command post, while the captain launched into a long barrage about who were we to be checking up on him, whether we didn't have our own work to do, why we were concerning ourselves with his business, and so forth. He said he was simply going about his normal duties. Had we come to accuse him of doing something awful? His tirade went on for maybe forty-five minutes, during which he accused us of having a private worship service in our house the night before when the priest came, and said we should not think we were doing anything behind his back, because he knew all that went on.

At that point I lost my temper, exclaiming, "Since when is it against the law to worship in your own home?"

"It is," he said. "That's what churches are for."

I pushed him further: "Are you trying to tell me that somewhere in the laws of this country it says a person is forbidden to have worship in a private home and with friends, and that worship can take place only in churches?" I knew by the looks my co-workers were giving me that they wanted me to keep quiet, but I couldn't control myself. I insisted on knowing exactly what the law was and where it was written, because I understood there was freedom of religious expression in Honduras and that Honduras was a democracy. I went on and on; I can't even remember all I said.

The captain did back down, first claiming that worship was only to occur on Sundays in churches, but then conceding that no such law existed, only it was understood that this was what churches are for. "In a situation like ours in the border zone," he continued, "with subversives everywhere, a military commander is allowed to make any laws he wants, and this is one that I am making."

I protested that he could not make it after the fact but rather had to tell us ahead of time. He said that was what he was doing right now; from now on, should a priest come, he had to go to the church beside the command post rather than hold worship in a private home. Then he started another tirade, saying that all the Honduran population had been excluded, and that a priest was supposed to serve all people, not just a small group. It was preposterous.

Finally, someone said, "What does all this have to do with Paolo? We came to find out what his crime is or what he is being charged with."

The captain laughed, saying we had better all be aware because his men were watching us, and he had found out that Paolo was going out to the villages to lead worship on Sunday morning, where he would start out talking about Scripture but end up asking, "How is the struggle going?"

Having made this ridiculous, unsubstantiated accusation, he asked us to leave his office, but maintained we should not concern ourselves because in due process Paolo would be released. Paolo was indeed set free this evening at about nine o'clock. He said the captain had not accused him of anything but had simply told him to sit on the bench and given him a lecture about preaching subversion.

The captain dropped another bit of information while we were there: "We [whoever that means] have been studying how El Salvador got to the point where it is now and realize it is the fault of the Catholic church. The ones who have taught Marxism to the people are the lay catechists and the priests, and those who are working in Catholic organizations such as Caritas. They tell people to organize. So first the people form unions, next they rob banks, and then they blow up bridges."

The captain interspersed his talk with phrases about "subversion" and "Cuban-style communism." Finally he said, "We are aware that the priests here in Honduras have already trained all of you lay catechists. You have even started blowing up bridges in our country. But we want you to know that it is stopping right here, and that we'll tighten security to keep it from happening. Even if elections need to be postponed, we will not let Honduras fall to the communists."

We finally left, realizing it was futile to try to talk with him. I was churning with anger and unexpressed frustration; yet at the same time I was relieved when Paolo came back to us right before I left to go down to the camp.

Just an interesting sideline: the woman who runs the dining hall for the soldiers and the captain said that before Saturday night's shooting the captain had been gone for two days to attend a meeting with Salvadoran military at the border; she implied that he had come back with some kind of plan to terrorize the population.

All is quiet tonight as I sit here in the clinic with two refugees. In a little while, if all remains calm, I will go to Graciela's and Ignacio's tent where they promised a hammock and a blanket would be waiting for me. I have slept with their family several nights. The tent is very crowded, since they share it with two other families, which adds up to a total of seventeen people; nonetheless, it is pleasant to experience a home environment and to be with the children in the morning when I wake up.

I especially enjoy the early morning hours when the older women gather, usually at 4:30 before dawn, to sing the rosary and recite their prayers. It is so restful and reassuring to hear the sing-songy voices and those words coming from the toothless old women I can't even understand. It gives all of us some peace. I have wanted to get up with the women some morning, but I can never get out of bed at that hour. So I just lie in the hammock and listen.

October 21

At 6:30 p.m. a soldier appeared outside our door and took up his post. Eduardo went out after a while to try to strike up a casual conversation with him. He would not comment at all on the fighting in town. When Eduardo asked him about his assignment in front of our door, he said he was there for our "protection." Protection! How can the captain tell us point-blank that he considers us the enemy and then have the nerve to send a soldier to "protect" us! It feels oppressive to know he is sitting out there while we are trying to relax inside.

Even listening to the radio is a strained activity because we cannot discuss what we are hearing. No one wants to sing or play games; we all feel subdued by the soldier's presence. We should probably carry on with our normal activities and let him hear that we don't talk about anything but school supplies and food problems.

October 23

This afternoon a truck with food supplies finally made it to town, the first in a whole week because the heavy rain had made the fording of streams impossible and had turned the roads into a muddy mess. As soon as the truck arrived, we opened up the warehouse to distribute the food. Our stores had dwindled down to just a few sacks of beans. Now we have corn again. Word spread quickly that food was available, and we all worked hard to distribute it before dark.

While we were in the warehouse, four soldiers arrived in brand-new uniforms and hard helmets with the inscription, "Municipal Police." This little mountain town now warrants municipal police complete with knee-high boots and billy clubs. One would think we were in Central Park in New York City! It is disgusting. They searched all the refugee men, looking for weapons, and demanded they show their identification cards.

Tonight I ate supper with Graciela's family in the camp. While we were eating, someone came to our tent to say that people from El Salvador had arrived claiming they intended to visit relatives; but after the guards who watch the camp had given permission to enter, some refugees recognized them as having come from their town and having worked with what is called the "*Escuadron de la Muerte*," the death squads. They asked for Miguel, the camp coordinator. This is the first instance I know of that Salvadoran military have come looking for Hondurans rather than refugees. Fortunately they left the camp when told Miguel was not around.

October 27

We were finishing supper tonight when a soldier knocked on the door to announce that the town had been put under curfew and no one was to go outside from now until morning. So we all stayed in the house, feeling the lack of space, oppressed by knowing we cannot leave. There has been gunfire already this evening. The uncertainty leaves me tense and frightened. It is much more difficult to sit here, wondering what is happening to friends, than to be out there with the people during a crisis. I have to force myself not to think about the situation, or the suspense will become unbearable; my stomach ties in knots as I imagine the worst, having heard the stories people tell. So I try to concentrate on other things, or play games with my co-workers for distraction.

October 29

A visiting journalist from Europe will be leaving tomorrow morning; so tonight the Caritas team gathered around the table with a cassette player and filled a tape with messages for Barbara. The journalist will put it in the mail in Europe when he gets home. It was fun to observe my co-workers, who had never made a cassette tape before, in their awkwardness and excitement as they talked into the recorder to communicate something to Barbara. After everyone had said what they wanted, there was still space left, so we played one of Barbara's favorite word games and recorded it to let her share in the fun.

I had a long talk with the journalist who has been interviewing different townspeople as well as the captain at the command post. How differently people talk to someone they know is leaving! For instance, our neighbor said he watches us and knows that the food from our warehouse is picked up not by refugees but rather by people from El Salvador who take it back across the border. Of course the journalist asked him how he could prove that, and he replied, "I have seen it with my own eyes." I tried to explain to the journalist why his statement couldn't possibly be true, considering that the border area has been patrolled by Salvadoran army since the July invasion.

Salvadoran soldiers roam this area freely now; in several instances they have come right into town to the Honduran military command post, talked to someone there, and then left. I myself cannot distinguish them from Honduran military because I have not been here long enough, but the children point them out to me.

I ask them, "How do you know they are Salvadoran soldiers?"

They reply, "They wear their hats at a different angle, and they carry an M-16 rifle rather than the FAL of the Honduran military."

With the number of Salvadoran soldiers patrolling the border area even at night, it is not possible for people to smuggle food across the border in fifty- and one hundred-pound sacks. And to say that Caritas is promoting it is totally unsubstantiated.

Caritas, through its volunteers in the villages, keeps a weekly census of the numbers of refugees here. Occasionally refugees pack up and return to El Salvador, only to come back a month later saying their home has been burnt, or they could not stay for another reason. So there is movement of refugees, and we cannot control that. But what we do control is the amount of food distributed. The figures are given at the coordinating meeting every week. We turn in the data on the number of refugees here and request the amount of grain we need to feed that number. There is no excess.

October 30

Some journalists came through today, and I took them to the camp to hear testimonies. I remain emotionally detached as I translate, as if it no longer affected me. A few people can tell their story very well, in a clearly organized way, without falling apart. So I go back to the same people time after time. My emotions are numb, not because their tale has become less terrifying or commonplace, but because I know I would not be able to continue to work here if I were to let myself feel everything. I often wonder whether journalists and other visitors who come through think that I am calloused, when in fact it is just a survival instinct.

One journalist had just been to the capital city where he interviewed staff who represent the different agencies at the national level. He reported that apparently discussions are taking place between the UNHCR and the government about relocating all the refugees away from the border zone by the first of January.

Just this afternoon I heard rumors which have come across the border with the arrival of new refugees: allegedly right after January 1 the Salvadoran army is planning a new military offensive against the guerrillas. The Honduran government apparently wants all the refugees and international workers out of here so that no one will witness their collaboration with the Salvadoran military. The captain already is having meetings every other weekend with Salvadoran army personnel. He does not try to keep it a secret; he even brags about it to townspeople.

I don't know how the refugees discover this kind of information so quickly. When I mentioned the relocation to one of the refugees, he had heard about it already. His comment was that the majority of the refugees would not voluntarily move farther inland but would rather risk going back home to El Salvador. "We are not stupid," he said. "If the Honduran soldiers don't like us here at the border, they will resent us even more once we are further inside their country. We won't move. If we are going to die, we'll die at the hands of the Salvadoran army."

I asked him how they could possibly go home, considering how many people's homes were burnt to the ground when they fled. He smiled and told me to go talk to Ignacio, Graciela's husband. When I did, Ignacio confided that he had gone home last weekend. He noticed my surprise and added, "I just had to go back and see how our town is." He had left in the morning for the all-day hike, stopping in each village on the way to ask whether any troops or any movement of soldiers had been observed recently. He was able to get through with no trouble, never encountering soldiers on the way.

When he reached his hometown, he saw many homes burnt to the ground, and others had been ransacked. "We expected this kind of invasion sooner or later," he explained. "Many of our neighbors and we ourselves prepared by burying some of our possessions in the dirt floor of our house. I went back to see if they were still hidden, and indeed some had not been found or destroyed. So now we have money."

"Who in your opinion ransacks the houses?" I asked.

"The only people who do not flee are those working for the military or ORDEN; they are the ones who ransack the houses."

"Would you tell me how much money you had hidden?"

"It was all my life's savings, about 400 colones."°

November 1

Willy left to go back to Europe this morning. Willy is a Belgian who has been coordinating the French doctors' team for over a year now. He has been a good friend and I am going to miss him. Willy left this morning announcing simply that he was going into the capital city to get some supplies and would be back. He was not able to say good-bye to people because of recent attempts to kidnap him.

Last week, when it became apparent that soldiers were out to

° The 1981 exchange rate was 3.5 colones to the dollar; his life savings for a family of seven was slightly more than $100.

get him, he started taking more precautions. It was the first instance here in this border area where we had seen open hostility against one of the international workers. The captain all but directly accused Willy of going to El Salvador and giving medicine to the guerrillas. He probably singled out Willy because Willy is articulate and has always stood up to the captain; also he had been here the longest and had gained the affection of the refugees. Whenever he walked into the camp the people smiled and waved, calling him by his first name and treating him like a friend.

Three nights ago it was Willy's turn to take the night shift at our little hospital. Whoever takes that shift usually spends the entire night there. When he left the next morning to return to his small room at the far end of town, he found the door standing open. The room had been completely ransacked. Interestingly, only his papers and notes were stolen—everything with the slightest bit of writing on it—whereas his clothing and his suitcases had not been taken. Even things that could have been sold, like his tape recorder, were left lying around the room.

Willy was convinced the captain had something to do with the event. The room Willy rented was in the house of the town mayor, who must have been in on the maneuver, since he claims not to have heard anything. Willy thought they took all of his papers because they were looking for proof that he had corresponded with Salvadoran guerrillas or was presently working with them.

Then yesterday a local Honduran who has been working with the captain came to Eduardo to warn him that the captain was out to get the French doctors, particularly Willy. The man mentioned a plan to kidnap Willy, take him to El Salvador, and interrogate him there with the Salvadoran military to make him confess he was working with the guerrillas.

Apparently last night the plan was to kidnap him, but they never considered the possibility that he might not be in his room. Since Eduardo's informant continues to work with the military, Eduardo could do nothing about the incident except tell the

UNHCR representative. Willy of course took the best precaution possible by departing this morning without mentioning to anyone that he was leaving for good.

Last night the French doctors had a party for Willy, talking as though it were just a general celebration without specific reason. All the Caritas workers were invited; but at 7:00 p.m. as we were getting ready to go, a soldier came to the door and told us that again a curfew had been imposed and no one would be allowed to go out after 7:30. Curfews are becoming so commonplace that we thought nothing of it and ended up staying in our house all evening.

Later Willy came by in the truck; he was going to the camp to spend the night there, but stopped by to ask why we had not come to his party. Bewildered, we exclaimed, "But there is a curfew on!" He said, "No, there isn't. We had a party, and we even invited some soldiers and townspeople. No one mentioned a curfew."

This morning our neighbors confirmed that none of them had been put under curfew either; so apparently soldiers have been coming to the Caritas house for almost a month now, imposing curfews for us alone. The people we talked to said there had been a general curfew, at most four or five times, whereas we have been forced to stay inside at least three times each week. Eduardo decided to mention this at the Tuesday night meeting of the agencies. We talked to the French doctors, and they apparently also had been told to stay inside much more frequently than the rest of the townspeople, but not as often as Caritas.

We should have discussed this earlier with the other staff who work with refugees; but the French doctors are always either in the clinic down at the camp or in the little hospital, where Caritas workers rarely visit because that is not our area of responsibility. Caritas workers are in the warehouses, the tents of the people, in the villages, or in the fields working on the agricultural program. Our work does not bring us together for casual conversation. And when we do talk, we discuss events of greater importance. There is no time to sit and chat. This is how a whole month passed before we realized what the military was doing. Now that we are aware of it, they won't be able to get away with the trick.

I am anxiously awaiting the radio news tomorrow that Willy got on his plane safely and is on his way to Belgium. I imagine the soldiers will be upset to discover he got out of the country.

November 4

The immigration officer continues to harass the refugees, especially the men. Whenever Caritas workers stop by the immigration office, he is cordial, polite, and helpful; but the refugees tell us that as soon as we leave, he begins his tirade against them. I have become more involved because several male refugee teachers have told me about their problems with immigration. Juan in particular has had several run-ins with them. Each month as he goes to renew his papers the officer asks him what he is still doing here, saying they don't want a single Salvadoran man in Honduras.

"We are not going to let Salvadoran guerrillas ruin our November 29 elections and subvert us," the officer says. "All Salvadorans had better get back to El Salvador before then. If you don't go on your own free will, you will be forced out by the men in green."

Juan seems to be having more trouble with the immigration officers than others, which may be partly my fault. Months ago we were having a teacher training course in town on the day Juan needed to renew his papers. Usually a refugee can count on spending three to four hours waiting in line outside the immigration office. Many refugees need to get their papers renewed on a given day, but the local immigration officer keeps irregular hours and takes breaks at will, going to the local cantina for a drink with his friends.

I went with Juan to ask the officer if he could renew Juan's permit right away because I needed him to be in a class I was teaching. The officer cordially agreed and told Juan to wait just five minutes outside the door. Once I had left, the immigration officer started calling Juan all kinds of names: "teacher's pet," "friend of the *gringa*," and asked him who he was to get a special request like that from the gringa. The harassment went on for several minutes.

Juan just stood there and took it all, not wanting to cause any trouble. Ever since then immigration has continued harassing him. Each time he comes in, they ask him why he is not back in El Salvador.

It seems ridiculous that these thousands of people have to come to immigration once a month for another permission stamp to stay in Honduras. When I asked about that in a meeting I was told the Honduran government doesn't want people coming and going across the border; if they give permission for more than a month, the military won't feel in control of the situation.

The debate about the elections gets more heated as the day draws near. A storeowner asked me last week if I would stay around here on November 29. I said of course; I would continue my work as on any other day. She seemed surprised that I was not leaving the country during the elections, claiming that nobody works on election day.

"Won't the refugees have to be fed regardless?" I asked. "Do you mean it is a holiday?"

"Nobody knows what will happen on November 29," she replied. "No one even knows whether the elections will come off."

When I tried to question her further she refused to talk about it any more and insisted on changing the subject. I had another conversation with the woman down the street who occasionally makes coffee cakes for the Caritas team.

"I'll vote for the National Party at election time," she said.

"Why?" I asked.

"Well, two of my sons are teachers in the school, and since this town has always voted conservative, the whole school board is conservative. If another party comes into power, those who have worked in the past under the National Party will lose their jobs. My sons would too."

"You don't mean that elementary school teachers in a small

town like this would be affected by a change in party politics?"

"Listen, they'll kill before they'll give up their power in this town."

"Do you want to vote for the National Party?"

"No, I think the Liberal Party would be better for the country and better for this town. But my sons are supporting me now that I am a widow. If they don't have their jobs I won't be able to eat."

I am getting a different perspective on what "democratic elections" mean here in Honduras!

The refugee teachers have told me they no longer want to come into town from the outlying villages for our Saturday morning meetings, saying it would be better to postpone meetings until after the elections. Until then I should visit them individually in their villages during the day. I asked what problems they had experienced.

Evidently they did not want to answer my question there in that large group, but at the end of our meeting a couple of the men followed me to my office saying they wanted to talk. One of them was Pedro, a nineteen-year-old man who on several occasions has confided in me his guilt and discomfort at not wanting to fight with either side in El Salvador. He clearly supports the resistance, but he does not think he could take up arms. That is difficult for him to admit when he knows that most other young men his age have joined the rebels. Pedro said one morning he had been a little late and was walking with just one other person when suddenly he encountered soldiers on the other side of Guajiniquil, no more than half an hour from town. The soldiers stopped them and asked Pedro for his identification, then threatened to tear his papers up. "You're a guerrilla, aren't you?" the soldiers said.

"No, I'm not."

"Then you must be from ORDEN," the soldiers shot back.

"No, I'm not from ORDEN either."

"Then what are you?"

"I'm a refugee."

The soldiers shook their heads, waved fingers at him, and said sarcastically, "Oh, no, there are no male refugees. Women and children, yes, but we don't accept you men. You better go home to El Salvador."

Then one of the soldiers launched into lecturing Pedro, "I'm one of the safest men in Honduras. You see this green uniform? This is what makes me safe. Nobody dares call me a guerrilla. Nobody dares call me any other kinds of names, or accuse me of anything. The safest thing to be in Central America is a man wearing green. If you want to be safe you better go home and join the Salvadoran army." Pointing toward El Salvador, he added, "I have connections right up there on the ridge. I can get you into the army with no trouble. Nobody will ask you about your past. You can get into a green uniform and then nobody will ever accuse you again of being a guerrilla."

The soldiers tried to talk Pedro into going with them right then, saying they were going up to talk to the Salvadoran soldiers at the outpost on the ridge. Pedro replied that he wanted to think about it, that he at least had to talk to his family and say good-bye. The soldiers mimicked him about having to go talk to his mommie, ridiculed him, and pushed further to make him go along. The only reason Pedro got out of it was that right at that moment some more people came down the road. If it had not been for those people Pedro thinks the soldiers would have taken him back to El Salvador by force. He was quite shaken as he relayed it all to me. After this incident he did not want to come into town again. He will return to his village and stay there.

At our weekly meeting of the agencies I mentioned the harassment the schoolteachers are feeling. The UNHCR representatives said they will discuss it on a national level. The colonel who represents the army at those national meetings also promised to look into it, but I doubt anything will change here at the border.

November 11

Most of the beans and corn have been harvested by now. I

enjoy hearing the refugees in the villages talk about their bountiful crops. When Caritas first started the agricultural project, the idea of working collectively was not well accepted; each family wanted its own small plot of land to farm its own way and make its own decisions.

Caritas helped the men agree to work the land collectively, explaining it was the best way given the situation we are operating under, with the UNHCR contributing money to rent the land and even purchasing the crops from the people so that the families can have a small amount of money at the end of their harvest. After these long months of work the people now talk excitedly about "our corn," "our harvest," and "our crops." They have developed a collective attitude about the work.

The harvesting of the corn is a rather long process. Over a month ago everyone went to the mountainside to turn the corn, bending each ear down so the husks would protect it from the rain. Now they are shelling the corn and cleaning it, which involves a process of laying down large mats and tossing the kernels up in the air and letting the wind carry away the dirt and the hulls. Then they bag the corn to store in the warehouse.

Since all the work is done except for the cleaning and bagging, we have started new handicraft projects. Already the refugees have begun weaving hammocks and making cooking pots and sandals. Caritas has bought several foot-treadle sewing machines so that the people can alter the used clothing to fit them. All the clothing left in the warehouse comes from the United States and is far too large for adults, so it must be remade.

Miguel, the Caritas coordinator for the camp, was called into the command post last Monday and held all day until supper time. We wondered why he was called in and debated several times whether we should go talk to the captain, but decided against it. Several times we walked past the command post and could see him sitting on a bench in the shade by the door. On being released, Miguel said the captain had not talked to him at all; he was just held all day long and finally let go at suppertime.

At the meeting of the agencies Tuesday night, Eduardo said

that it has been hard to do our work because so many Caritas workers seem to have to spend much time in the command post. He said it in a general, unthreatening way, almost as an aside. The captain laughed and apologized, explaining it had been a mistake; he had had a radio communication from the Salvadoran army stating that they had taken a picture of Miguel in a guerrilla group in El Salvador over the past weekend and wanted the captain to hold Miguel until they could get the proof over to Honduras. Later they allegedly called him back saying it had been a mistake and he should let Miguel go.

It is ridiculous that the army would call back and say it was a mistake. They do not care enough, even if they have no proof. Second, the captain openly admitted that he has regular communication with the Salvadoran army. I wonder whether he realized he was admitting that to us!

Eduardo's diplomacy amazes me. He can ask questions in a totally unaccusing way. I find myself boiling with anger in those meetings, wanting to provoke an open confrontation with the captain or the UNHCR representatives. We go to meeting after meeting, week after week, telling them the problems we are confronted with, and their response is always the same: "We'll look into it and do all we can." Nothing ever comes of it.

The captain openly lies, but no one challenges him. Sometimes I am tempted to call him a liar in front of the whole group. I get so angry that I walk out of the meetings, knowing how damaging it would be to attack the captain or the soldiers verbally. It is less dangerous to show anger with the UNHCR representatives, and so I do, even though I realize it won't help. A couple of times Eduardo has spoken to me about the potential damage I could cause. I am almost to the point of not going to any more meetings, because I get too furious with them all.

My frustration with the UNHCR representatives is so great that I can hardly be civil in our conversation. They are not doing anything at all to offer protection to the Caritas workers. I feel deeply about it because my co-workers are my friends and are harassed while doing good work. The UNHCR would not be able to carry on this work if it were not for the labor of all the Honduran volunteers. The Caritas workers have asked for a UNHCR identification card which would allow them to say, "I am working with the United Nations and should receive the same protection as an international worker." The UNHCR initially agreed, but now they seem to be stalling.

Many months ago we asked for Caritas identification cards with a picture on it and the bishop's signature. They finally arrived, but at a time when they had become virtually useless; in fact, at this point it is detrimental to be identified with Caritas. For instance, when we go to Santa Rose to renew our papers, and soldiers at a checkpoint ask what we are doing in the country, I never say I am working with Caritas. If we have to explain more about our work with the refugees, we say we work with the UNHCR. The attitude toward Caritas continues to be that we are aiding the guerrillas.

Apparently the UNHCR members do not take the threat against the Honduran volunteers seriously, and therefore are not pushing the ID cards. We would be satisfied if they could at least assure us that the Honduran military will be told the Honduran volunteers with Caritas and CEDEN are under United Nations protection like the international workers, yet the UNHCR remains unwilling to do that.

November 12

This evening I am writing by candlelight in Los Hernandez where I shall spend the night. It feels good to be out in the villages again. The Caritas team decided to change the decision to return to town every night, because many villages are experiencing such harassment by soldiers that they desperately want someone to stay with them in case there should be a confrontation. We realize we run the risk of being accused of aiding the guerrillas, but the people's protection is more important than those accusations.

I run less risk since I, like the French doctors, am an international person; so we are the ones who sleep in the villages, while our Honduran co-workers return to town. I will be sleeping in the recently erected grain storage tent. It's my favorite place in Los Hernandez, a simple A-frame structure open on both ends, built on a hill under a mango tree. A refreshing breeze comes through, a delight after having been crowded together in a closed-up house.

I arrived in time for supper and was pleased to be invited to eat with Ramon from our team, and his wife, Maura. I helped Maura make *pupusas* for supper, a special Salvadoran treat which consists of a tortilla stuffed with beans or cheese. Ramon's family has a cow, and so we had a type of cheese similar to cottage cheese for the pupusas. We also had fresh fish which Ramon had caught from the river Lempa. It is hard to imagine that something as good as this fish could come out of that river which for me only holds memories of death and fear. Ramon says that when the river goes down, it is a nice place to swim; some day we ought to go back and swim there.

Less than an hour ago, as I was picking up my pen to write, rumors came to us that soldiers were in the village. The people immediately panicked, saying, "Let's go into the house, close the door, and bolt it." Instead, two men and I walked from house to house asking who had heard the news and from whom. We finally discovered that two young boys had been sent out of the village about 3:00 p.m. to get the family's cows. They had seen three soldiers out there, but by the time they had rounded up the cows and returned home it was 5:00 p.m. They had told their mother who perhaps an hour later had told her neighbors. In fact no one had actually seen soldiers enter the village.

Situations like this fill the people with fear and keep them awake at night as they wait for something to happen. The fear drives the men out of their ranchitos to stay either in a house with more walls for protection or just out in the ravines. Some even go into the cornfield, saying they would not want to be in a house when a soldier comes there. They say if the soldiers decide to start shooting, they'll shoot at the ranchitos, but not into the open grass. Therefore it is safer in the fields.

November 13

Prudencia came into town from her village this morning. It was so good to see her again! We eagerly exchanged the latest news. She had not been to town for over a week, afraid to leave her family alone. I am so happy when she comes in to work with me! Prudencia is rapidly filling the void Barbara left, both in the work and in the desperately needed companionship and friendship.

We are getting ready for the end of the school year. The plan is to give basic literacy exams to the children at the end of the month. The children are excited about a written test, which seems so formal and official in their present disorganized, temporary living situation.

Last Saturday the teachers came to La Virtud for a final meeting. It was difficult to convince them that we needed to meet, but I told the immigration officer as well as the captain that all the teachers would be coming, stressing perhaps too forcefully that I was expecting them to have no problems whatsoever. The teachers did arrive without harassment from soldiers. We developed the tests with the teachers working in small groups, deciding the test questions themselves.

I was proud to see the teachers assuming leadership and working together. In the area of group process and leadership their growth has far exceeded my expectations. Not my test, but theirs will be handed out to the children in a few weeks. They made up the questions for reading, writing, and arithmetic, and today Prudencia and I copied the questions onto stencils. Tomorrow I will take them to Mapulaca, where a schoolteacher lets us use the mimeograph machine from their Honduran school.

Prudencia says the children are talking constantly about the testing; they are nervous with anticipation and have even asked for sample questions. In the past many children and adults felt the education was not all that serious because of our constant improvising—having no textbooks, sitting under trees, working with a chalkboard nailed to the tree, sitting on stones instead of benches, and using buildings that were little more than stables.

The talk about the testing is now helping to correct their attitude. We think that over 80 percent of the children in the schools have learned to read and write during the past eight months.

Late this afternoon I left the refugee camp to sit on a rock by the river and relax, away from the hubbub of the Caritas house. I stayed to have supper with Graciela and Ignacio, visiting until almost dark. A few months ago the distance from the camp to town would have presented no problem; but now as we get delayed in the camp, the short walk becomes filled with anxiety and dread.

I am afraid I will meet a soldier on that isolated stretch of road; worse yet, I am afraid they will see me from a distance and suspect me of some "subversive activity" because I am out at this hour. The common practice is to shoot without asking questions. I took the shortcut straight up the hillside, which we often prefer during the daytime not only because it is faster, but also because the path is shaded by trees along the way. It is a steep climb, but I knew this time my rapid heartbeat was more from fear than physical exertion.

With a sigh of relief I entered the Caritas house, only to be greeted by a scene of chaos. The room was in total disorder, as if we had just moved in an hour ago and were yet to be settled. The others were talking agitatedly, telling me I had missed the excitement by just a few minutes. Five Honduran soldiers had entered the house and searched the entire premises from top to bottom— through all our boxes of clothes, under the beds, in all the kitchen and cooking supplies. They did not leave a corner unturned and untouched, saying they had received word that the Caritas team had been distributing boots to guerrillas earlier that day and that they had come to pick up the evidence.

While allegedly looking for boots, they also searched every notebook and scrutinized each scrap of paper. Of course they were told we had never distributed shoes to the refugees.

"We are not asking you," was the short reply. "We have our orders to search your premises." Obviously they were frustrated at not discovering the evidence they had been looking for.

After they had finished the search, they announced the cap-

tain wanted to see Rafael and Teresa at the command post. This is
the first time a woman has been called in. My mind goes wild,
remembering the stories Salvadoran women tell of the treatment
they receive from Salvadoran soldiers. I doubt any of us will be
able to sleep tonight, filled as we are with anxiety. Powerlessness is
a terrible feeling, and it overwhelms me more each day. My initial
thought on awaking at dawn is no longer, "What shall I do today?" but rather, "What will happen to us today?" My stomach is
tied in knots from nervous tension. I wish I could cry to relieve
some of the tension, but tears don't come these days.

November 14

Rafael and Teresa are okay. Teresa was held only for about an
hour at the command post last night and not harmed physically,
only questioned at length about what kind of work she does and
why she makes so many trips to the villages. She and Rafael were
questioned separately. The captain gave Teresa a lecture about
getting too close to the refugees, saying they will only warp her
mind with lies, and indicated that for the sake of her own safety
she should return to her hometown. Then he allowed her to go to
the Caritas house.

Rafael was held overnight and had to sleep on a hard wooden
bench in the hallway of the command post where the night guard
could watch him. He was not harmed physically either, thank
God, but the captain did threaten him several times, warning him
not to be flippant with him and referring to Rafael's service in the
military a few years ago when he had chosen not to stay in the
army where he could be "secure." The captain pretended to take
Rafael into his confidence on the basis of his having served in the
army. He said he had evidence that many Caritas workers are
collaborating with the guerrillas and preaching subversion to the
refugees in the villages and the camp, and that Rafael had best
have nothing to do with the team. He told Rafael that the DNI is
keeping files on all of us, recording our actions and movements.

Again the captain mentioned that he knows the team is holding secret meetings and that he does not like it and will find out

when they are. He suggested several times in an offhand way that maybe Rafael has softened because of being away from military discipline for too long, and perhaps he should do some military calisthenics in the command post. Rafael had the distinct impression that the captain was threatening him with torture. But then this morning at nine o'clock a soldier told him the captain had said he could leave. When Rafael walked into the Caritas house I felt weak with relief at seeing him unharmed and smiling.

We certainly don't need any other problems with Honduran soldiers but we've got them. Two soldiers were killed and one was wounded in the Guarita area last night. The story is jumbled and confused; several versions have already run through the town. As I piece it together, the three soldiers were in civilian clothes, and had caused trouble at a small general store where they said they were Salvadoran guerrillas.

It's probable that local Hondurans shot them thinking they really were the guerrillas they pretended to be. But the captain said he believed they were shot by guerrillas. He is covering up the fact that the soldiers were in civilian clothes, a fact which the doctor who attended them confirms. The captain is trying to stir up more anti-refugee sentiment among the local Honduran population. We are concerned because soldiers in La Virtud are saying they will get revenge for those two lives.

Delia and I are spending the night in Mapulaca. We came over this afternoon to use the mimeograph machine in the local school. It was a long process to run off three pages of tests, both beginning and intermediate levels, for over one thousand children. We had supper with Delia's family and then went over to the radio to find out if any cars might give us a ride back to town. On the radio we picked up communications with the capital city. Once again Salvadoran soldiers have come into La Virtud. Later we heard from Eduardo that another curfew has been imposed and we should not plan to return because we would not be allowed in there after dark. I am enjoying my evening away from all the hassles and worry.

On Saturday evening the Caritas team usually gathers for

worship. It gives me an empty feeling to miss out on that tonight. Delia and I both commented on it and decided to read the Scriptures together; but it is not the same with just the two of us. In our Scripture reading we seem to turn most often to those passages which offer words of assurance and console us now that we have come under persecution.

I notice that my co-workers and I come to worship with an almost desperate hunger. We devour each reading, seeking consolation time and again, needing the certainty that our work is in fact following the example Christ set for us and is in line with Christ's teachings. "Feed the hungry, clothe the naked, visit those who are sick; whatever you do to the least of these my brothers and sisters, you do it unto me."

With the assurance we gain from the Scriptures comes a deep joy that undergirds all our days. Yet we need to reunite because we have fears, despite the assurance. How can we be both assured and fearful at once? My human side tells me to fear. I fear tonight for my co-workers, and I want to be with them because I know they are in danger. I wake up in the morning with the question, "What happened during the past hours? Which villages did the soldiers search and harass last night?"

My prayers at night as I lie in my hammock are fervent and often desperate. "God, protect the people out in the villages. Accompany those who may have to flee their homes in El Salvador tonight. Give them peace in their hearts. May they feel your comforting presence, whatever they have to endure."

The answers to my nighttime prayers come immediately. In La Majada this week, soldiers have come through three different nights before dawn, awakened families in their grass huts, and searched for weapons; but they have not taken a single person, nor raped any of the women, nor forced any of the men to return to El Salvador. These are the deep fears of the people.

God help us. God help the UNHCR representatives who are responsible for the security of these people. It is beyond me why an institution as powerful and as big as the United Nations cannot demand that the Honduran army cease the hostility against the refugees and tell the Salvadoran army that incursions into Honduran territory will no longer be tolerated. How much power does the UNHCR have? How much pressure can they bring to bear on the Honduran government, especially in the light of the U.S. military and economic aid to Honduras and U.S. wishes that Hondurans help the Salvadoran government in any way they can to stop the guerrilla warfare?

At what point does guerrilla warfare become legitimate? How many thousands have to flee the country, how many thousands have to say they support the guerrillas, before the guerrilla movement becomes a legitimate force in the country? One tenth of El Salvador's population has sought refuge in a dozen different countries, and many of them say they believe the rebels are fighting for their freedom.

November 15

Today was to be a relaxing day for the Caritas team. We had agreed to take the afternoon off to rest. As it turned out, we did take time off, but not as expected. Right after lunch Elpidio came into town, a Caritas volunteer who lives with his wife and children in the small village of Mescalar on the other side of the main road and down into the valley from La Majada. The village is located fairly close to the border, but has not had any refugees living in it since the July invasion of the Salvadoran National Guard. The people moved because they felt they were too close to the border.

Elpidio stopped by our house this afternoon to say he had received a note from the captain's sister who is a schoolteacher in Valladolid, far away from here. The note said the captain wanted to talk to him and he should come to the command post. Why would the captain's sister send such a note? If the captain needed to see Elpidio on official business, he could have sent a soldier or could have told him himself.

Elpidio hung around our house for a bit, unsure what to do; then he talked with some friends who don't work with Caritas and who know the latest gossip from the soldiers. Those people told Elpidio not to go to the command post, saying the captain had been "*muy bravo*" (irate and belligerent) for several days, especially since the report of the two Honduran soldiers killed in Guarita.

Against the advice of both the Caritas team and his other friends, Elpidio went into the command post. An hour later, at about 3:00 p.m., a local girl who sometimes volunteers with Caritas came by our house, obviously upset and nervous. She reported that the captain, another soldier, a refugee, and Elpidio had just left the command post in the captain's truck and had driven out of town in the direction of La Haciendita. Two hours later we saw the truck return, without Elpidio and without the other refugee. It can only mean that the two men have been killed.

Since a UNHCR representative was here, Eduardo asked him to go with him to the command post, Eduardo told the captain that he was looking for Elpidio, since they were scheduled to work together that evening. The captain replied, "Why are you asking me? I don't know who he is. I have not seen him nor talked to him today." That was the end of the discussion.

"Why Elpidio?" I keep asking over and over in my mind. If the captain wants to accuse anyone of working with the guerrillas, Elpidio is the last one he ought to accuse. There are no longer any refugees in his village. He is a quiet, shy man, and he served in the Honduran army when he was younger. It does not make sense to me.

None of us ate supper tonight. We weren't feeling hungry to begin with because of the situation, but the cooks had prepared supper, and we reluctantly sat down at the table. Just as we were taking our first bite, Celio walked in—I should say he stumbled through the doorway. We jumped up to help him to the table and got a wet cloth to wipe his dirty face. He said he had come from the command post.

Celio is a refugee from the village of Guajiniquil, a relatively calm place until now, even though it is fairly close to the border and in a direct line between the Salvadoran army outpost and the camps. Celio coordinates the refuge work in Guajiniquil for

Caritas. His position is difficult because of the mixed feelings of the Honduran families in his village. While some families show a generosity toward refugees that goes beyond everyone's expectations, others show hostility toward them.

Three soldiers appeared at Celio's door this morning and took him to the command post. Inside the post he was beaten on his back and legs with a stick and forced to do push-ups while being kicked; then he was hit in the head with heavy rubber tubing, forced to do calisthenics, and pushed around with the butt of the soldiers' rifles. When he was not tortured, he was forced to sit in the hot sun. He was not offered anything to eat or drink all day long. Beatings and torture went on intermittently the whole day. He showed us the lumps on his head and his back which is already swollen with welts. When the captain released him, his only remark was, "This will teach you a lesson."

We asked Celio what he thinks is behind the captain's actions. The only explanation he could think of was that some Honduran in his village might have accused him of something; other than that, he felt as bewildered as the rest of us about why he should be singled out.

November 17

Tonight I am sleeping in a hammock hung in the nutrition center down in the camps. Again I brought a candle with me to be able to write late into the night, wanting to record every detail of the nightmare of yesterday that we have miraculously survived. Sunday night, the fifteenth, the captain once again imposed a curfew, so we stayed in our house all evening. It was a quiet night, without a sound from outside.

The next morning we were just getting up and making our beds when Eduardo came in and quietly said, "Come outside and look at the front of the house." We found the front completely desecrated with slogans in red paint, saying, "Here we distribute food to the wives of guerrillas so that they can take the food up to the mountains."

Eduardo said the house of the French doctors had also been

painted. We went around the block to the front of the plaza to find the same red paint covering the windows of the doctors' jeep and the front of their house: "Here we give medicine to refugees and Salvadoran guerrillas, but not to Hondurans." The slogan on the house of the CEDEN workers around the corner said, "We are communists and we work with the subversives." All the slogans were signed MAACH, which stands for the Honduran anti-communist movement, recently organized in this country.

Charles, the UNHCR representative, and a military colonel happened to be visiting and had spent the night here too. But neither had much to say about the desecration of our houses. They had planned to leave by plane that morning, so I agreed to take them to the airstrip. When I returned to the Caritas house to get ready, I found Eduardo and Rafael already busy painting the front of our house with blue paint. Eduardo explained his own interpretation of the painting was that someone wanted to distinguish our houses from the others in town and that perhaps the plan is to bomb those which have been painted. This possibility had not even occurred to me. He also noted this happened on a night when soldiers were patrolling the streets and a curfew was on; the soldiers either did it themselves or gave permission for it to be done.

We left in the jeep at about 7:00 a.m. to drive to the airstrip which is on the road to Mapulaca, about twenty minutes away. But we had no more than gotten into the jeep and driven across the plaza when we were stopped at the command post for the most thorough and yet sloppy inspection we have ever received. The soldier went through every single paper, searched each person's bag, leafed through the French magazines the pilots had in their overnight bags, and spent a good fifteen minutes on every single passport pretending to read page after page of a language he could not understand.

Throughout all this, the soldier kept looking at his watch, giving the distinct impression that he was not so much searching us as trying to delay us until a designated time. It seemed curious to me that the colonel with us did not request that the process be speeded up, but instead remained very patient. At one point I sat down beside him on the steps and commented, "It seems an insult to do this to a colonel." He responded, "They are only doing their job."

An hour had passed before we were finally given permission to continue. We drove as quickly as we could to the small landing strip, when a peasant from a nearby village came running toward us with the news that he had found the plane on fire. We leaped out of the jeep and ran up to the airstrip. The ground under the plane was still smoldering. The person intending to sabotage the plane apparently did not have much experience with arson; all the person had done was uncap the gastanks in the wings, take some gas out, and sprinkle it on the grass underneath the plane. Of course the grass on the landing strip was cropped short, leaving little to burn away.

The peasant who saw the smoke and came running up was able to extinguish most of the fire underneath. He also threw dirt and grass on the wings, thinking the wings might catch on fire; so there was dirt in the gas tank, and the pilots had to syphon out all the gas and strain it before they could take off.

I drove on into Mapulaca which has radio communication with La Virtud, and radioed the team to tell them what had happened. They said another plane would be landing there shortly, and we should wait for it to pick up a new group of journalists. I finished some other business I had to do in town and was just about to head back to the landing strip when another call came over the radio. It was one of the French doctors saying they wanted the UNHCR representative to stay because they were worried something drastic might happen that day. I said I would do my best and rushed back toward the landing strip, only to hear the plane taking off. I had just missed them.

The other airplane arrived shortly afterwards, bringing a large group: a U.S. Congressional aide, two men from OXFAM America, representatives of the Presbyterian church, a French doctor, and celebrity Bianca Jagger. It added up to quite a carload.

We crammed all the luggage into the jeep, squeezed in ourselves, and drove back to La Virtud. Significantly there was no check as we came by the command post, except for a disinterested glance over the luggage. Nothing had to be opened; the soldier merely asked all the guests to go across the street to immigration and present their papers, a formality that had not been required before. It was almost noon by the time we arrived at the Caritas house, after a trip which normally takes forty-five minutes at the most. Today it took five hours, and I felt as if the day should have been ending instead of just beginning.

I got back just as the Caritas team was gathering around the lunch table for an emergency meeting. They saw a connection between Elpidio's abduction, our houses being painted, and the deaths of the two Honduran soldiers. The majority of the team insisted we should leave because the house had been marked; since the UNHCR was not offering protection, we were in too great a danger. Eduardo alone disagreed; but then, as I pointed out, he was under UNHCR protection as the coordinator. I myself was confused, having no idea what the others meant by "leaving" or what I should do as an international person.

As we were discussing and many were saying, "I am going to leave; Eduardo can stay if he wants," a little boy came running in, reporting that ten Salvadoran soldiers had come down the hill and walked into the command post. A few minutes later they had come out and gone into the captain's dining hall. We asked the boy to return to the plaza, keep an eye on them, and let us know about any changes.

We had continued our heated discussion about what to do when suddenly the boy burst in again, announcing the soldiers had gone into the camp. For a moment we sat in stunned silence. Then everyone jumped up as if one body. Eduardo told me tersely to run and get the journalists and get them down to the camp. The rest of the team members said, "Let's get out of here."

I ran to the house of the French doctors where the journalists were eating lunch, burst into the room, and shouted in Spanish that the Guardia had entered the camp. One of the journalists repeated in English, "The National Guard is in the refugee camp."

The group reacted quickly. They jumped up from the table without a moment's hesitation, rushed out the door, and headed toward the camp—some on foot, others in the jeep. I stayed behind in the French doctors' house to comfort their cook, Angelica, who is Graciela's sister. Angelica was beside herself with fear, knowing all her family was down there. She cried uncontrollably. I held her, desperately trying to think of what I might say to console her, but knowing that in this situation nothing could be said. I knew she needed to be with her family, so I suggested she go on down to the camp.

I returned to the Caritas house where a remnant of the team was hurriedly packing up their things. I could not bear it, unable to understand why they were leaving, still unaware that they were in even greater danger than the refugees. Miguel turned to me at one point and said, "Look, Elpidio is gone, and we are next."

"What should I do?" I asked him.

He replied, "They won't hurt you. You are not Honduran. Get down to the camp and help."

I obeyed. As I hurried around the bend of the last hill, I saw the jeep of the French doctors parked in the middle of the road and a large group of refugees standing at the entrance of the camp wringing their hands and crying. They said that soldiers and some ORDEN men in civilian clothes had walked through the camp and collected a group of about thirty people, including men, women, and children. They had not meant to take that many, but family members had protested their loved ones' being taken, and those who had objected were simply taken also. A woman told me that Graciela had been taken along with her mother Marcelina, an eighty-year-old woman. Graciela's children found me, hung on to my skirt, and we all stood there crying. The refugees, I was told, had been led out of the camp with their thumbs tied behind their backs.

When the journalists arrived in the car, the soldiers were in the process of leading the refugees across the road and up the hill in the direction of El Salvador. One soldier knelt down and aimed his rifle at the jeep, telling them to halt. People stayed in the truck and did not move while the gun was pointed at them, watching all the refugees being led across the road and into the riverbed out of sight. But as soon as the soldier left, the journalists jumped out of the car and started running after them.

This was all we knew. We stood around waiting, praying that those internationals along with the refugees would not be taken prisoner and disappear into El Salvador. Suddenly, after about ten minutes which seemed like an eternity, a few of the refugees appeared at the bend in the river, greeted by hugs, tears, and a flood of questions. They were exhausted and obviously in shock, but they related that the journalists had caught up with them and had begun shouting and pointing at their cameras: "We are the international press. We are taking your pictures. Tomorrow the whole world will know what you are doing and see the crime you have committed. Let the people go! Let the people go!"

The soldiers were so surprised by the journalists following them that they did stop short for a moment, but then continued walking. At the insistent cries of the journalists they stopped again, undecided for a moment. Then they let their prisoners go. The journalists stayed until the last refugee had been released and until the last soldier had headed up the mountain toward El Salvador. Only then did they follow the group back down the riverbed.

What excitement! It was a chaotic moment of tears and hugs and explanations and disbelief that everyone was still alive. People pointed to the red marks left on their thumbs caused by the string which had bound them. Regina, a fourteen-year-old girl who works in our schools, found me and sobbed in my arms. She had been so frightened, thinking she would be killed. A thought ran through my mind, "We all know the ORDEN people don't kill the girls. They keep them for their own sexual gratification." Thank God she was back, alive and unharmed.

It seemed like the event was over when it had hardly begun. But suddenly a little boy tugged at my skirt saying there were more soldiers inside the camp. I looked in the direction he pointed and saw another seven men tied by their thumbs, being led away at gunpoint by four soldiers who wanted to take them up the mountainside. Patrick, one of the French nurses, ran right up to the group of soldiers and pointed his camera at them, again shouting that he was taking their picture and they had better stop. One soldier turned around and pointed his gun at Patrick who immediately said, "I'll give you my film if you give me the people. Let's make a trade. You can have my camera if you give me those men."

The soldiers hesitated, but on seeing a crowd gather around them and noticing many people taking pictures, they became more disconcerted. They insisted on taking the film out of all the cameras they had seen; but two people succeeded in concealing their cameras, so I think several pictures will get out of here as evidence. On gathering up the film the soldiers did release the seven men and began walking up the hillside toward El Salvador.

While everyone else had rushed into the camp to stop the second group of soldiers, Bob, a U.S. Congressional aide, and I ran to the other side of the river across the bridge in the direction the soldiers were going. Dear God, I don't know why we thought we might be of help over there. I guess we thought we would get one more chance to confront the soldiers in case the others should not manage to stop them. Our idea was to be between the soldiers and the border if they came that way. We hid in the corn, ready to confront them, until it was obvious that they had let everyone go. Then we crawled through the corn down to the camp along the river's edge where they would not see us. As I look back on our maneuver, I wonder what on earth we thought we were going to do to four armed soldiers.

Two of the internationals made a smarter move. They went in search of the captain to report the presence of ORDEN people in the camp. Much to all our surprise, he responded that he could not send his soldiers to protect the refugees because he had already lost two men (referring to the two soldiers killed in Guarita on Nov. 14).

Now as I reflect on today's events it does not seem possible that all the refugees came through alive. When the episode was over I climbed the hill back to the Caritas house. It was practically empty. Our truck driver Arturo sat in the pickup ready to take off with Rafael and Teresa. They are going back to their home, about seven hours away from here, and are taking Reina and Manuelito, the orphans who stayed with us. All their belongings were piled into the back of the truck. When I asked Arturo what he was going to do with the truck, he said he would leave it at the headquarters of the diocese in Santa Rosa.

I am worried about my co-workers. Will I ever see them again? They have been my family here for many months. The fact that I don't have to flee because of the color of my skin and the passport I carry is painfully unfair. I keep wondering whether I should have gone with them. Where is my first loyalty—to my co-workers or to the job? Deep inside I know that while I want to be with them, someone has to stay here and continue the work.

Delia, the cooks, and I locked up the house and went down to the camp. We found the people still traumatized, needing to talk and remain near each other. Graciela told me in detail about her experience. The ORDEN men had come to their tent, grabbed Ignacio, and tied his thumbs behind his back. Graciela angrily protested, pulling at the arms of the paramilitaries. They shoved her roughly to the ground, which brought frightened cries from the five children.

Graciela jumped up and tried to block the way, a futile effort against so many opponents. The men simply dragged her along with Ignacio, leaving all the children with their grandmother crying and shouting from the entrance of the tent. When the toddler broke away from his grandmother to run after Graciela, the other children followed, although Marcelina tried to stop them. Graciela snatched the two youngest children up in her arms while the ORDEN men pushed Marcelina into the group of prisoners, one making a remark that they preferred their whores younger, but she would serve as well. Graciela was forced to march with the two infants in her arms.

"Why did you argue with the paramilitaries?" I asked her. "Weren't you afraid to confront them?"

"This wasn't the first time I have been treated badly by soldiers or paramilitaries," she replied. "After a few times it is better to risk death than to lose one's dignity. I cannot stand by silently when they take away the people I love."

Graciela is not the only one badly shaken and needing the comfort of the large group. Tonight the refugees whose tents are in the outside rows brought their blankets to the center and lay down together on the ground between the rows of tents. The crowdedness feels safer in case the soldiers should return. All the international staff are down here as well, spread out among the people. We may lie down, but few will sleep tonight.

A large group of refugees gathered a while ago in their chapel tent to recite their rosaries, to pray for the people in the villages, and to reaffirm their faith in the midst of fear and desolation. The words of their songs are comforting. "I will sing unto the God of the children of Israel, the God of Moses who led his people out of slavery and bondage. The same God will give us courage and strength and be our guide on the way to liberation."

November 18

After weeks of insisting that La Virtud needs a permanent representative from the UNHCR, we finally saw him arrive today from Costa Rica, a Swede named Ingmar. I hope things will change with his presence here. We all feel encouraged after talking with him; he seems able to stand up to the games the military are playing with us.

Late this afternoon word came that the Salvadoran National Guard, who were roaming through La Haciendita, had gone back to El Salvador; so Eduardo and I, along with Patrick, Ingmar, and one of Elpidio's brothers, walked to La Haciendita to meet with people willing to talk about what they had witnessed.

In the first house people told us that last Sunday the captain and a soldier had parked their truck in front of their home and left the village with two men, one of them Elpidio whom someone knew personally, and the other a Salvadoran refugee whom several recognized as living in La Virtud. They were obviously led away as prisoners, each with a large sack of powdered milk on his back.

We walked through the town and out into the countryside in the direction of El Salvador, talking with Honduran families along the way. They continued to point in the direction the soldiers and their prisoners had gone, until we reached the last houses on the Honduran side of the border. The people willingly and openly pieced the rest of the story together. They said the captain had led the way; then came two blindfolded prisoners, and finally a soldier who kept prodding the prisoners with the point of his gun.

They were in front of the last few houses of the village when the refugee prisoner stumbled and told the soldiers he could not go any farther with the blindfold on. So the soldier removed it, but as soon as he did, the refugee threw the heavy sack of powdered milk off his back into the face of the soldier, ran toward the refugee homes where a group of maybe fifteen children stood, and disappeared behind the children. The soldier fired in the general direction but did not hit anyone. The refugee ran into the thick underbrush along the trail. Rather than go after him, the soldier put the second bag of powdered milk on Elpidio's back and forced him to keep going.

The people continued their story saying the group had been out of their sight for only a few minutes when they heard gunshots. Some time later the soldier and the captain returned by the same path, got into his truck, and drove off. The people knew Elpidio had been killed and dragged for some distance. They could tell by the blood on the ground and the signs of something heavy being dragged. Also, one of the bags of powdered milk had spilt and left a trail. The soldier had kicked dirt over it to cover up the trace.

We asked if anyone had found Elpidio's body. No one was ready to commit himself, but many made references to the vultures flying around. After much discussion we found two boys willing to lead us in the direction where they had seen the vultures. We hiked the mountain paths for maybe half an hour, then stopped to catch our breath while Eduardo pointed out where Honduras ended and El Salvador began, at the beginning of the sloping valley before us.

The stench and the vultures led us to Elpidio's body. The sight of his flesh, torn apart and picked over by the vultures, was nauseating. As we looked at the lifeless form in silence, I said over and over in my head, "This is Elpidio. This is Elpidio." I was somehow trying to connect the friend I remembered with this form, but did not succeed. The vultures had already eaten most of the flesh off the head and upper torso. The bones of both arms were picked over and flung a few feet from the body. There was little flesh left on the rib cage, but the lower half of the body was still intact. One boot was flung to the side, the other still in place; and it was by the boots and the pants that Elpidio's brother identified the corpse. He picked up one of the boots and put it in his small backpack to keep as evidence.

We did not speak much—there was nothing to say—and we did not stay long because of the stench and the huge vultures who were obviously upset at being interrupted in their meal. Most nauseating was the presence of a dead dog which had been tied next to the body and shot. The act seemed so senseless and con-fusing. The dog's body had not been touched by the vultures and had not begun to decay, so it probably had been killed more recently.

"Why would anyone do that?" I asked, bewildered. No one seemed to have a response, until one of the boys mentioned that for the last three days Salvadoran soldiers had been patrolling the area. It was their way of saying, "This man was a dog." The boy also said Salvadoran soldiers who had come to their house asking for food had mentioned to each other that they were drinking milk—apparently the supply Elpidio had been forced to carry on his back.

We began walking back to La Haciendita, stopping here and there to talk to some more Hondurans and asking whether they would be willing to testify against the captain to prove he killed

Elpidio. The Hondurans readily agreed. We drove back to La
Virtud and went into the house of the French doctors to discuss
what to do next. We decided we would ask for a meeting with the
captain to question him specifically about Elpidio.

November 19

I am so angry and full of other emotions tonight that I can
hardly collect my thoughts and put them on paper. I spent the
entire day hiking to different villages to talk with the Caritas coordinators and the refugees. Eduardo sent me because I am the only
one left from the team who knows all the villages and the rest of
the committee workers. I was to tell them that we will have no
more meetings for an indefinite period, and they should carry on
their work as well as they can, coming in only on days of food distribution for their village and finding some time to talk during
these distribution hours. It will be best to make it appear that
Caritas has completely fallen apart organizationally.

Talking with the refugees was difficult. I am full of anxiety
and uncertainty myself, and find it hard to reassure anyone else.
Our future is entirely uncertain here; in no way can I promise
them that our situation will improve. I asked in several villages
whether they have any idea where the Caritas workers have gone;
no one knows anything. I am so preoccupied with worry about
them that I can hardly think of anything else.

I came back to town late this afternoon only to find the camp
in an uproar. A representative from the UNHCR, along with the
Honduran colonel who was the government representative to the
refugee program, had flown in and called a meeting with the
refugees to tell them they have two options: voluntarily be
relocated to a new camp fifty miles away, called "Mesa Grande,"
or voluntarily return to El Salvador. No one will be allowed to
remain in La Virtud.

The discussion became heated and intense. Apparently after
the two officials had made their speeches they asked whether
there were any questions, and were surprised to find that the
refugees had not only questions but also opinions. They inquired

about the living conditions in the new area and about the attitude of the surrounding Honduran population concerning them; they asked whether this was a short-term solution, and whether they would be allowed to stay together as one large group or would be scattered; and they brought up the sensitive question of security, asking outright what guarantee the UNHCR would give that the present harassment by the Honduran military will cease in the new camp.

The UNHCR representative responded that the new camp will be much less crowded, with a tent allotted to each family and with more space between the tents; that there will be land for the refugees to cultivate; that the Honduran population near them is cooperative and amiable; and that this particular group of refugees which comes from one area of El Salvador would not be broken up.

The question of security was the most explosive issue discussed. The colonel calmly tried to explain that the Honduran army feels defensive and hostile because of the difficult location so close to the border and the presence of the Salvadoran military just over the mountain ridge. He maintained that when the refugees get away from the border there would be no further reason for the soldiers to feel such defensiveness, and the situation would improve. The UNHCR representative went even further, saying the new camp will be considered United Nations territory rather than Honduran territory, because it has been purchased by the United Nations.

One of the refugees responded, giving his own interpretation. "The Honduran military consider us guerrillas. None of us has any confidence that they will change their opinion; therefore we want definite assurance from the UNHCR that we will be given more protection in the new location. If the UNHCR cannot promise that, most of us will choose to go home to El Salvador." His final statement was almost a slap in the face of the colonel: "If we are going to die, we want to die in our own country and not in a foreign land at the hands of a foreign army." The colonel chose not to respond to the speech, obviously angered by it.

Tonight I suggested to my co-workers that the three of us who are left should continue to meet, plan, and strategize. Eduardo's bitter response was, "How can you call three a team?" I am sure he feels hurt and very alone, but so do Delia and I. It would help so much if we could continue to support each other. But Eduardo has closed himself off, giving orders without explanations. I asked his opinion on several issues, including the meeting down in the camp, but his replies were terse, cynical, and bitter. He must be angered and frightened by the continual threats we hear through the rumor network in town, most of which are against him as coordinator of the refugee work.

I try to understand and not take it personally, but it is painful to realize he has rejected Delia and me. He says he has been trying to contact the Caritas committee in Santa Rosa but has received no response all day. Part of his bitterness stems from the fact that not a word of support or caring has come over the radio from other priests or the bishop. It was only in this part of our discussion that Eduardo allowed his emotions to show, angrily explaining he had made it clear on the radio that the Caritas team had disappeared and that they immediately needed a priest up here, or someone who could speak from an authoritative position. It has been two days, and we have heard nothing from Santa Rosa. Delia and I comfort each other by being together, but we are too preoccupied with anxiety over the welfare of the rest of our team. The uncertainty is difficult to live with.

November 20

Eduardo came over this morning saying that a news team from the U.S. had arrived who wanted to be taken to the place where Elpidio was murdered. Eduardo preferred not to be seen taking people to La Haciendita, but I was still so angry with the captain that I felt reckless and said, "Yes, I'll take the group out there." The news team came to the Caritas house, and we were just exchanging names and shaking hands when Victoria, Elpidio's wife, walked in and introduced herself: "I am *'la viuda'*—the widow." She wanted to go along with us to see

Elpidio's body also. We borrowed a jeep from the French doctors and set out for La Haciendita.

Upon arrival in the village, people went into their houses and closed the doors, obviously not wanting to have anything to do with us. The few who did not shut us out were reluctant to talk to us. I asked if any soldiers had been in the area during the last day or two, and when they shook their heads, I asked if the children who had accompanied us on our first visit could go with us again to make sure we found the right path. The little boys did not want to go with us; it took quite a bit of persuasion before they finally agreed.

We repeated the long, dusty hike through the hills and again watched for the vultures to be able to locate Elpidio's body. Elpidio was killed five days ago, but I was not prepared for the extent to which the body had decomposed, nor had I expected the destruction the hungry vultures had brought about in just five days. When we came out here two days ago, the legs were fully intact. Today we found that the leg bones from the knee down had been picked clean. I imagine in another two days nothing will be left except the skeleton.

I ached for Victoria, regretting that she had not been able to come with us earlier. The journalists asked her if she was sure it was her husband. She said yes, but all she could recognize were the pants. There was nothing else to go by—no shirt, no facial features. It will be difficult for her to accept his death. In no way will we be able to give this body a proper burial, and because of that there is no finality to his life. All Victoria will feel is his absence from her family.

We stayed only a few minutes before we were driven away by the odor of the decomposing flesh, and we made the long, hot hike back home in silence. When we came upon some Hondurans living at the edge of the village, the news team wanted to interview them. Their unwillingness to comment on what they had seen and heard last week stood out in stark contrast to their talkativeness when we came through a few days ago. I am sure they have been threatened by someone.

Back in La Virtud I offered Victoria a cup of coffee. Neither of us said much, still numb from the day's experience. Before she left, I asked her what she would do now, and to my surprise she said, "I'll carry on with the church work my husband was doing." Her response gave me new courage and hope. The soldiers are trying so hard to intimidate us, but they haven't succeeded in scaring away Victoria and her children.

This evening we heard on the ham radio that the refugees from Valladolid are being relocated to Mesa Grande. We didn't think this would happen until after Christmas, and now that they have already started in Valladolid, I wonder whether we won't be relocated sooner also. The rumors about Mesa Grande are running rampant and frighten many people here.

I, too, am worried. Mostly the rumors are discouraging descriptions of the living conditions. Allegedly there are not enough tents for the newly arriving refugees, so that people have to sleep out in the open. They also say that there is not enough water or food. I feel pressure from the refugees to try to calm their fears and answer their questions about the unknown future, but I am reluctant to do so because I don't want to be lying to them. It may be as bad as they say it is at Mesa Grande.

November 21

I have been eating breakfast with the French doctors lately. The past week's events have brought us all closer together, and now that my co-workers are gone, I need their company. When I walked into their house this morning, I found them frantically packing to leave. Surprised and bewildered, I asked the reason. They answered that their program director in the capital city had called them to Tegucigalpa for a meeting because he was contemplating pulling out of the country. I could not believe the doctors would leave the refugees in this time of crisis, and I found myself desperately trying to convince them to stay, despite the request from their director.

"Couldn't you ask the director to come here?" I asked. They responded they might be gone for only a few days but felt they needed to pack up everything in case the director decided to pull the entire program out of the country. It is such a letdown. After all the talk of not letting the military scare us away with threats, accusations, and harassment, the French doctors were now giving in. As they loaded their last suitcase into the back of the jeep and drove off, I felt the tears welling up. I walked into the empty house and wept. How will we manage to keep the clinics running now?

In the afternoon schoolteachers came into town from the villages seeking advice, reassurance, and some clarity as to what the future holds; but I myself was so needy today that I did not offer them much. It must have been disappointing for them. The schoolteachers wanted to know what we would do about the final exams we had planned to give the day after tomorrow. I could hardly care less about final exams and schools. To try to carry on as if nothing is wrong seems so futile to me! But I did my best, and although none of the villages had been able to hold classes this past week, we decided the teachers should try to give the exams; so they all took copies of the tests back with them to the villages. I seriously doubt the children will come to school on Monday. They are too frightened to leave their parents, even though in most cases their grass huts are in sight of the school building.

November 23

The refugees are more adept at coping with chaos and uncertainty than the rest of us are. They have filled the gaps of leadership left by the departing international workers and the Caritas staff. In the midst of this crisis, when we needed to continue the refugee food distribution that Caritas had been in charge of, the refugees stepped in and completed the task without any difficulty. I am amazed at the smoothness with which the camp is running on its own leadership. The men, with no outside help, have organized groups to continue the harvest of corn and beans which are dried and ready to be collected. Perhaps living in a war-torn country has taught them to go on as best they can, even in emergencies.

I feel I am getting more directions from the refugees on what needs to be done than from Eduardo, who virtually has ceased to function as the coordinator. I understand how Eduardo feels. We still have heard nothing from the regional office in Santa Rosa or from any of the other priests. The volunteers from the other agencies all received word from their national directors and were advised about how to proceed, but Caritas has had no communication. I have been going to the villages on my own, knowing this needs to be done. But I wish Eduardo would give more direction, in spite of his disappointment and the sense of abandonment we all have. I was grateful for the few times he gave me a concrete assignment, because these days it helps just to obey, without having to think.

November 24

Last night someone tried to set Eduardo's house on fire. A stack of lumber, still waiting to be made into school benches, had been piled up outside of his house. Someone poured gasoline on it and set it afire during the curfew hours. Badly shaken by the experience, Eduardo stated today that he wants the UNHCR representative to sleep at his house or else he will resign from his position.

People in town say the leaders of the National Party, the most conservative party, have been boasting that they are the ones who set the wood on fire. The town is getting more and more tense as we approach election day, particularly since those of the conservative party insist they will make sure that the area is cleared of refugees before the elections.

This afternoon we risked having a meeting with a representative from each village and gratefully were not interrupted by soldiers. The major point of the meeting was to discuss what was to happen on election day. Eduardo gave simple instructions: "On November 29 no refugee is to be out walking through the hills or to try to come into town. Everyone should stay home. If refugees are seen, this may easily provoke accusations that one party expanded their number of votes by getting refugees to vote in their favor. All refugees living with Honduran families here in La Virtud are to spend election day down in the refugee camp, so we can be assured that no refugees will be around when people go to the polls. Do you have any questions?"

Of course the people had no questions about those instructions in particular, but they had many questions about the future: when would the relocation begin; what would they be able to take along to the new camp; what was to become of the projects like the crafts and the agricultural program? Eduardo could not answer them. He asked for an update on what had been happening in their villages. Almost all had reports of harassment by Honduran soldiers and of regularly sighting Salvadoran soldiers walking through their areas. The place we are most worried about is Mescalar, Victoria's village. Salvadoran soldiers have come through almost daily, searching the huts of the few remaining refugee families. The people are fearful. After the meeting I asked Eduardo if I should go spend the night in Mescalar. He responded, "No, it's too dangerous. The people will just have to do the best they can."

November 27

Two priests of the diocese finally arrived yesterday. Eduardo, Delia, and I spent the better part of the afternoon with them. I found it difficult to talk because of my anger. "Why did it take you so long to come?" we asked. They said that twice they had tried to come, but both times Honduran soldiers had stopped them and forbidden them to go any nearer to the border. The first time they could not even get out of Santa Rosa. They were told in no uncertain terms that any priests who tried to go into the border area would be killed. A few days later they attempted to leave without asking permission, but got only as far as Vallodolid until the military stopped them again.

I found it difficult to see their perspective. All I could think was, two times they tried to come in the past week and a half. What were they doing all the other days? Why didn't they at least communicate to us that they had tried to come but were unable to get through? Couldn't they have radioed us? True, the military listens in on our radio communication, but that should not have stopped the priests from sharing the necessary information.

We discussed unfinished tasks and the division of work among those of us who are left. We are in better condition now regarding security than we have been for several weeks. Jon Alpert and his television crew have offered to stay through the elections to lend an international presence. In addition, the National Council of Churches in the U.S. has sent four international observers, all of whom speak Spanish and have had years of experience in Latin America. We have been sending them out to sleep in a different village every night.

With the quick person-to-person communication in these mountains, even Salvadoran soldiers seem to know when foreigners are present in a village and might witness their coming. While the Salvadoran military is intent on persecuting the refugees, they are deterred by anyone who can make an international issue of what they are doing. Aside from the TV crew and the representatives from the NCC, the CONCERN staff also has two visitors here, so we feel we are well-covered for the upcoming elections. I am going away for a few days' rest. What I want more than anything is to sleep through an entire night without hearing gunfire.

Two members of the Caritas staff, Julia and Paolo, have returned from hiding. Five others have sent word that they are safe but will not return. Early yesterday morning someone came in from Los Hernandez with a note addressed to Eduardo and me. It was from the rest of the team who said they wanted to talk with one of us. Would we come to Los Hernandez to meet them? Eduardo sent me, refusing to go himself. He has not gone more than two blocks from his house since the attempted arson, saying he feels his only security is to stay within arm's reach of the UNHCR representative.

I returned to Los Hernandez with the man who had brought the note. He took me to a house I had never been to before, and in a back room I found Miguel. The relief that exploded inside me on seeing him helps me understand the trauma Salvadoran families go through when one of their family members disappears. To live day in and day out not knowing whether a loved one has been killed or is suffering from torture must be even worse than the anguish I felt not knowing where my co-workers were.

Miguel and I talked for a long time. I shared what had happened since the team left, and he told me where they had been and what they have decided. They sent a message back with me stating that they feel their lives are in danger in La Virtud and they will stay in hiding until they know whether the church-at-large in Honduras, and particularly Caritas at the national level, supports their work. The church still has not made a public pronouncement condemning the killing of Elpidio. The five who are in hiding, as well as the more than fifty Caritas volunteers in the villages, all feel the church's betrayal. Not a single word of support, defense, or encouragement has come.

The message my co-workers sent back with me stated that the team would return only under two conditions. One, the church must issue some statement to defend the Caritas workers against the lies and accusations flung at them. Two, the UNHCR must offer them the same security they offer the international workers and give them identification papers which would put them under the jurisdiction of the UNHCR.

One bright note in today's meeting: Caritas of Belgium has sent a volunteer to work with us. Her name is Helena. She is here for six months, and she has been sent to work with the education program. How ironic that just as the school project falls apart, Caritas finally responds to our pleas for more help! Helena's contract was arranged long before our crisis broke, but she seems to be coping very well as we have tried to fill her in on the last week's events. I am most grateful that she seems able to take over what little is yet to be done on the education project and work with Delia, so that I am freed to carry on the work of my co-workers out in the villages.

Late this afternoon, as we were in the office trying to give her an overview of the school project, teachers began arriving from the villages with the tests the children had completed. In most cases the teachers were disillusioned that our hard work and preparation for the exams had seemingly been for nothing. Less than half of the children showed up to take the exam, and they were so nervous that they jumped every time a twig snapped. So we doubt that we will get any kind of conclusive data from the tests. Nevertheless, Helena and Delia will begin the evaluation tomorrow morning.

Eduardo told me tonight that this morning the few remaining refugee families from Mescalar were loaded onto trucks and sent to Mesa Grande. He said he didn't want to tell me yesterday because he knew how upset I would be. He went out to the village this morning with the UNHCR and CEDEN staffs, after relocation of refugees from Guarita to Mesa Grande. Mescalar was relocated early for two reasons. First, the relocation in the Guarita area was completed two weeks earlier than the UNHCR staff had expected, because more than half of the refugees chose to return home to El Salvador rather than risk going farther into the interior of Honduras. Accordingly, our projected date for relocation had been moved up. Second, the refugees left in Mescalar felt so threatened by Salvadoran soldiers that the UNHCR decided to relocate them right away. So the move we have all been resisting for months is now a reality.

I had no personal opinion about the relocation, but the people I am here to serve, the refugees, always adamantly opposed moving further into Honduras. I, along with the rest of the Caritas staff and the French doctors, felt I should support the position of the people. The tactic of the military has been to let events convince us that relocation is our only choice. I despairingly admit that the tactic has worked in Mescalar, because the people see the relocation as a lesser evil than the psychological trauma they have been suffering closer to their homeland.

December 2

I am back after four marvelous days at the seashore on Honduras' Atlantic coast. Four nights without gunfire or mortar shelling! Accompanied by a friend from home, I walked the sandy shore and talked and played in the sparkling aqua-blue waters of the Caribbean. We stayed in a beach house owned by some priests, a simple one-room house with a screened-in porch, kerosene lamp light, and an outhouse. A hand pump supplied water for drinking and washing off the salt water. The beach house is in a small coconut grove. We hung our hammocks between coconut palms and soaked in the silence, broken only by the songs of the birds and the occasional thud of a falling coconut. The sun and salt water worked their healing touch on the flea and mosquito bites covering my legs. The silence and good company soothed my taut nerves. The fresh saltwater fish, fried in oil just squeezed from coconuts, was a delightful change from beans and tortillas. And the four-day rest also gave me time and space to grieve.

I thought about the Caritas team, how good it would have been to take a retreat together. It was difficult to fight off the momentary stabs of guilt which came each time I thought of the refugees. I feel a deep oneness with them in their suffering, but I can leave at any time. They cannot. I thought about Caritas, too. Should I resign to protest the way my co-workers have been abandoned by the organization? It has been two weeks since Elpidio was killed. The church is silent. What is wrong? Is it unrealistic to expect the church to respond within two weeks? Am I too quick to judge in my pain?

The bishop and other church leaders call people to do the works of mercy, but when these result in persecution, the church does not stand by them. The institutional church is so rigid that it has difficulty being the true church. Everyone talks about the church helping the refugees, but in fact it is the other way around. The church comes to minister to the poor, and there, in the midst of the poor and the suffering, the church encounters God and finds salvation.

Honduras made it through the elections without a military coup. On the national level the Liberal Party won by a large majority, but here in La Virtud, as predicted, the National Party won.

Election day passed without any major incident between the refugees and the soldiers or the townspeople. The few potentially explosive moments passed without problems. On Saturday night before the elections, the National Party brought in a film called *Attack on the Americas*, made by the American Security Council in the U.S.° The local party showed the film on the wall of the municipal building in the plaza. Just the excitement of having a movie in this town where nothing happens on weekend evenings was enough to bring out a majority of the local people.

The movie is a right-wing analysis of the Central American conflict, basically portraying the conflict as caused by Soviet-style communists who are invading the region and brainwashing people with plans to take over one country after another, slowly moving north and gradually arriving at the southern border of the United States.

Bringing in this film was a sly move on the part of the National Party. The people are already insecure about the war in El Salvador. Their fears offered fertile ground for all the reactionary messages the National Party brought. After the film, the National Party members gave speeches in the plaza, reiterating the main points of the film and criticizing the Liberal Party for having what they called "communist tendencies." They said the National Party will make sure that Honduras does not fall to the communists.

December 4

Helena and Delia have started Christmas clubs for the children in the camp. This was Helena's idea, and it is a great one.

°The American Security Council grew out of the Mid-American Research Library, founded in the mid-1950s. Initially its focus was on internal security matters, and it inherited the files of Senator Joseph McCarthy. Now its membership of mainly retired military personnel, defense contractors, and politicians focuses on foreign policy issues. In 1978, the ASC set up the Coalition for Peace Through Strength which actively lobbied against the SALT negotiations and the Panama Canal treaty. The ASC has been called the "heart and soul of the military-industrial complex." Its motto is, "We have to win the cold war." Its headquarters are located in Boston, Virginia.

The children desperately need something to keep them busy now that school is out for the month. It is not good for them to sit in their tents listening to their parents' talk about the uncertain future. The clubs are just right to get them excited about Christmas and to keep them out of mischief.

Harassment by Salvadoran and Honduran soldiers continues in most villages. The incidents are small, such as a few soldiers being sighted walking around the edge of the village or coming in to ask for a certain person whom the refugees may or may not know. The harassment is just enough to wear away at people's determination to stay close to their homeland. The Honduran soldiers are expressing more and more hostility toward their own people, the Honduran families who either work with Caritas or have opened their homes to the refugees.

The hostility is expressed subtly; for example, soldiers talk to families who have not helped with the refugees and make slanderous remarks about their neighbors, creating tensions between people who previously had had cordial relationships. As the refugees see their Honduran friends becoming isolated in this way, they begin to fear what might happen to the Hondurans once all the refugees have been forced to leave the area. In Guarita, from which all refugees have been moved, the military is threatening and harassing Honduran families who previously opened their homes to the refugees. It seems as though they are guilty by mere association with Salvadorans.

The only village in our region that has been relocated so far is Mescalar. Most families left there are related to Elpidio. Victoria, his widow, has been threatened several times by Honduran soldiers. Their aim is to stop the investigation against the captain by the UNHCR. Soldiers told Victoria that her family will see more of its blood spilled if the investigation continues. They have maintained an around-the-clock surveillance of her house for several days, telling neighbors they want to see if Victoria will speak to any more UNHCR representatives or journalists.

The soldiers also warned Elpidio's brother that Victoria had better not testify. The local judge who had to identify Elpidio's body has also been told by soldiers to drop the investigation. No one in La Haciendita will talk to the UNHCR representative now that their testimonies are needed, so it appears that the captain will never be brought to trial. The UNHCR representative here seems to have resigned himself to seeing his investigation obstructed. He is so unassertive that the soldiers, rather than being warned not to repeat this crime, now clearly know they can get away with it.

December 5

The captain has been replaced by a lieutenant. It is not a significant change for us. We know the lieutenant from several months ago when he was assigned here. I would characterize him as a sly and conniving man, definitely disagreeable. I am sure the captain was pulled out because of the investigation against him. This is the way the judicial system works in this country.

The soldiers are getting more brazen every day. This morning ten Salvadoran soldiers came down the mountainside, walked right through the middle of town in broad daylight, and entered the command post. Later they left with the lieutenant and headed up the path to La Cuesta, which is also the return path to El Salvador. Whenever this has happened in the past, a crisis has followed, so we are all worried.

Sister Irma, the regional coordinator of Caritas, came today from Santa Rosa. Finally we have a sense that someone at the national level does care about what is going on here. Irma brought the news that on December 10, Bishop Rodriguez from Santa Rosa will come to visit us, along with the national Caritas director and the bishop from Tegucigalpa who is also the national president of Caritas. Irma called a meeting for all the volunteers who have been serving in the villages.

By midafternoon, a large group had assembled. Irma talked about Caritas' indecision on whether to continue the work or not, and about some of the difficulties of making a statement at the national level regarding the situation at the border. She did assure us, though, that other Caritas groups around the country have heard of Elpidio's death and of the persecution we are suffering.

Her update on the living conditions in Mesa Grande was depressing. At the national level several of the agencies are trying to convince the government that the relocation must slow down, although Irma made no predictions about the government's or the UNHCR's response. She encouraged the volunteers to describe the situation in their aldeas and asked how they felt about the Caritas leaders having fled.

"Do any of you feel such danger that you would like to go to Mesa Grande or another part of the country?" Irma inquired. I was surprised to hear only two families express such concern over the danger in their village that they wanted to move. One was Victoria. Irma promised her she could go to Mesa Grande with her two children when the next group of refugees is relocated.

Irma explained the move would mean living as the refugees do, receiving the same food allotment, living in a tent, and basically joining the refugee society. The other person who wanted to move with his family was Lucío Aguirre. I don't know Lucío very well, but his wife, Santos, has been one of our schoolteachers, volunteering to teach Salvadoran children even though she is Honduran. Lucío is a lay catechist, and I have always enjoyed going up to their village for Sunday worship because of the way he draws out the people's reflections on the Scripture lesson of the day.

Lucío shared with the group that his house is just a stone's throw from the border with El Salvador. Ever since July, when the Salvadoran National Guard built a command post within sight of his house, he has been afraid to stay in his home. Accordingly, he moved his family down the mountainside about a quarter of a mile to his brother's house. When Salvadoran soldiers come down the mountain into La Virtud, they always walk right past his house. The soldiers also steal pigs and chickens and anything else they find when no one is keeping watch. In recent weeks those visits back and forth from El Salvador down to La Virtud have become so frequent that Lucío feels he should get out of the area completely. Irma assured him that if he and his family could be ready to go to Mesa Grande next week, she would see to it that they had transportation to the new camp.

This evening as I was thinking about Lucío and Santos, I remembered that during a worship preceding one of our meetings a month ago, Lucío asked us to turn to Hebrews 10:32-39. Reflecting on that Scripture was one of the most powerful sharing times we have had in all these months. I looked up the passage again tonight.

December 7

Lucío was killed this morning by four Salvadoran soldiers. I came up from the camp at noon and found Eduardo's house filled with neighboring Hondurans. Eduardo said that around eleven o'clock two of Lucío's sons had rushed into his house, breathlessly saying that the soldiers had killed Lucío. Arne, the UNHCR representative, and Eduardo agreed to tell the Honduran authorities this time and make them go along to be witnesses. So just fifteen minutes earlier the lieutenant along with two soldiers and Arne had left in the direction of La Cuesta.

"Did you send anyone from Caritas to be with the family?" I asked Eduardo.

"No, I haven't, and I certainly am not going up there myself. They have declared open season on Hondurans," he said bitterly.

I said I would go. Another visitor had just arrived, Blake, a representative of Mennonite Central Committee. Blake was on his way to Mapulaca, but he immediately offered to go along as soon as he heard what had happened. La Cuesta is located exactly where its Spanish name suggests—straight up the mountainside; but we walked as fast as we could, barely catching our breath to be able to talk. I shared with Blake the events of the last few weeks. We had gone only about a third of the way when we met the lieutenant coming back down the mountainside, panting and sweating. He grinned and said he couldn't go the rest of the way—his heart was bad—but that he had sent three other soldiers on ahead. I couldn't help but wonder if he had already been drinking, since that seems to be a daily pastime for him.

We continued the hard hike until, coming around the last bend, a few feet beyond a dried-up creek bed, we found the soldiers with Lucío's body. Arne was there also. He said Lucío had been shot seven times. Were it not for Lucío's clothes, I would not have recognized him; two of the bullets had hit him in the back of the head and come out through his face, rendering it completely unidentifiable.

Only a few hours had passed since the murder, but hordes of flies already buzzed around the dried and matted blood. In addition to the bullet wounds to the head, there were several to his arms and back. His body lay twisted and stiff among the rocks in the creek bed. Arne said he had sent Lucío's sons to get some men who could bring a hammock made into a stretcher in order to take the body to the house of Lucío's brother. They arrived within a few minutes, and right behind them came a CEDEN worker bringing Jon, Karen, and Carlos with all their TV equipment. We watched as they set their cameras rolling and began questioning the boys about what had happened.

The older son related that he had gone with his father to their old house to sort out the beans they wanted to sell before moving to Mesa Grande. They were inside working when four Salvadoran soldiers came down the path from El Salvador and entered the house. They asked Lucío what time it was, and Lucío replied the radio had just said it was a little after 10:00. Then the soldiers said they were looking for the path to El Salvador and demanded that Lucío come out and show them the way. Lucío responded he did not know, but they as Salvadoran soldiers certainly should. They began harassing him, saying he should go with them because they knew he went across the border to talk to the guerrillas all the time. They took him by both arms and forced him out of the house.

The little boy began to follow them. On the path the soldiers turned on the boy and angrily asked why he was following. They ordered him to go back into the house and stay there. While the soldiers had their backs to Lucío, the boy said, his father took off running down the path in the opposite direction. He fled through the underbrush and had reached the dried-up creek bed when the soldiers began shooting at him. The boy huddled in the house until he was sure the soldiers had returned to El Salvador and then he ran down to his uncle's house where his little brother and mother were. His mother sent him down to La Virtud to tell Eduardo.

Jon picked up a spent shell, turned to the Honduran soldiers, and asked them whether it was the kind Honduran or Salvadoran soldiers use. The young soldier was obviously uncomfortable and did not want to comment. He looked about fifteen years old. The cameras continued to roll as the neighbors lifted Lucío's body and put it on the hammock. We all headed down the mountain, a somber parade.

They took the body to the house where Santos stood waiting along with other neighbors. Santos was hysterical with grief and rage. Tears streamed down her face. She cursed the Salvadoran soldiers. Neighbors took the body into a room where they covered it with a sheet. Santos kept weeping uncontrollably. After seeing that she was well-attended by family and neighbors, we left.

This evening they brought the body to La Virtud to the house of one of Lucío's uncles. Eduardo took coffee and sugar from the Caritas warehouse for those who would sit with the body all night long. We all spent several hours down there; I returned right after midnight. Lucío's is the first wake I have attended. I found it somehow comforting to sit for a couple of hours in the semi-dark room lit only by candles, look at the crude wooden coffin, and give myself time to come to grips with the reality that Lucío is gone.

Most of the wake was spent in silence, but intermittently someone began a song and others joined in, or someone read a Scripture that came to mind. Eduardo, Delia, and I sat together on a bench weeping at the loss of our brother. We found comfort in mourning together. As we walked back to Eduardo's house in the moonlight a little while ago, Eduardo mentioned that last night two international visitors had slept in La Cuesta. They left shortly before 10:00 a.m. to return to town. He wondered if the

Salvadoran soldiers had kept vigil on the visitors, thereby knowing exactly when they had left and when to go after Lucío.

Only a few hours are left until dawn. All of us are sleeping on the floor in Eduardo's house tonight. I must put out my candle and get a few hours of sleep. What will tomorrow add to our nightmare?

December 9

I am sleeping in Los Hernandez tonight, where I have come to meet secretly with Miguel so we can exchange news of the past few days. He brought word that the team members in hiding were mobilized by Lucío's assassination. Paolo went to his home six hours from here by a roundabout route, completely bypassing La Virtud, all the way on foot. Nemecio left word with his family here that they should join him at the home of his uncle who lives clear on the opposite side of the country. All the team members said they will not consider coming back to work with the refugees until Caritas has clarified its position.

Miguel is the only one left here. He is in a difficult position because his wife gave birth two days ago and he feels he cannot leave her, the newborn baby, and the two other children. He and his wife, Rosita, are trying to decide where to go since he has no relatives in other parts of the country. He asked me to talk to some of the priests about helping him and his family relocate to a different part of Honduras. Meanwhile he will hide, but stay close to his home and family. He told me he would sleep in the cornfield above his house to avoid being caught off guard in his home the way Lucío was.

It will be best for him to leave as the others have done. I told him what Irma had said in our last meeting about Hondurans working with Caritas being able to take their families to Mesa Grande if they are willing to live as refugees, and receive the same provisions and housing the refugees receive. I also shared that the UNHCR has refused to grant Honduran workers in Mesa Grande extra protection as United Nations workers. The statutes of their charter state that the UNHCR offers asylum only to those seeking it in a foreign country; therefore, Hondurans will not be protected in Honduras.

December 10

Irma and two of our priests brought three special visitors today: Bishop Rodriguez from our diocese; Bishop Dominguez, the bishop of Tegucigalpa and also the president of Caritas; and Chico Meráz, the national director of Caritas. Their visit was emotionally exhausting. From the moment they arrived, it seemed a whirlwind had caught hold of us. While they rested from the journey, brushed the dust off their clothes and washed their faces, we rang the church bells announcing that mass would soon begin. The bishops visited briefly with Santos and her family members at the house where the wake had been held. Then they carried Lucio's coffin to the church which was already packed to overflowing with people. All the volunteers who had worked on our committees in the villages came in earlier this morning.

The funeral mass was a moving eulogy for Elpidio and Lucio. Although soldiers lounged in doorways of the church building, Bishop Rodriguez spoke powerful words in his homily. He called Lucio and Elpidio martyrs of the gospel and martyrs of the church in Honduras which is seeking to be faithful to the message of Jesus. He said their deaths are the sad result of suspicion lodged in the hearts of men, allowing them to see their compatriots as enemies.

I looked at the faces of the volunteers, faces which showed a hunger for reassurance that all these years they had not been misunderstanding the gospel message nor the teachings of the church. The bishop encouraged us all to be steadfast in our continued work with the refugees during this difficult time. He assured us that an attack on any one of us would be considered an attack on the church-at-large and therefore an attack on him as our shepherd and spiritual leader. As we moved through the eucharist and began the funeral procession to the little cemetery at the edge of town, most of us let the tears flow—tears from the pent-up emotion of the past several days, but also tears of relief at the encouragement we had heard in the bishop's message.

Immediately following the burial services, we returned to Eduardo's house to meet with the bishops and priests as well as new Caritas members who had just arrived. It was a painful meeting in which I keenly felt the absence of the rest of the team. It was difficult for me not to blurt out that the others were absent precisely because the bishop's visit had been delayed so long and his words of reassurance had been so slow in coming.

Eduardo suddenly seemed uncommunicative; Delia and Julia were their usual shy selves; and so I did more than my share of the talking, mostly in an emotional fervor rather than calmly and objectively. Sister Irma and the priests must have felt caught between their loyalty to the bishop and loyalty to their parishioners and lay catechists, the people who are now suffering.

The bishop said Caritas wants to keep working with the refugees, but he questions how much longer it can put the lives of local Caritas workers in danger. A confrontation with the Honduran military could result in Caritas being forced completely out of the refugee work and should therefore be avoided. Eduardo, Delia, and I as well as some of the newcomers responded that unless some pronouncement comes from the church, the soldiers will continue their rampage of killing. They feel they are insuring that the conflict in El Salvador does not spill over into their country and that the guerrillas who operate in El Salvador do not "contaminate" Honduras. As long as the soldiers consider the Caritas workers guerrilla supporters rather than church workers, they will continue on their present course.

Accordingly, we made two specific requests. First, we asked the bishop to make a public statement, to be published in all the newspapers, saying that the two armies in collaboration are responsible for the deaths of our two co-workers and that the church will not tolerate this attack on its people.

When it seemed clear that the bishop was unwilling to make this public statement, we next asked to be allowed to attend the meeting of all the priests and nuns in the diocese which will take place in just a few days. Some priests and nuns are unsympathetic to our situation, and some would even call us leftists and dangerous elements in the church; we therefore felt that the meeting of the presbytery would provide the opportunity to share our perspective of what has happened at the border.

On this second point, the bishop was equally adamant, refusing to let us send a representative to the meeting. He promised to share our concern, but gave no indication that he had even heard our message. Our meeting ended abruptly, with the group divided into two camps. I am ashamed to admit that I became so frustrated at the close-mindedness of the bishops that I left the meeting in tears before it ended.

At supper tonight, the Caritas team discussed what to do. We decided that since we have not been given permission to attend the presbytery meeting, we will draft a letter and send it to those attending. We discussed the points we wanted to include in the letter, and then three of us stayed up late writing it. Even the mechanics of composing the letter were difficult. Since we did not want to have a light burning late at night in the Caritas house, we went over to Juanita's house two blocks away.

Juanita graciously opened the door to our knock in the darkness, and we went into the back room off the courtyard where we whispered and wrote by dim kerosene light. Twice we were forced to extinguish the light because we heard footsteps along the road beside the courtyard wall. The picture of the early church in the catacombs came vividly to my mind, and I wondered if they had been as frightened as I was tonight. We finished our letter late before returning to Eduardo's house to sleep. It was the first time in weeks that any of us had risked walking around town after dark.

Tomorrow morning at breakfast we will read the letter to the entire team and get their approval. Diego will take the letter with him when he leaves on the bus tomorrow and make copies for everyone at the presbytery meeting. I fervently hope they will hear what we want to communicate. I hope the bishop is not too upset by our action, but I am sure he cannot imagine how devastated we were on being told that the presbytery agenda had already been set and they would be discussing something entirely unrelated to the border zone. Right there he contradicted everything he had said in his funeral homily, leaving us more isolated than we had felt in months.

December 12

This has been an awfully long day. It started at 4:30 this morning when Padre Guillermo and I left the Caritas house to drive to Mapulaca. On this side of La Haciendita, where a footpath comes down to the road, we found Miguel waiting for us with his wife, Rosita, and their newborn baby. A dozen or so of their neighbors followed behind, carrying the other children and a number of bundles and boxes. The men loaded the boxes into the back of the pickup and handed the sleepy children to ride with Miguel, while Maria and I got in front with Guillermo. After emotional good-byes from the neighbors we were off, heading out of the border zone.

To avoid La Virtud for Miguel's sake, we chose a roundabout route to reach Santa Rosa but with three fewer checkpoints on the way. We bumped and bounced along for eight hours. Before each checkpoint Guillermo stopped the car and traded places with me, feeling that a foreigner driving through was less likely to have difficulties with the military. In Mapulaca Miguel got out of the truck, walked through town on foot, and waited for us on the other side. Thank God it turned out to be an uneventful trip, with no problems at the military checkpoints.

December 13

I just arrived back at La Virtud. Miguel and his family are safe, living with the family of a seminary student on the other side of the country. Miguel will look for work and for a small, obscure town where the family can settle. It was difficult to say good-bye. Will I ever see them again?

Back here everything seems calm. The soldiers should be calm—they have achieved a major victory. The day before yesterday all refugees from La Cuesta were relocated to Mesa Grande.

Lucío's family has packed up and left. Santos, the young pregnant mother who is now a widow, moved with the four children and all her possessions to the home of a relative in the interior of the country. Lucío's brother moved also; no one seems to know where, except somewhere into the interior. Elías, the other Honduran lay catechist from La Cuesta, moved his family to Mesa Grande along with the rest of the refugees.

Now La Cuesta is free of Hondurans who would protest Salvadoran soldiers' setting up camp here. That was their goal. They are probably celebrating their victory. The day after tomorrow El Carrizal, the village closest to La Cuesta, will be relocated also. Thus the Honduran territory between La Virtud and the Salvadoran military outpost will be vacated, giving the soldiers freer access to the camp below town and easier communication with the Honduran command post in La Virtud.

December 14

For at least three weeks the refugees in Los Hernandez have been saying that new refugees want to get across the border at the river Lempa. We have kept close contact with the village, trying to have someone in Los Hernandez at all times should word come from the river that help is needed. Several international visitors have gone out and waited. Honduran Caritas volunteers from Los Hernandez have risked their lives numerous times by making trips to the river to check. I know at least two refugee men who have gone back into El Salvador to search for those who are trying to cross over.

The crossing seems a simple procedure but is actually quite complicated. Salvadoran and Honduran soldiers are patrolling the banks of the river. The people hiding in caves and ravines on the Salvadoran side are afraid to risk coming down to the river unless they are sure someone will be there to receive them. Few people can swim and therefore need assistance with the actual crossing. Since three or four miles of land between Los Hernandez and the river are uninhabited, one always runs the risk of meeting soldiers on patrol.

The Caritas volunteers in Los Hernandez frequently hike down to the river and by chance have encountered small groups huddled near the cliff-like rocks on the other side. One volunteer related she had walked along the Honduran shoreline so that anyone on the other side could see her, when suddenly three lone figures emerged from behind rocks and waved at her from the opposite bank. Her husband then took a tire inner tube and swam across to get them, asking the people to hold on to the tube while he swam back to the Honduran side. The three people said they had been waiting for two days, always keeping vigil for soldiers, and having no idea if or when help might come to get them across the river.

The Salvadoran and Honduran soldiers appear without warning, so on any given day when soldiers are sighted in the general area of Los Hernandez, no one tries to go down to the river. We have found three cadavers in the area between Los Hernandez and the river, that of a woman and two small children. But it does no good to ask the UNHCR to talk to the army about this, because we can prove neither that the dead were Salvadorans seeking refuge nor that Honduran soldiers killed them. The soldiers refuse to be responsible for the lives of anyone who ventures into the area, arguing they are on patrol to make sure guerrillas do not cross the border.

Yesterday at noon one of the volunteers from Los Hernandez came into town saying this time they were sure many people were waiting at the river to get across, and that Honduran and Salvadoran men were ready to help if they could be accompanied by international visitors. The camera crew—Jon, Karen, and Carlos—immediately volunteered to go down and take all their equipment with them. The feeling was that soldiers seeing the camera equipment would be less likely to expose themselves and be caught on TV camera in the act of patrolling the border area. Diane, from CONCERN, also offered to go down. Until this month Diane has only worked in the camp with the nutrition program, but she has willingly added extra work to her schedule and gone out to Los Hernandez several times recently.

The hike ahead was long, so we hurriedly organized ourselves and set out for Los Hernandez. We rested only a few
minutes in Los Hernandez while we talked to the men who would
lead us to the river and assist the refugees in crossing over. We
chose a path I had never walked before, through a low jungle-
type terrain and up and down a steep rocky cornfield mountain.
One of the men told me we would come out at a point about four
miles downstream from where 3,000 people crossed on March 18.

We arrived at the river bank, and sure enough, seven women
and children huddled on a cliff-like ledge on the Salvadoran
shore. Diane and I watched while the TV cameras were readied
for action and the men stripped down to their underwear and
swam an inner tube across to the other side. The frightened cries
of the children broke the silence as they were lowered into the
water in the middle of the inner tube. Then began the slow, labo-
rious work of swimming them all across.

We were there to receive them, lifting them out of the inner
tubes and getting their feet on firm ground again. One of the
Honduran men had thoughtfully packed a bag of tortillas, filled
with beans, which we distributed to the children. They hungrily
stuffed their faces as the TV crew tried to question them about
how they had been living these last few days. "Eight days without
eating," said one of the children, "only drinking water and eating
plants and flowers around us."

After the second trip one of the new arrivals said she knew
where more refugees were hiding. If we promised to wait, she
would take someone to find them. So we did wait for more than
half an hour, during which time we explored the Honduran
banks, coming upon many spent shells from FAL rifles which
Honduran soldiers carry.

Someone noticed that about ten feet up the steep hill behind
us the rocks looked artificially arranged. We climbed up there and
discovered a mountainside barricade. Big stones had been stacked
about three feet high and space had been cleared behind for three
to four men. Trash littered the area: K-ration labels "made in the
USA," empty sardine cans, and other military food containers,

some with labels printed in English, French, and German as well as Spanish. We were all sobered to think that the very moment we were down at the river's edge, we could have been under military observation.

Movement on the far banks brought our attention back to our task. Once again we began helping the people out of the inner tubes, comforting the frightened children, and distributing the few remaining tortillas. Into the midst of it all, frightening us momentarily, walked Charles, the UNHCR representative, along with two CEDEN workers and a Honduran who had showed them the way. We had been so absorbed with the events before our eyes that they seemed to appear out of nowhere. I was afraid Charles would be angry with Diane and me for bringing journalists into dangerous territory, and felt relieved when he seemed more interested in assuring himself that this new group of refugees came across safely.

I wondered if Charles, like myself, was fearing a repeat of the March 18 exodus. Interestingly enough, all that Charles said directly to me was that the UNHCR is willing to give Caritas the education program in Mesa Grande if I go and coordinate it there. What a strange way to greet me down at the river's edge! I expected him to ask me what I was doing there, but no such question came.

Dusk was upon us as we finally began the long trek back to Los Hernandez. We were grateful that the additional men had arrived because the refugee adults were far too weak and exhausted to carry the children. So each of us, including those carrying camera equipment, found ourselves shouldering or cuddling infants or small children, most of whom struggled in our arms and cried for their exhausted mothers. Since we hadn't thought of bringing flashlights, the walk became difficult as darkness fell. It must have taken us twice as long to make the return trip. It was probably good that we had no flashlights, for if we had seen the rocks we had to climb over, we probably would not have attempted the walk in the darkness. I am amazed at how strength and stamina are given when they are desperately needed. The fast-paced hike to the river's edge had exhausted me, but the return hike, burdened by a child, was no more difficult.

When we arrived at Los Hernandez, the family of one of the Caritas workers had hot beans and tortillas waiting for the new arrivals.

December 17

We brought 46 refugees from Los Hernandez to the camp today. The UNHCR insisted the new arrivals be moved from Los Hernandez since it is so close to the border. The refugees, in their fear of meeting soldiers on the way to La Virtud, would have refused to make the trip had it not been for the internationals. They were still weak from the ordeal they had lived through before finding safety in Honduras. The hike was slow, dusty, and hot. Fortunately they had no bundles to carry since they crossed over with nothing but the clothes on their backs, and the internationals again helped carry the children.

The arrival in the camp was a touching sight to behold. People eagerly came out of their tents in search of family members or neighbors. In less than an hour every person had found a familiar face and had been invited to live in an already overcrowded tent, which nonetheless seemed like a luxury to them after eight days in the open.

The experiences of some people have indeed been nightmares. One woman's entire mouth, chin, and cheeks are blown off. Another woman was hit when she was cradling her infant in her arms; the bullet went right through her arm and killed the child. A twelve-year-old girl walked eight days with half her foot blown away.

Eight-year-old twin girls were at home with their father and baby brother when the military invasion hit their town. They fled with neighbors, but both the father and baby were wounded. The family got lost from the rest of the group, but found a cave to hide in. For several days the girls scavenged plants and flowers to eat while attempting to find the others. Their daddy "went to sleep and wouldn't wake up," they said. Other refugees finally found them because of the baby's cries, but the baby died before they were able to cross the river. The girls are in shock. The first sign of emotion they showed was when they found an aunt in the camp. On seeing her they both began to cry.

December 19

The villages of San Jose, El Pilon, and El Campo were relocated to Mesa Grande this morning. Prudencia's family was among them, but I didn't go to say good-bye. The preparation for relocation is a difficult and tiring task. The names of the families are called one by one, and the soldiers search all of their possessions. Then family after family are loaded into large, open-air cattle trucks, until each truck holds about fifty people. International visitors assist in most of this work, under the direction of the UNHCR. They accompany the refugees on the long trip to Mesa Grande, one riding in each truck. By having an international on each truck, there is less chance that the Honduran soldiers will harm anyone during the long trip on those isolated mountain roads. I have not helped with the relocation so far, finding it unbearable to participate in something the refugees are forced to do against their will.

I don't even want to visit Mesa Grande. The reports brought back by the international visitors are sobering. They say Mesa Grande is located on a high flat plateau surrounded by mountains, at an altitude with a climate different from La Virtud. While it gets hot during the day, the nights are cold and drizzly. There is a shortage of blankets and building material. People are forced to put their efforts into building more tents, so the construction of other things like a cooking area for each family has been delayed. Communal kitchens feed over a thousand people at each meal.

The refugees are trying their best, but everything is disorganized. The internationals reported that on the day they spent at Mesa Grande, breakfast was not ready until nine o'clock, lunch was served at 3:00 in the afternoon, and supper an hour after dark. When the trucks arrived bringing over five hundred new people on a six-hour trip, neither food nor tents were ready for them. The biggest problem is apparently the lack of water. When the last group of refugees arrived, there had not been enough water to wash the pots and pans from the last meal and accordingly they had been unable to begin preparing supper.

The refugee men are working long, hard hours either constructing tents and communal kitchens or digging holes for latrines. The ground is limestone rock, so it takes hard work to dig the holes for the tent posts and the latrines. The men are complaining that they cannot continue to do this kind of work and then receive only a tortilla with beans at each meal.

The refugees in the few remaining villages and the camp are trying to decide what to do. Many of them want to talk with me about it. I feel placed in a difficult position, unable to help them decide whether to return to El Salvador or go to Mesa Grande. Neither option offers them a secure future. The people are being radicalized by this forced decision. Many are saying if so many Salvadorans go to Mesa Grande there will never be a resolution of the problem in El Salvador.

"In Mesa Grande we may face death at the hands of the Honduran army. If we are going to risk our lives, it would be better to go back home and try to change things there. We have towns to rebuild, crops to plant, unions to organize, and laws to change," they say. And yet on remembering the repression from which they have fled, they hesitate. These are hard decisions. What the people want more than anything is peace.

December 20

We had a Caritas meeting tonight. It feels strange to think of this new group as the Caritas team. Only four are left of the old team. In addition to Helena, three people from Caritas of Spain have arrived: two doctors, Mercedes and José, and one teacher, Carmen. We received a radio call from the team members at Mesa Grande saying they need a teacher to begin the new school program there. Tonight at the meeting it was decided that I must go rather than Helena or Carmen. The group gave two reasons. First, the teachers I worked with have all gone to Mesa Grande, so

I know the people and can reorganize the same program. The second reason was more painful to hear. The soldiers are aware that I am one of the few remaining who know all the villages and people in them, so they watch me closely. In addition, I am still so angry with the soldiers for the deaths of two friends and with the UNHCR for giving in to the repression and relocating, that my comments at meetings cause more harm than good. We decided tonight that I will stay here through Christmas, but on December 26 I must leave for Mesa Grande and stay for at least a week to begin the initial preparations for the education program there.

December 22

The refugees from La Majada were relocated today. I went out for part of it, not so much to help load people into the cattle trucks as to be with Juanita. La Majada has always been our most crowded village, and the refugee work centered around Juanita's house because it's at the very entrance of the village.

Juanita and I watched as the boxes and odd-shaped bundles were piled into the trucks. The refugees are so fearful of scarce resources in Mesa Grande that they try to take everything with them—chickens and pigs, firewood, homemade clay pots, crude beds made of young tree saplings roped together, even pieces of plastic from their grass hut roofs. After the dust had settled from the last truck pulling out, Juanita and I walked through the village, so awesomely silent where there used to be laughing children.

Most huts had been torn apart to take the supporting poles. What remained looked as if the wicked wolf had huffed and puffed and blown the houses down. Juanita will be lonely out here. Since she and her husband, Luis Alonso, have always worked with Caritas, we will try to send international visitors out to visit here and stay overnight occasionally.

Tonight at suppertime the UNHCR representative Arne stopped by to say that no more refugees will be relocated until after Christmas. From the way he talked, I got the impression that were it up to him we would keep on relocating, but none of the truck drivers wants to drive again until after New Year's since this is traditional vacation time in Honduras.

Christmas night, December 25

Never have I experienced such a powerful Christmas celebration, nor have I ever worked so hard, been so unconcerned for myself, and had such fun. It has truly been a Merry Christmas. We began making merry two days ago when we saw the gifts which arrived from a U.S. group called Mission International. For a couple of months now the refugees had been weaving wide shallow baskets, one for each family, which Salvadorans use to hold their warm tortillas in much the same way we would use a bread basket. But no one knew why we wanted to have the baskets distributed by December.

Oh, the sense of excitement in the air as each mother came to the Caritas truck with her basket! The gifts they received were simple and unadorned: five pounds of flour, one pound of margarine, three pounds of sugar, spices, tomatoes, potatoes, eggs, yeast, banana leaves. Their excitement reminded me that some families have had nothing but rice, beans, and tortillas during these long months.

The rural custom is to eat pork tamales and sweetbread at Christmas. Within an hour of the food distribution on the twenty-third, women were firing up the adobe oven. On into the night women took turns baking their sweet cinnamon bread. At 3:30 a.m. the men began the hard work of butchering hogs for the tamales. I had so looked forward to witnessing the butchering, but I had stayed up late the night before, so on hearing the first squeal I pondered getting up less than a few seconds before falling back asleep until dawn. They were more than half done by the time I awakened.

The refugees did all the butchering themselves and decided how to distribute the meat. I enjoyed listening to their decision-making process in the cool dawn hours. The honesty and integrity of these folks never fail to impress me. With the squeal of hogs resounding through the river valley, our Christmas Eve began.

Before the breakfast beans and tortillas were ready, the men were distributing meat tent by tent. It was important to cook the meat as soon as possible in this hot climate.

While the women made tamales wrapped in banana leaves, we kept the children busy putting the final touches on their nativity scenes, one for each of the three sections of the camp. The nativity scenes were part of the Christmas club project Helena initiated for the children. Using clay from the riverbed, the children made figurines to illustrate the nativity: Mary, Joseph, baby Jesus, sheep, shepherds, and cows. Their imaginations put Jesus into an environment similar to theirs; so along with the traditional animals, there appeared pigs and an armadillo, and baby Jesus was sleeping not in a manger but in a hammock. They painted corn and beans in bright colors, strung them into garlands, and used them as adornment for a dead tree branch painted green.

They hung other imaginative things on their tree—tiny empty medicine boxes, figures shaped from the tin foil from the margarine sticks. I even saw brightly colored discarded margarine boxes used as decorations. Last Sunday during catechism class the children were given paper and colored pencils and invited to draw what they heard in the Christmas story. We posted their artistic efforts all around the nativity scene tents. Everyone enjoyed passing by to admire their artwork.

The other major project of the clubs was to prepare a traditional Christmas drama. It was a modern adaptation of a thirteenth-century epic poem with long orations and songs detailing the events surrounding the Christmas story. The production was directed by Maria Santos, an old but energetic woman who teaches most of the catechism class and can recite the long rosaries from memory. Under Maria Santos' direction, the children memorized their lines and made imaginative colorful costumes for each role.

At dusk the troubadours began their program, walking between the rows of tents and stopping every so often. Several of us followed them, wanting to hear the entire program, but many of the words were new to me and it was often difficult to understand their singsong voices joined in unison. I remember that one section told the event from the shepherds' perspective, another gave the impressions of the townspeople of Bethlehem, yet another related the musings of the three kings as they journeyed to the birthplace of the babe. There was a fascinating conversation between Mary and Joseph as they marveled at all these visitors to their stable door, and a touching solo from Mary as she spoke of giving birth to her first son, far from home and in a strange place.

Two parts of the program were particularly imaginative. One was the animals' narrative of their experience on that glorious night. The burro told how he had offered his gift to the Christ child in the early dawn hours. As Mary searched for some cloth to wrap the baby in, he breathed his warm breath on baby Jesus to keep his tiny body warm. The other part was the journey of the wise men as they traveled the many miles, sleeping by day and following the star by night. Each time they stopped at homes along the way, they were offered food provisions: tamales, sweetbread, and coffee.

Needless to say, the troubadours were the highlight of our Christmas activities. The next afternoon, Christmas Day, the children were invited to repeat the performance at the church in La Virtud for all the townspeople.

Everyone stayed up late on Christmas Eve, relaxing and visiting. The international staff stayed in the camps, and we consumed enough tamales, sweetbread, and sweet coffee to sustain us for several days. At midnight the lay catechists led us in worship. Their simple, moving Christmas reflection was not that Christ is with us, as I had expected, but rather that we are with Christ, accompanying him in his first days of life: born in a strange town, forced to flee and take refuge in a foreign land at only three days of age. It was a sincere identification with Mary and Joseph and the new baby.

While the refugees did their hard work on Christmas Eve, we worked hard on Christmas Day. The Caritas team organized a game day for children and adults. We placed ourselves at various locations throughout the camps, and people moved from one place to another playing a different game at each place. Most games were well-known favorites: pin the tail on the donkey, musical chairs, and three-legged races. Our grand finale was the long anticipated breaking of the piñatas. The children had made the colorful animal figures in their clubs. Amidst the clamor of excited voices, we organized the children according to age and strung the piñatas in the trees; then dozens of children took their turn being blindfolded and swinging their stick at the piñata to break it and release the candy hidden inside.

Our Christmas celebration would not have been possible without the generous donations from church groups in the U.S. and Europe. Sister Irma said most people who give money designate it specifically for emergency medical and food provisions. But this year, a few groups, like Mission International, had designated their gifts for celebrating the Christmas holiday. The refugees were also deeply grateful for the presence of the international visitors who had chosen to accompany them in a time of great need. The Salvadoran people are family oriented, so they recognize the sacrifice of others spending the holidays away from their own families.

January 2, 1982

I am writing from Mesa Grande where I have spent the last week. This is the most despairing and depressing place I have ever seen. The refugees agree with me. Everyone is scrambling to organize on a massive scale what should have been organized long before people arrived. For many months the refugees in each geographic region along the border were attended by a different agency. Now, all the agencies and all the refugees have been flung together and no one seems to know which end is up.

The relatively simple task of basic communication seems monumental here. CEDEN is in charge of all the transportation, the radio communication and the water system; Caritas takes care of food and clothing distribution; World Vision supervises construction; and the Mennonites are in charge of building latrines and locating new arrivals in each tent. While Caritas must distribute food, CEDEN has all the vehicles, so Caritas is continuously hounding them for the use of the vehicles to transport food. World Vision takes care of construction, but since Caritas is in charge of the communal kitchens where food is cooked, World Vision must continually seek out someone from Caritas to tell them where and how to build the kitchens. CEDEN has the radio communications, so sometimes they receive word that five hundred refugees are coming from La Virtud; but they neglect to pass it on to the Mennonites who must receive them and assign tents to them, nor do they pass word on to Caritas who must see that a meal is prepared for them.

It sounds complicated on paper, but the reality is even more confusing. Tension and frustration seem to be the common denominators here. The interagency turmoil is nothing compared to the turmoil among the refugees. The environment is new, frightening, and crowded. People from literally hundreds of different villages in El Salvador have been thrown together in one large camp.

Trusting relationships do not develop overnight for these rural people. The arbitrary placement of two to three families per tent has resulted in difficult situations where people with long-standing conflicts are suddenly living side by side or, at the other extreme, complete strangers share crowded living quarters. While out in the villages the refugees separated themselves according to like-minded friends, here at Mesa Grande people with different political perspectives have been thrown together. That too undermines any efforts to build trusting relationships.

The physical aspects are even more despairing. The nights are very cold here, cold enough to need warm clothes. Of course the people have neither shoes nor socks. There isn't even one blanket per person, and one blanket is not enough. To keep warm at night in the Caritas tent, we eight workers lay a piece of plastic on the ground, put blankets on top of it, and sleep in a long row. That way we share both body warmth and the blankets. Julia, one of the Caritas workers here, commented to me, "Sure, you like it after only two nights. But we've been here three weeks and it's getting tiresome."

The water situation is the worst. This high plateau does not have its own water source. They had to go several miles away to find a river strong enough to be tapped to supply water for the whole camp. But planning and constructing a water system takes time. How can the UNHCR relocate thousands of people to a place that doesn't have an adequate water source? There isn't enough water for cooking, let alone for bathing or washing clothes.

The cooking situation is desperate. The women are spending most of their time standing in lines at the scarce water spigots which sporadically dry up, sometimes both morning and afternoon. Cooking corn, beans, and rice requires large amounts of water. We've eaten suppers as late as ten o'clock at night. Women are getting up at 3:00 a.m. to catch water for the breakfast meal. The men complain they are not getting enough food to do the hard work on the construction teams.

The only place for washing and bathing is a rather small river a half mile beyond the entrance to the camp. To get there, one has to pass the military command post, cross the road, and walk down a twisted path. The people don't mind the walk, but the soldiers sometimes refuse to let the people pass or they go down to the river to watch the women bathing. Sporadically they demand that the refugees present their papers. The harassment has gotten so bad that no one wants to go down to the river unless they can go in large groups, accompanied by someone from one of the agencies. We don't mind going along, but it does get frustrating having to bathe in a group of thirty to forty people, and there are far more groups of refugees than there are staff workers. All the agency personnel agree that, given the present conditions, especially the faulty water system, the relocation must be slowed to allow more time for organizing.

Giles, the newly arrived UNHCR coordinator, complains that we are working inefficiently. He lives five miles away in San Marcos, visits the camp for an hour or two each day, and says the conditions don't seem so bad to him here. He's never spent a night here, nor has he stood in a long line to receive a meager meal after hours of hard physical labor.

It angers us that while the UNHCR pushes the agencies beyond their capacity, it will not admit that it is being pressured by the Honduran military. Why won't the UNHCR use its international authority and say to the army, "You win. The relocation is happening as quickly as is humanly possible, but we will not tolerate further abuses to the refugees." The unwillingness on the part of the UNHCR to take the stand in keeping with its role here is almost more difficult to accept than the actions of the military itself.

Given all these problems, I do not understand why everyone feels an education program is urgently needed. We have had lively arguments among the Caritas workers. I feel I could better contribute my time to some other area of work, but the other staff members insist that the most helpful thing I can do is get all the kids out from under their parents' feet.

Together with some of the former teachers we took a census of the children, tent by tent. There are over six hundred school-age children, and at least that many preschool and infant children. I will need to take at least twenty adults out of other work areas in order to get the school started. Most of the former teachers from La Virtud are in a leadership capacity for other important tasks. Prudencia and Rosa Angelica coordinate the kitchen teams; Juan is in charge of a food distribution tent.

And where would we hold classes? In La Virtud we started out sitting under trees. There are no trees here. Giles says that schools are not a priority, and lumber cannot be used to build school tents; but all the other staff say that because the idle children cause trouble, the schools must be made a priority. While the French doctors agree that idle children are a problem, they adamantly insist that no schools be built until they have enough clinics.

I find it hard to adjust emotionally to this new situation. I'm living in two worlds—the world of La Virtud where, in spite of the repression, we were basically happy because of the unity felt between the Caritas team, the French doctors, and the refugees; and this other world, confusing and impersonal, encouraging people to be selfish and competitive. I resent being here.

In spite of my resentment, I will return to La Virtud, finish up my work, pack my things, and move to Mesa Grande permanently. It is no harder for me than it is for the refugees and the rest of the Caritas team. We will find comfort in being together. Of the team members who fled last November, Alejandro, Reina, Julia, and Paolo, all came here to work after the bishop published his letter in the newspaper. These four, along with several former volunteers from the villages, form the new team. We will try to rebuild the relationships that disintegrated at the border.

It's also good to be with the schoolteachers again. Prudencia and I have spent long hours together, talking over all that has happened since December 18 when her village was relocated. Her family is fine, although naturally they find it difficult to get used to a tent after living in a grass hut. The Caritas team has agreed that in all of our tasks we will find a refugee to share leadership with us. Prudencia has agreed to coordinate the education program with me. Working closely with her will be a joy.

January 5

I'm back in La Virtud. It feels good to be hot again! The two weeks I was gone were relatively quiet here. A new UNHCR representative has arrived, a tall, thin Swede named Andres. As often as they change, it's no wonder we feel no continuity. Tonight at a meeting we discussed the next relocation. The refugees down at the camp have formed a committee to discuss the relocation with the UNHCR. They asked for reassurances on three points: that there be land to cultivate at Mesa Grande, that a reception center be built at Los Hernandez for new refugees, and that a small group of refugees be left at the reception center in order to justify maintaining a small international staff which in turn will insure that refugees are not turned back at the border by Honduran soldiers.

Andres was outraged by the idea of a refugee commission. "Who do they think they are to put stipulations on us?" he stormed. Andres acts as though the refugees are nonpersons without opinions. He finally consented to the points in the refugees' request, but his voice lacked interest and conviction. We discussed the request from Mesa Grande to delay sending more refugees. Andres visibly chafed at the delay, which is understandable. He is the one who must tell the lieutenant.

January 7

Yesterday morning Andres told the lieutenant that further transfer of refugees to Mesa Grande would need to be postponed until the physical conditions improve there. The lieutenant did not take it well, insisting that the remaining villages (there are only three: Guajiniquil, Los Hernandez, and El Amatillo) be moved immediately. He allowed a postponement only for the refugees in town and those in the camp. We should have expected that he would "convince" us to see things his way.

January 8

We are beginning to see a pattern in the soldiers' behavior. Whenever they get impatient with the slowness of the relocation, they target the group to be transferred next. Where the refugees previously expressed reluctance to move, the emotional strain of persecution becomes so great that they docilely accept their fate as the only alternative to regain their peace of mind. Yet at the same time they resent being forced to relocate. This makes it so confusing for journalists who hear first from the UNHCR that the refugees willingly go to Mesa Grande and then hear the refugees say, "We didn't want to come, but were forced to."

My belongings are packed. Tomorrow I go to Mesa Grande.

January 30

On January 22 I went back to La Virtud to accompany another group of refugees to the new camp. The trip was hot and exhausting. We went through the routine calling out family names, waiting while soldiers completed their senseless search of all the bundles, then piled into the trucks and drove off. Each truck carried one soldier and one international representative along with its refugee cargo.

Most of the children were excited since few had even been in a vehicle before. But the excitement ended in the first ten minutes as motion sickness overtook both children and adults. The creaky cattle trucks tossed us about, swaying over the rocky, mountainous road. Dust filtered in, the sun beat down on us, and very little air moved to relieve the stench of vomit. Six long hours. . . .

We stopped once when the driver got out to eat a fast meal. I asked him for a ten-minute break for the people. He acted as though he wanted to refuse, but then relented and let down the back gate. The other trucks in the caravan followed suit. If the internationals did not accompany each truck the people would not be allowed even one brief stretch.

We arrived at the camp anxious for food, drink, and a bath. The welcome was refreshing. Refugees at the camp entrance greeted us by waving a welcome. It helped take away the fear of the future which occupied most minds during the long trip.

These few weeks at Mesa Grande have had their positive and negative aspects for me. After so many months of preoccupation with soldiers and security, it has felt good to get work done without interruptions. Prudencia and I have drawn up a program budget on a monthly basis and done an annual estimate. After days of lobbying the construction crews, we got a large tent for an education center. A week later, more lobbying procured us two tables and benches. We've prepared a requisition for school supplies and expect to see the first sheets of plywood to build chalkboards in about two weeks. We have to keep watch for every truck bringing lumber into the camp to make sure the plywood gets to us. I chafe at this competition for scarce resources.

Caritas is in charge of all schooling except health education which the French doctors and CONCERN nutritionists will do. Necessity has dictated that we begin activities with the old people. The upper camp area holds two thousand people, one hundred and fifty of whom are over sixty-five years of age. The activities program started when a Honduran doctor became concerned about the frequent cases of hypertension he was finding in these *ancianos*, as they are called. So he and a temporary volunteer social worker from CEDEN did a census of those over sixty-five and brought them together to talk.

The ancianos feel worthless here. Back in the villages they maintained their position as the family authority. Now the internationals tell their sons and daughters what to do and where to work, but for the elderly all the jobs are too hard and exhausting. They are cold. They point to their calloused, wide feet that have never known shoes and say their feet are freezing. Many stay in bed until 11:00 a.m., until the sun raises the temperature in their tents to warm their bones. But by afternoon the tents are like ovens, so they are forced out to seek a more comfortable place. There are no trees in the tent area, no place to escape from the hot afternoon sun.

More than anything, these old folks are depressed. They have resigned themselves to the fact that they will never see their homeland again. "We're going to die here in Mesa Grande," they say. Back at the border people could decide if they wanted to return to El Salvador and walk the half day to their former homes, even though the war continued. Now that choice has been taken from them. They will be here until the UNHCR decides when they can go home, which means they will be here until the conflict is over. But how many years will that take?

When the CEDEN volunteer left, I took over the work with the elderly group. We have organized afternoon activities where all of the ancianos gather for a short but enthusiastic program which includes playing a game and discussing a topic of their choice; then they line up to receive a glass of *orchata*, a ground rice and sugar drink, along with a vitamin pill.

We all enjoy the hour of fun each afternoon. The old folks are as uninhibited as children in playing games. The topics they choose for discussion have included everything from health and nutrition to Bible reflection centering on the theme of preparing to meet one's Maker. Many ancianos have expressed the feeling that no one cares about them. But now that we've started this group, they sense a growing friendship with the various international workers who participate in the program.

The anciano group has been a positive aspect of the work here. The hardship of daily existence in this environment is the negative side. Living in tents is difficult, especially when they have been built one on top of the other. In some instances, three families must share a single tent. With fifteen to seventeen people in a tent, illnesses spread quickly. The noise of the children is constant. How often I have longed for the silence offered by thick adobe walls. Infants in nearby tents seem to cry all night long, keeping me awake. Sometimes in frustration I want to get up and grab the babies away from their mothers. I should be more sympathetic, knowing that many mothers do not have enough breast milk to last through the day and night, but it's hard to be patient when I'm losing my sleep.

The continual noise gets on everyone's nerves. Privacy is a thing of the past. Everyone hears everyone else's fights and conversations. It is so hard to relax here, or to take a break. There are few benches to sit on and not a single chair with a real back to it. In the Caritas house at La Virtud, we would play the guitar to relax; but around here the people hear it and crowd around until one feels like a performer.

There's no place to go to write. The kitchen table for the Caritas team is in public view of half of the camp, and people come and interrupt me. I could go to the education center, but to take a light in there at night arouses everyone's curiosity. The tent walls are made of plastic, so the light shines out; and the children are so undisciplined, they stick their fingers through the plastic to make a hole in order to see what's going on.

The water system is another big problem. Bit by bit, the meals have gotten more organized and many of the people are finally cooking as individual family units. But there still is not enough water for bathing or for washing clothes, so we must all make the long trip down to the river. It's an extra hassle we don't need, given all the hard work and other frustrations.

Construction in general has almost stopped for lack of lumber. I'm not sure where the holdup is and we all have mixed feelings about the delay. On the one hand it means that the relocation will be postponed because there are no tents to receive new people; therefore refugees and international observers will stay at the border area longer, protecting the Honduran population. But on the other hand, we can't go on with our work here. As long as the tents don't get constructed, we will not be able to build schools, benches, clinics, or nutrition centers either.

In addition to all our troubles, we continue to feel the burden of the suffering that continues at La Virtud. We did not realize how much the repression would escalate as fewer and fewer refugees are left in the area. The international observers bring us reports of the latest events. The soldiers have begun throwing rocks on the tents at night. They come right into the camp, as do the immigration authorities. They demand to see everyone's identification papers and then search the tents for weapons which they never find. Life in the camp has become so dangerous that the refugees dare not go out more than a few yards. Two refugees, a woman in her seventh month of pregnancy and her sixty-five-year-old father, were killed on January 12 right outside the camp.

Since reports of the depressing conditions in Mesa Grande trickle back to the people, new complications have developed. Mesa Grande could receive only two new groups of refugees during January, one on January 22 and one on January 26. The waiting period has given the refugees time to think and weigh their options. Despite the terror they live with at the border, many have decided not to move further inland; but neither do they want to return to El Salvador. Their choice is simple, to stay where they are. On January 22, when El Amatillo was scheduled for relocation, only thirty families of the eighty-six who live in that village presented themselves at the trucks. Then on January 26, when the trucks were ready to take the people from Guajiniquil, not one of the seventy-eight families there came out of their ranchito with their belongings packed.

The resistance to the relocation had been spontaneously decided by the refugees; in fact, the groups in Guajiniquil and El Amatillo did not even talk to one another or know that the other group had opted for resistance. Still, Andres is furious. He has accused the Caritas workers and the other international visitors in the refugee zone of instigating and organizing the resistance. Of course, this is not true. The Caritas team talked for months about what our position would be, agreeing to let the refugees decide themselves and then support their decisions because we are here to serve them. Andres, rather than confront the Caritas workers to their faces in La Virtud, has voiced his suspicions at a national meeting in front of all the other agency personnel as well as representatives of the army and the government. It's causing a real problem.

February 28

The atmosphere in the camp makes it impossible to rest or write. We have decided that each person on the Caritas team will take three days each month to get away from Mesa Grande for rest. I will have time to write only once a month. Working in Mesa Grande holds little of the joy and fulfillment that working in the villages held.

I am critical of the way the other agencies carry out their work. Caritas tried so hard at the border to develop a high level of refugee participation in the decision-making process. In contrast, the other agencies did not use this approach previously, nor are they doing it now. Consequently, those refugees who were in the Guarita sector under World Vision want handouts, are extremely individualistic, and feel content to be told what to do. Those from the La Virtud sector, however, are discontented with their sudden forced passivity.

The UNHCR has assigned the Mennonites the undesirable task of constructing permanent frame houses. The people want to go home. The very presence of those wooden houses taking shape at the edge of the camp tells them they won't be going home very soon. The men are reluctant to help with the construction. No one complains about the Mennonite volunteers; they are doing fine, given their situation. It's just that those houses symbolize everything the refugees do not want to accept, and therefore the refugees' cooperation is often irresponsible and unenthusiastic.

I talked with one of the Mennonite college students who's volunteering for three months here. It saddened me to realize that he had gained the impression that Salvadoran people are lazy. I wish he would come over to the education tent to see the enthusiasm of the school teachers there.

CEDEN continues to do a slow, poor job with the water system. They have never thought to ask the opinions of the refugees, either. We were sitting around the fire outside Prudencia's and Carlos' tent one night, talking about the water. A man commented, "Several of us worked with some Peace Corps workers once on a water system in our villages. We could help plan an adequate system here, but nobody asks us. CEDEN has its own professionals with their university diplomas."

CEDEN is also in charge of agriculture. The men are loaded into trucks early each day and ride some twenty-five kilometers to the site of the cultivation. But here again, the CEDEN workers decide what, where, and when to plant. How can they expect the people to develop enthusiasm and a sense of responsibility when they're never made to feel like they're doing the work for themselves and their own community?

The refugees are depressed for another reason: They have no news from home. Back at the border an amazing amount of news traveled back and forth through a kind of people's mail service. Hondurans still crossed over to Salvadoran towns to do their business, making purchases, and selling their wares. They often brought back a letter for a refugee family, or at least news of where soldiers, guerrillas, and ORDEN people were. They reported which towns were calm, which ones were not. The people could keep track of their villages and hear from relatives. A friend came to visit a refugee for a day or two occasionally. Now there is no contact.

Those who know how to write have the option of sending letters through the regular mail service. This has become possible only because one CEDEN worker has taken the initiative to distribute free writing paper and stamped envelopes for letters she then collects and drops in the mail. But who knows if the postal service can be trusted with letters carrying the return address "Mesa Grande Refugee Camp"?

Some of the refugees have decided the life here isn't worth enduring. Twenty-one people, including two entire families, have left. We were completely unaware of it until they didn't show up to collect their weekly food provisions. The rest of the refugees kept their secret. It took them two days and nights of walking over the mountains to reach La Virtud. They've done their harm there, staying in the camps for two days and painting a grim picture of Mesa Grande to those who are yet to come.

The situation at La Virtud doesn't change much. The persecution continues with new names and faces. When Mapulaca's turn came for relocation, only 250 of the 700 refugees showed up with their belongings. Andres ordered the Mennonites in charge of that sector to close the warehouse, leaving 450 people without aid. A Honduran army colonel went to Mapulaca with Andres and told one of the Mennonite workers that the soldiers will force the refugees out of the area. Andres also cut off all food and medical care for the refugees who resisted relocation in Guajiniquil and El Amatillo. He said they no longer come under UNHCR security.

The administration and military leadership in the border area continue to shift. Andres left, to be replaced by a Frenchman named Sergio. An army captain left and was replaced by a lieutenant, who has been even more belligerent than the men before him. And with his coming, collaboration with the Salvadoran army increased. Last month he announced that the relocation had to be completed by February 15, which was an unrealistic demand and which, of course, was not met.

By now we've learned that whenever such a request comes from the military, it means some kind of military operation will begin in El Salvador. Sure enough, on February 20 La Virtud was put on a seven o'clock curfew. Some of the international visitors kept watch and witnessed about 200 Salvadoran soldiers enter La Virtud from one direction, congregate in the plaza with Honduran soldiers, and leave town in the other direction on the path to La Cuesta and El Salvador. Shortly thereafter, distant shooting began which continued all night long.

A new development this month has been the frequent attacks on internationals associated with the refugees. Honduran newspapers have published inflammatory articles accompanied by political cartoons. We are accused of harboring guerrillas in the refugee camp, of channeling supplies to El Salvador, and of teaching subversion rather than providing humanitarian aid. The political cartoons portray Mesa Grande as a bubbling caldron of communism being stirred by the various agencies.

The immediate result of these articles was that Hondurans in the towns nearby and elsewhere in the country showed heightened suspicion toward us. We noticed it even in San Marcos, five miles from Mesa Grande, where store owners were much less cordial and in some cases hesitant to serve us. When we go to the larger cities for supplies or to renew visas, we no longer feel safe in striking up a casual conversation on the buses or in the taxis. Rather than saying we're in Honduras to work with refugees, we must make up some story or play the role of the tourist.

Back at the border a shocking incident happened in Guarita. Padre Juan was in church after mass, preparing to celebrate two marriages. The church was empty except for a few old women kneeling in prayer at the statue of the virgin. The army captain in charge of both La Virtud and Guarita came into the church, intoxicated and belligerent. He walked up to Juan, who was still dressed in his cassock, grabbed Juan's beard, and hit him in the face. Then he struck him again, knocking Juan to the floor, and continued beating him. The screams of the women brought townspeople and soldiers running, the latter taking the shouting captain back to the confines of the command post.

The captain shouted something to the effect, "I told all you foreigners to get out of here with the refugees, and I meant don't come back."

Juan is bruised and sore but not seriously harmed. The bishop excommunicated the captain and placed the Guarita church under Holy Interdict, which closed the church's doors to the public. The message from the military is clear! You foreigners have caused us enough trouble. We will put a stop to it.

Another of the refugees' relocation fears is becoming a reality. At Mesa Grande the Honduran soldiers who guard the camp's entrance have become more overt in both their surveillance and harassment. At night they come into the camps and stand vigil in the communal kitchens. Even more frightening is their vigilance at the latrines located at the very edge of the camp, partway down the ravine. It is so isolated there that a soldier could kidnap a person and no one from the camp would hear any cries for help.

The soldiers claim they are looking for suspicious nighttime activities and meetings. We had initially been told that this piece of land was purchased by the UNHCR and therefore considered international territory, but when the issue of soldiers patrolling inside the camp was brought up at a staff meeting, Giles contradicted the former UNHCR representative, saying the land is sovereign Honduran territory and the military has every right to enter as it pleases. He did agree to talk to the commander about the fear the military is causing.

The repercussions are small but not insignificant. No one wants to go out to the latrines at night, so people just step out between the tents and squat on the ground. This would not matter so much if it were just one or two people, but in a crowded tent city with thousands of people, all of whom walk around barefoot during the day, it creates a potentially serious health problem, not to mention the stench that we must all endure when the hot sun bakes that contaminated soil.

The role of UNHCR representative Giles is that of protection officer. He repeatedly reminds us that all security matters are to be referred to him. But he sits in his comfortable apartment in San

Marcos, and never spends enough time in the camps for the people to feel they can rely on him for security matters. Out of necessity the international staff has become his security patrol. The refugees tell us what's happened to them, and we relate the incident to Giles.

In a recent meeting, he requested that we give him the time and date of the incident, a description of the site where the incident took place, and the refugee's name and tent number. Does he think we have no work of our own? Doesn't it occur to him that if the refugees had enough confidence in him to give him their name and tent number that they would come to him directly? For all we know, he might pass that same information on to the Honduran military.

At the same meeting, representatives from La Virtud were discussing the continuing security problems with both Honduran and Salvadoran soldiers. I finally asked him if the UNHCR would state point-blank to the Honduran military that they must not allow the Salvadoran military free access to the border area. Giles' response surprised all of us: "That is a complex question involving the politics of this entire hemisphere and we will not discuss it here because it is beyond the scope and interest of this meeting."

How can the UNHCR effectively carry out its duty to protect the refugees if it can't even make such a request? Is the UNHCR passively accepting the repression at La Virtud because it encourages the refugees to accept the UNHCR policy of relocation to Mesa Grande?

March 31

Prudencia and I led a teacher training course this month, along with a Honduran teacher from San Marcos. Forty refugees participated in the two-and-a-half-week course. It was exhausting work—not just the full day of planned schedule, but the individual help many participants asked for each evening. But it was fun. The group was enthusiastic and inquisitive throughout the course, and now they are anxious to begin classes. As soon as the school tents and benches are finished, we can begin. The parents are visibly relieved that their kids will soon be out from underfoot.

A week after the teacher training course, we organized a program for the whole camp and presented it late one evening from the wooden platform that is used at general assemblies and worship. We hung gas lanterns around the platform for our stage lights. The teachers sang songs and presented a series of funny, but thought-provoking skits about school life. This was our chance to let the parents know who has been trained as teachers, what the classes will be like, and where and when instruction will take place. The program ended with a song a few teachers had written, adapting music from a Salvadoran folk song:

> For you, child, who has never known the security of home;
> For you, infant, born in a tent in a strange land;
> For all the children who pass their days playing barefoot in the mud;
> For you we will teach, for you there will be schools.
> For this humble woman, who gives love when there seems nothing else;
> For you who shoulder all the uncertainties, all the pain;
> And when no tortilla can be found, it is you who suffer most;
> For you we will teach, for you there will be schools.
> For all those whose hearts carry the justified dream of a better tomorrow;
> We bring together your pain, your ideas, your dreams;
> And tomorrow you'll see these capable children making those dreams come true.
> For this we will teach, for this we will teach.

Moments like those, where the vision we all work for stands out so clearly, are few. Normally camp life is too intense, too involving to leave the tasks at the end of the day and relax.

The Caritas tent is the worst place to be because that's where people come to ask questions or favors. It's also where all the journalists visit. After two months of having the supper meal interrupted three and four times each evening, I started avoiding the Caritas tent and eating supper with different refugee families.

To my surprise, the refugees are helping me adjust. There is something relaxing about getting absorbed with the menial tasks of fixing the meal and washing dishes. With the refugees, I forget the day's list of "jobs yet to do" and relax by the fire. We watch the brilliant stars and observe the moon go through its stages. Those are the moments of peace. The people are great philosophers, teaching me much about keeping work and rest in balance.

Suffering continues at La Virtud. News from the border is heartrending and paralyzing. The relocation has kept us in a continuous state of emergency. Five trips were made this month, each bringing about 400 people. Los Hernandez was emptied. The refugees living with families in La Virtud came, as well as about one third of the camp below town.

The new arrivals brought reports of the military's latest savage actions. Soldiers focused their surveillance and harassment on each locale as its date for relocation drew near. As the size of the remaining groups shrank, the soldiers became more severe. They targeted the men, saying men were not welcome in Mesa Grande and should all go back to El Salvador. The incidents of arrest, torture, and disappearance escalated to daily occurrences.

Some of those who remain unaccounted for were young men in their late teens and early twenties. The lieutenant denied ever having taken them, or said they were caught carrying a concealed weapon. Among those who have disappeared is Celso, the carpenter who helped to build all the school benches in La Virtud for us last year. He is sixty-five years old, one of the most gentle men I have ever met. When he was taken prisoner, a little boy climbed a tree behind the command post wall to see what would happen. He reported seeing Celso nude, his clothing thrown to one side, and a huge rock on his shoulders, balanced with his hands. He was forced to do deep knee bends while being beaten with a leather belt.

Soldiers began demanding ID papers of everyone they met. Those without papers were accused of having just come across the border and of being guerrillas. Even in instances where they had left their papers in their tents and family members brought the papers to the command post, the lieutenant did not change his mind.

The soldiers have enlisted the assistance of townspeople for the harassment; one man in particular is operating in the manner the civilian paramilitaries operate in El Salvador. He has boasted of having been given a list of "wanted persons" from the Salvadoran army. Time and again, whenever the Honduran soldiers raided a grass hut or tent to take a man prisoner, Chungo, as he is called, has been present at the arrest.

The camp below town is now under constant military surveillance. As dusk falls, the soldiers allow themselves to be seen on the surrounding hills, and on several occasions during the night the camp has been stoned. Refugees cannot go out even for firewood. On March 20, an eighty-year-old man left the camp to urinate in the underbrush. Soldiers beat him up and took him prisoner.

Both La Virtud and Mesa Grande had a particularly depressing visit this month. On March 23, Eugene Douglas, U.S. White House Adviser on Refugees, came with several State Department Latin America Desk officials. Douglas and company arrived in a military helicopter, spoke only to the UNHCR officials and not to any refugees or other international staff. At La Virtud Douglas acted like an imperial commander, saying he would make sure the relocation was completed quickly. At one point, when people attempted to speak to him about the repression, he brushed them aside, saying he had not come to hear sad stories, but rather "to kick the UNHCR's ass into gear." If anyone wonders who runs the UNHCR, Douglas apparently thinks the U.S. does.

The other major event this month happened on March 24. The refugees at the La Virtud camp called a meeting with the UNHCR representative Sergio to request that they be relocated to another country—not farther inside Honduras. They said they fear for their future if sent to Mesa Grande. They presented a petition with hundreds of signatures, saying an earlier UNHCR representative had told them that the UN Statute on the Rights of Refugees includes a provision for this request if they fear for their security. Sergio ignored their request. He implied that the international staff was responsible for the petition. When the issue was brought up at one of our joint meetings in San Marcos a few days ago, Giles was even more adamant than Sergio had been, stating flatly that relocation to a third country was out of the question.

April 30

School has finally begun! The people are happy. It puts a structure into the daily life of the camp that helps everyone feel more settled. How can humanitarian aid agencies say that schools do not fall into their emergency care priority and therefore not fund them? They should come and see the difference it has made at Mesa Grande.

The last group of refugees from the camp below La Virtud packed up April 15—five months after the relocation was begun. Many of us went back to put closure on that part of our lives and to ride the trucks with the people. It was painful to see that barren river valley which once teemed with life. An earthquake could not make one feel more devastated. The refugees took everything with them except for twenty tents, one clinic, and one warehouse, all of which were to serve as a reception center should new refugees come across the border.

A group of international observers stayed behind with Sergio, a UNHCR representative, mainly to see what would happen to the few remaining Honduran families who once worked with Caritas, but also to see if any remaining refugees wanted to go to Mesa Grande rather than try to return to El Salvador. The group should have stayed in the so-called reception center, but gave in to the soldiers' demand that they go up to town while soldiers guard the camp. Almost before the dust of the last truck had settled, Hondurans from town came down the hillside to the camp and began to take apart, board by board and nail by nail, what remained. The soldiers turned their backs and stood by silently while the so-called reception center disappeared.

Nothing is left there now. A week later, Sister Irma went back to see if Caritas could take up where it had been three years ago, before the first refugees arrived, when church people were simply helping poor Hondurans. Several persons said they would like to try starting up the old milk project for Honduran children. Everything stopped before it really got started. Two more Caritas volunteers were killed, accused of giving powdered milk to the guerrillas. The zone is militarized.

Eduardo is also gone from there but did not leave of his own choosing. On April 12 when he was in San Marcos for a meeting, he had lunch at the church rectory and stepped outside for some fresh air. A pickup truck pulled up, men jumped out, threw him in the back, and drove off. Alejandro, who was standing on the opposite corner at the market, witnessed the kidnapping and immediately notified the UNHCR. Since Eduardo was an agency coordinator, both Bishop Rodriguez and Charles from the UNHCR intervened and demanded his safe release. For three days we waited anxiously for news. When news did come, it was horrifying.

The DNI had taken Eduardo to Tegucigalpa where they held him three days. He was tortured and interrogated continually during that time. They threatened that he would never see his family again if he did not answer their questions. They reinforced the threat by covering his head with a thick hood which they tightened at the neck. They held the hood tight until his body so desperately needed oxygen that his muscles went into spasms and, in the torturers' words, he "jumped like a frog." Then they questioned him about virtually every person working in the refugee program, demanding that he admit each was a communist.

The torturers even told him to confess that Bishop Rodriguez was a communist. They intermittently beat Eduardo with a piece of thick rubber hose which bruised him deep in the muscles so that he was unable to control them, but did not leave visible scars. At one point, he could tell by the conversation and other sounds that new soldiers were being taught torture techniques on him. When one soldier failed at an assignment, he was beaten up by the other torturers.

We cannot help but be deeply affected by all of this. The

fear which Eduardo's experience plants in the hearts of the other
Honduran workers is especially strong. Death would be preferable. Caritas has sent Eduardo to Panama. Alejandro is particularly devastated by all of this; he and Eduardo had worked together for three years at the border.

I am not feeling well. For two weeks I have had intestinal
and lower back pain. It is time for a break. I will ask for a two-
week rest, see a doctor, and then try to look toward the future at
Mesa Grande.

June 15

I have been gone six weeks. When I left, the population at
Mesa Grande was 8,000; it now is 8,500. On the weekend of May
28-31, the Salvadoran and Honduran armies launched a coor-
dinated encirclement operation in Salvadoran territory all along
the border area of Valladolid, La Virtud, and Mapulaca. It was
reported in El Salvador as the largest offensive ever mounted
against the guerrillas. It might have been a weekend attack, but
civilians fled from soldiers for fourteen days, finally getting
through to Los Hernandez on June 11. A group of internationals,
on hearing of the extent of the attack on the local radio, insisted
on going from Mesa Grande to La Virtud to be available if
needed.

When I arrived yesterday, Guy, the new UNHCR representative, greeted me exultantly: "The reception center at La
Virtud is working, and you said it never would!" I listened to his
version of how the internationals went to the border and five
hundred refugees were gathered up and trucked to Mesa Grande.
Then I did what he should have done before bragging. I went to
talk to the new refugees and hear their testimony.

I cried on seeing them, feeling transported back in time to
the March 1981 Lempa crossing. The people are skinny and
gaunt, with sunken eyes, protruding bones, and skin infections.

Their testimony is a long one and I will not record it in detail.
They gave the names of many Salvadoran towns where they
sought refuge only to meet more soldiers. Still inside El Salvador,

they saw Honduran and Salvadoran soldiers fight side by side. At the border, almost the entire length from Valladolid on back to La Virtud, they tried to get past Honduran soldiers who fired on them, threw grenades, and shouted obscenities at them, accusing them of being guerrillas. With the help of a Honduran farmer, in whose cornfields they hid, they miraculously met the international staff and were saved. The people said about 1,800 lived in the area from which they had fled. Only 500 are safe at Mesa Grande. How can Guy call that a success?

The military has truly won. They limit the numbers of refugees who come across the border, and they are free to help the Salvadoran army at their own discretion, which has been their goal from the beginning.

Prudencia's older sister and brother-in-law arrived among this new group of refugees. They are so skinny. Prudencia says they spent fifteen days without food. They are silent and just stare out into space. Prudencia broke down weeping when she told me that their three children were killed during the invasion. "Guerrillas!" she said mockingly. "They were all under ten years of age." When the people were hiding, the soldiers listened for the cries of the children, and that is how they found the civilians.

In spite of all the grief around us, coming back to Mesa Grande feels like coming home. I love these people. I visited the schools in session and jokingly called the teachers "maestro." They stand so tall and proud of their achievements. I feel proud of them too.

I am going back to the U.S. Six weeks of rest was not enough and I need further medical care. It is hard to leave. Only the fact that I cannot keep working forces me to accept the inevitable. Most internationals go home sick and exhausted after six months. It was bound to catch up with me, too.

The future here is uncertain. On May 12, Guy told the refugees that all but two thousand of them will be sent further into Honduras. He did not know exactly when, perhaps in a year. The refugees are adamantly opposed to it. What will happen at the border? Will the UNHCR eventually provide the security it is supposed to? What if that security contradicts U.S. interests in the region? Can the people go to another less hostile country? Will they ever get home? A journalist asked Prudencia this last question and she replied immediately, "Not as long as the evil and unjust government in my country is propped up through military aid. There will be no peace until there is a change."

I slept in Prudencia's tent one last time so we could prolong our good-byes. I told her how guilty I felt to turn my back on human suffering and walk away. Like she has done so often this past year, Prudencia offered sound advice. "You are not turning your back," she comforted me. "It's all right for you to go home. You can keep us in your heart and accompany us from there. Witness to what you have seen, and share our story."

Epilogue

At Christmastime 1983 I journeyed back to Honduras. A year and a half had passed—exactly the same amount of time I had spent as a volunteer with the refugees—and the changes I found were immense. I wish I could report a happily-ever-after ending to the story of my dear friends. But during my brief holiday visit, I learned that the refugees' hope to return home to a country at peace seems further from fulfillment than ever.

Our emotion-packed reunion began at the airport where Alejandro, my former Caritas co-worker, met me. The long truck ride to Mesa Grande revealed the drastic changes in Honduras, and also offered us a chance to reminisce and prepare me for the changes in the camp. Despite Alejandro's description, the visual impact made me feel I was a first-time visitor to Mesa Grande. The majority of the tents have been replaced by more permanent zinc-roofed structures; water flows adequately from many spigots; laundry areas made of cement have eliminated long hikes to the river; trash barrels stand at frequent intervals; community buildings abound. The harshness is understandably still there: overcrowding, noise, dust which becomes mud with the rains. But the infrastructural improvements are gratifying. The people told me it represents financial aid channeled through churches and the UNHCR along with months of hard work by the refugees themselves.

Prudencia's children eagerly pulled me along by the hands to show me the camp's handiwork: clothing sewed on a treadle machine, hammocks woven in bright colors, simple wooden furniture (even some wooden toys), shoes and sandals, metal kitchenware,

267

and most amazing, a shop to repair the agency vehicles. I saw familiar faces at every turn as we toured the workshops. Most of the teachers have switched to new jobs, "to learn another skill while there is opportunity," they said smiling. What was most gratifying was to see how they have applied their teaching skills in new areas; many hold positions of leadership and responsibility. I found Juan among the tailors where he was coordinating the entire shop. Graciela was in the nutrition center, and Prudencia works in a clinic. Our former star pupils now teach the youngest children, and the former teachers now supervise the entire teacher-training program.

We spent long hours catching up on our personal lives. I shared my year-long struggle back to health; they had their own stories. The Gonzales youngest grandchild died. He was the only tie they had with their own daughter who was killed by the Salvadoran National Guard. Chema's wife came across the border and is now united with her husband and children. What a joy to see them all together, remembering back to the days of Lempa. Prudencia had a baby—her fourth; Graciela's mother was repatriated back to El Salvador by the UNHCR; she wanted to be in her own land when she died.

The hours we spent in conversation were not all on such a personal level though. Catching up on changes in their lives over the past year and a half meant hearing mostly about their ever-present concern for the future. The threat of yet another relocation has hung over them like a dark shadow ever since they arrived at Mesa Grande. These simple farming folk consistently turned the subject of the conversation to the political and military alignments throughout the region, for they perceive correctly that their future will be decided not by themselves but by international developments.

There has been little change in the situation in El Salvador during a year and a half. The U.S. strategy of sending massive amounts of arms and advisers to train troops has resulted only in more death and in a larger, but no more efficient army. Desertions stand at an all-time high, and the territory under guerrilla control (with a basically sympathetic civilian population) has been impenetrable except by aerial bombardment. These air attacks only terrorize the civilian population and produce still larger numbers of refugees fleeing into Honduras.

When I left Honduras in June 1982 Mesa Grande held 8,000 refugees, and another 5,000 Salvadorans lived in camps near the Honduran town of Colomoncagua, a 12-hour journey from Mesa Grande. Now, Salvadoran refugees in Honduras number almost 19,000 and more arrive following every anti-guerrilla operation by the Salvadoran army. Each new group of refugees brings the same horror stories of brutality by the Salvadoran army, National Guard, and death squads.

But the figure of 19,000 represents only those who have successfully arrived to the refugee camps, itself a feat close to miraculous. Recently arrived refugees to Mesa Grande recounted to me their efforts to evade Honduran soldiers who now control the mountainous border area. They had to seek out a Honduran peasant sympathetic enough to risk his or her life by contacting the UNHCR protection officer in charge of refugee reception. Then, with planning worthy of a spy novel plot, the UNHCR would find the new refugees who were hiding out in the hills. Eventually they would get to Mesa Grande.

The UNHCR attempts to maintain reception centers in the border towns, but they are not always functional. The Honduran army is the ultimate authority and twice in the last year, during Salvadoran military operations, the army has ordered UNHCR officials out of the area. The Honduran army has militarized the border to stop the flow of refugees and to collaborate with the Salvadoran military in its operations. The UNHCR says it is powerless to challenge the military's decisions in Honduras, as it is present there only by invitation of the government. Many among the aid agency staff feel UNHCR officials accept the army's orders too meekly and do not do enough to protect the refugees.

For two years there has been constant, unsettling talk of relocating the camps to the interior of Honduras. The UNHCR states humanitarian motives for the proposed relocation. It says the refugees will have increased freedom of movement with access to Honduran markets, land to cultivate, and better security. These goals are laudable, but simply unachievable. The U.S. embassy in Honduras has publicly doubted the feasibility of these goals; Honduran government officials forthrightly state that the relocation is for political reasons. Honduran papers carry an ever-increasing number of accusations that the refugees are guerrilla supporters. The U.S. embassy describes the refugee camps as "guerrilla R & R centers," implying that guerillas leave El Salvador to rest in the camps then return home to join the fighting again. Yet two years of tight military surveillance around the refugee camps has not provided any substantial evidence to back these accusations.

Instead, refugees have been dragged out of hospitals and even a dentist's chair, imprisoned, tortured, and forced to sign blank papers which later were produced as confessions of refugee-guerrilla collaboration. Other refugees who attempted to return to El Salvador on their own have been apprehended, killed, and labeled as guerrillas. Cadavers cannot defend themselves, so the charge stands. It is against this backdrop of unsubstantiated accusations and overt Honduran hostility that the refugees fear greater security problems if they are moved into the interior of Honduras.

Beginning in 1983 the United States chose Honduras as a new base for military operations in the region. Airstrips, training bases, munitions warehouses, military hospitals, roads, and radar communication to monitor the entire region's activities have been built. To myself and other visitors in Honduras, it definitely looks like preparation for a protracted war, all done under the guise of "routine military exercises." The initial two phases of the military operations were carried out along Honduras' southeastern border. Phase three has been announced for the border shared with El Salvador. It stands to reason that the U.S. would find a large refugee population and the accompanying international staff in the way of these military operations. This is part of the reason behind U.S. embassy pressure to relocate the refugees, especially those at Colomoncagua which is much nearer the border than Mesa Grande.

The relocation site proposed by the Honduran government, near Olanchito, is far from the Salvadoran border; it is also near the Puerto Castillo military base where U.S. advisers train Salvadoran soldiers—too close for the refugee's peace of mind. The relocation proposal has exacerbated tensions between wealthy Honduran landowners and their poor neighbors. The former stand to gain by charging the UNHCR high rent for the land; the poor see the refugees occupying land which should be redistributed in agrarian reform. When the refugees were moved to Mesa Grande from the area around La Virtud, they were promised land to cultivate, freedom of movement, and greater security. Why should they now be convinced by the same promises? They fear for their lives and for the lives of potential new refugees if the camps are moved into the interior. The border area would be militarized making it less likely that new refugees could get through. Throughout my visit, the refugees' conversations returned to the impending relocation. Singly, and as a community, the refugees repeatedly told me that they will resist the relocation. Many said they would return to El Salvador rather than be moved further inland.

As the U.S. militarization escalates, the UNHCR becomes still more a pawn. In the face of challenges to be assertive in carrying out its role as refugee protector, the UNHCR consistently claims that its power is limited. Honduras is not a signatory to the international accord justifying United Nations protection for displaced peoples, so many UN staff feel the agency could be thrown out at any time. The refugees repeatedly asked, "Is it possible to bring international attention to our situation and increase international support for the UNHCR so that it can fulfill its assignment to guarantee our safety?"

The U.S. military maneuvers in Honduras are still legally called "exercises," but months ago on-site advisers were speaking of a "permanent presence" in Honduras. The next phase of the operations is scheduled to include the border with El Salvador. The people of this book will be the immediate victims, along with the family and friends they left behind in El Salvador. The same scenario seems destined to repeat itself throughout the villages and *aldeas* of Honduras.

Rafael and Teresa, the Caritas couple who adopted two refugee orphans, went back to their hometown, far from the refugee population, but the stigma of having worked with "suspected guerrillas" was not so easily removed. Honduran soldiers came to their home late one night and dragged Rafael away despite the efforts of his wife and children to intervene. The house was torn apart, with no explanation given. Shortly after, soldiers brought a body to the La Virtud cemetery, buried it beside the grave of Lucio, and told some townspeople it was a "subversive Caritas worker." I learned at Christmastime that Teresa had written to me, pleading with me to help her find her husband. Her letter never arrived.

As we talked about the incident in the camp, I despairingly said there was very little I could have done. But the same Salvadorans who evangelized and challenged me in times past, once again had a response: "The deaths in our country will not end so long as U.S. policy continues on its present course. You can help us by working to change U.S. policy."

—Yvonne Dilling
March 1984

Appendix

Historical Background on Central America

By Gary MacEoin

Central American history did not begin with the misnamed discovery of America by Columbus in 1492. Mayan cultures had flourished for several thousand years, achieving remarkable triumphs in mathematics, architecture, and other sciences and arts. Earlier empires had disintegrated into tribal settlements by the time of the arrival of the Spaniards who found people speaking many languages, cultivating their land in common, and creating beautiful works of art in metal, clay, and cloth.

The Spaniards found little in this region to attract them. They quickly depleted the gold mines and other easily accessible mineral deposits, in the process forcing many Indians into slavery and largely destroying their cultures. Greater fortunes were to be made in Mexico and in South America. But it was important to secure Central America against the European enemies of the Spaniards. Accordingly they gave large land grants to Spanish adventurers who established plantations with Indian labor that served as control points. The entire region was divided into administrative units that today have become the countries of Guatemala, Honduras, El Salvador, Nicaragua, and Costa Rica. The Spaniards intermarried with the plantation Indians. Known as *mestizos* or *ladinos*, their offspring adopted European lifestyles and learned Spanish, producing the peasant class that constitutes the majority of the inhabitants today in all countries except Guatemala. Other Indians living on poor land or in the mountains retained their languages and tribal dress and customs and continued for many years to hold their land in common.

Gary MacEoin, a Roman Catholic from Tucson, Arizona, has authored several books on Latin America. He has reported from every country in the Americas during the last decade, and since 1980, has visited Central America seven times.

Independence from Spain in the first quarter of the nineteenth century opened these areas to business and commercial relations with the industrial countries of Northern Europe, especially England and Germany, and also to the United States. The result was a gradual incorporation into the capitalist world economy. The ruling families who had earlier governed on behalf of Spain and now monopolized power in the new republics found it advantageous to act as middlemen in trading with the industrial countries. Since the second half of the nineteenth century the subsistence economy has been radically transformed to produce coffee, sugar, bananas, cotton, and beef for export.

Economic activity increased enormously, but the benefits were confined to this small oligarchy which spent its wealth mostly in conspicuous consumption, and to the foreign investors who gradually acquired possession of much of the most fertile land. Indian communal lands were seized without compensation, often with genocidal killing of the people, as in El Salvador in the late nineteenth century. The situation of the peasants similarly deteriorated. Few of them had legal title to the small farms adjoining the estates for which they supplied labor, even when they had lived there for generations. Greedy landlords dispossessed them, using their private armies to deal with any who attempted to protest. As more good land was allocated to export crops, city workers had to buy imported food; and as import prices always tended to rise faster than wages, the living standards progressively declined.

By the early 1900s the United States business investments in Central America had become substantial, and with the decision to build the Panama Canal the strategic importance of the region also grew. Economic and political concerns consequently coalesced to create an image of Central America and the adjoining Caribbean as the United States' "backyard."

On the basis of this image a unique policy for the region was gradually developed. Much earlier, in 1823, President Monroe had enunciated the Monroe Doctrine for all Latin America, declaring that the American continent was no longer a field for colonization by European powers, and that the United States would look with displeasure on intervention by any European state in the affairs of the American republics. The Roosevelt Corollary enunciated in 1904 claimed for the United States the right to intervene to maintain or restore order in any country of the hemisphere. The Taft Modification a few years later softened the language but retained the content. Taft advised using the dollar to achieve United States policy objectives, while backing it up if necessary with the "moral value" of naval power. These principles have been consistently applied in Central America by all subsequent presidencies.

Central America should enjoy the benefits of the United States system, in the opinion of President Wilson, even if it called for force to impose them. The Good Neighbor policy of Franklin Roosevelt, according to a Mexican newspaper, transformed the region "into a league of *mestizo* dictators, with the United States destined to guarantee their slavery." The right of intervention by the United States in Central America was formulated in 1950 as the Miller Doctrine by Assistant-Secretary of State Miller, and it was updated and applied by President Johnson for the 1965 invasion of the Dominican Republic.

The Landless Majority

The dominant characteristic of Central America today is the grossly distorted access to land in a society where those without land literally starve to death. The reason is not population pressures in excess of the capacity of fertile land. Even in El Salvador, the most densely populated country on the American mainland, more than enough land is available to allow the entire rural population to grow the basic foods required for an adequate diet. But the concentration of land in few hands, begun by the Spaniards and accelerated in the late nineteenth century with the development of export crops, still continues. Simultaneously, the region has experienced the same population growth as other parts of the world during the past century, meaning more people with access to less and less land.

As peasants were dispossessed from fertile valley lands, they subsisted by cultivating the rocky, infertile mountainsides or succumbed to pressures to work in slavelike conditions as seasonal labor on the plantations. Some tried sharecropping, a system under which half the meager corn and bean harvest they extracted from tiny infertile plots had to be turned over to the landowner. A bad year meant more than tightening one's belt. It meant starvation or heavy indebtedness to the landowner that could rarely be paid off by seasonal work on the plantation. United Nations statistics graphically present the downward process. In El Salvador the proportion of peasants without access to any land either as owners, renters, or sharecroppers rose from 12 percent to 40 percent between 1960 and 1975.

Ironically, probably as much as half the land in the possession of the ruling classes was not put to any productive use. If the ruling classes allowed the peasants and Indians to grow their food on this idle land, the ruling families correctly reasoned, they would no longer have an endless supply of docile labor ready to work at starvation wages and under appalling conditions. In Central America this policy has produced the scandalous situation of widespread hunger and malnutrition in the midst of potential plenty.

One attempt to remedy this situation took place in Guatemala. In 1945 after a long period of dictatorships, Juan José Arévalo was elected president with more than 80 percent of the vote. In 1950 Jacobo Arbenz Guzmán succeeded him, again with an overwhelming mandate. Building on the modernizing reforms of Arévalo, Arbenz in 1952 signed an agrarian reform law expropriating the uncultivated portions of farms larger than 223 acres. One of those affected was the United Fruit Company which stood to lose 387,000 idle acres, receiving in compensation the value it had placed on the land for tax purposes. United Fruit turned to two members of the United States Administration with whom it had long-standing business links, Secretary of State John Foster Dulles, and his brother Allen, CIA director. Thanks to their action, as President Eisenhower describes in his memoirs, the CIA masterminded and funded a plot that overthrew Arbenz and canceled the proposed land reform. Since that date, Guatemala has groaned under ever more savage dictatorships, with genocidal attacks on Indian villages, slaughter of thousands of women and children every year, and massive displacement of population as internal and external refugees.

Explosion of Peasant Frustrations

Why did the United States use force to block the Arbenz land reform proposal but now sponsors land reform in El Salvador? Why has this failed? A brief look at the history of El Salvador during the twentieth century will help to explain the present situation.

The Mexican Revolution and the commitment to greater justice in the world contained in President Wilson's Seventeen Points and other statements of the victorious Allies in World War I had their echo in El Salvador, as elsewhere in Latin America. During the 1920s peasant organizations began to form and to agitate for land reform and for better working conditions for plantation labor. With the Great Depression that began in the United States in 1929, however, the situation changed drastically for the worse. The collapse of demand in the United States and the other industrialized countries for the export crops of El Salvador and other similar countries meant a drastic decline in the demand for plantation labor and a general decline in all economic activity.

Acting out of desperation and without any overall strategy, the peasants in El Salvador revolted and proceeded to seize the land they needed to stay alive. The revolts were quickly suppressed by the army, with the loss of at most a few thousand lives. Then the Fourteen Families (as the small, tightly interlocked group that controls the country is known) took a decisive step. They sent their armed bands throughout the country to kill everyone identified as an actual or potential peasant leader. There is understandably no official record, but the commonly accepted number is 30,000, a figure enshrined in the popular mind by a line of poet Roque Dalton: "Behind every Salvadoran stand thirty thousand dead."

Everything that has since happened in El Salvador, and what continues to happen today, cannot be understood without reference to this traumatic experience, one imbedded in the folk conscience of Salvadorans in the same way as is the Great Famine of the 1840s in that of the Irish. From the viewpoint of the Fourteen Families, the action was a success. It brought forty years of submissive tranquillity. It is consequently logical to try it again, using the barbaric techniques of intimidation and slaughter of innocents described by Yvonne Dilling from on-the-spot observation. From the viewpoint of the people, the slaughter established an unbridgeable gulf between them and the Fourteen Families. There can be no peace in El Salvador until the power of this group is broken.

Organized Resistance

Salvadorans suffered in silence for years following the 1932 massacre, but the determined seeds of hope for change were only dormant, while the people chafed under years of oppressive rule by the Fourteen Families.

The climate was right to seek reforms through the electoral process in the early seventies. Two new political parties had formed, both modeled on parties that had come to power in Western Europe after World War II. The Christian Democrats and Social Democrats secured a mass following immediately after organizing. For the presidential elections of 1972, they formed a coalition to challenge the monopoly of the Fourteen

Families, with Christian Democrat José Napoleón Duarte as presidential candidate and Social Democrat Guillermo Manuel Ungo as his running mate. Blatant fraud negated their overwhelming victory, and Duarte was forced into exile.

Time after time, attempted reform through elections was squelched through fraud and violence, and a growing number of Salvadorans turned to peaceful civilian protests in their efforts to secure justice. The government responded with oppression. The National University was closed for several years. Trades unions were taken over, their leaders imprisoned or exiled. Church leaders who identified with the popular movements were harassed. Tanks and armored cars fired on a peaceful demonstration of students in San Salvador in July 1975. Ambulances picked up the dead, so that the number of casualties was never known. In April 1977, Rutilio Grande, a Jesuit priest, was machine-gunned on his way to an outlying church. Two months later, a death squad (the White Warriors Union) ordered all Jesuits to leave the country "or face extinction." These events radicalized Archbishop Romero of San Salvador who became the spokesman for peaceful reform until he in turn was shot to death while celebrating mass in March 1980.

Long before that momentous event many Salvadorans had realized that the electoral process would never achieve the reforms they needed, as long as the process was controlled by the traditional ruling group. They abandoned the political parties, some to form peaceful protest movements, others to actively oppose with armed resistance the attacks by the Army, National Guard, and death squads. In 1980 the civilian protest movements coalesced to form the Revolutionary Democratic Front (Frente Democratico Revolucionario), or FDR. It incorporated the major part of the Popular Social Christian Democratic Party, reconstituted as the Christian Democratic Movement, the Social Democratic Party, the major trades unions, including the unions of teachers and of professionals and small businessmen, the directorate of the National University and of the Catholic University, and many small parties and movements of the left. The FDR thus represents the entirety of organized national opinion except for the right wing of the Christian Democrats and the ultraright fronts for the Fourteen Families. The various military resistance groups later came together as the Farabundo Marti Liberation Front (FMLN) which today is the rebel military force that controls large portions of the country. In 1980 the FDR and FMLN formed an opposition political-military coalition. The FDR-FMLN's stated goal is to oust the Fourteen Families and their military supporters from power, and to set in motion real reforms to allow full participation of all citizenry in society. The FDR-FMLN's target is military-economic; the target of the ruling oligarchy on the other hand, is the civilian population.

Widely respected independent monitors of human rights, including Amnesty International and the Legal Aid Office of the Roman Catholic diocese of San Salvador, have documented that 80 percent of the killings in El Salvador are civilian casualties of air and ground attacks by government forces and right-wing death squads, the two often working in concert. The other 20 percent constitute military and guerrilla casualties. Total violent deaths since 1980 exceed 30,000. A Salvadoran bishop recently commented that it is unusual today for a Salvadoran to die from natural causes.

As the guerrillas become more powerful, government forces increase their desperate brutal attacks; and the United States provides them with ever more deadly weapons and devices. More people join the guerrillas because they will not live under a government which practices genocide against its own people.

Land Reform in El Salvador

When the Sandinista government ousted Nicaragua's U.S.-backed Somozan dictatorship in July 1979 and began a series of radical reforms designed to end the U.S. domination of the economy and the society, Washington moved quickly to prevent a similar outcome in El Salvador. In October 1979 it maneuvered a military coup and installed a junta that promised modest reforms designed to take the edge off the popular pressures for revolutionary change while retaining intact the relationship of dependency with the United States.

Early in 1980 a land reform project was announced. A first stage was to convert big estates into cooperatives. When the owners were compensated, they promptly removed all their livestock and equipment and transferred their money to Miami. The decapitalized cooperatives are already in large part bankrupt. The second stage was designed to break up the middle-sized coffee farms (the main agricultural base of the Fourteen Families). The constitutional assembly dominated by this group effectively eliminated that part of the project. The third stage, based on the Vietnam hamlet model, was to transfer rented land to the tenant. To the extent that this has been implemented, it tends to consolidate *minifundismo* (uneconomical small holdings) and as such is an obstacle to meaningful land reform. Implementation of these programs was in the hands of the armed forces who used them to identify and kill peasant leaders, while rewarding farmers who are members of ORDEN and other death squads in the employ of the oligarchy.

Guatemala, Honduras, Costa Rica

The thrust for liberation and self-determination that ended a century of tyranny in Nicaragua is also at work elsewhere in Central America. In Guatemala the traditional unwillingness of the Indians to cooperate with the *ladinos* long slowed down the consolidation of the popular forces. That situation has changed radically in the past few years. The Indians under their own leadership have now established excellent working relations and coordination with the ladinos.

The government forces and the death squads, relying on the same U.S. military advisers as those of El Salvador, have no answer other than slaughter of noncombatants, burning of the villages and crops, and driving hundreds of thousands from their homes. The violation of human rights has been so outrageous that the U.S. Congress imposed severe restrictions on military aid. Successive administrations have, nevertheless, found ways to continue the flow, in part directly, in part by providing money to pay for arms and planes shipped by Israel. In 1984, the Reagan administration openly renewed military aid. And thus the bloody stalemate is prolonged, as in El Salvador.

In Honduras, the level of popular organization and militancy is lower, but the basic conditions are the same: widespread poverty, unemployment, malnutrition, gastrointestinal diseases, illiteracy, economic dependency on U.S.-based multi-nationals. A brief return to civilian government in late 1981 after a decade of military dictatorship has been effectively undermined by the U.S. military buildup and support of General Gustavo Alvarez, head of the armed forces. Alvarez, on the payroll of Castle and Cooke banana company while on active service, has far more power than the president of Honduras, and his power grows as the United States builds military and naval bases in Honduras and subsidizes former members of Somoza's National Guard who infiltrate into Nicaragua to terrorize, kill, and sabotage.

In Costa Rica a more equitable land distribution has long ensured social stability and provided the bases for democratic institutions. Nevertheless, in the past century it has been progressively affected by the decapitalization that results from dependence on export crops and raw materials. Its external debt is one of the highest per capita in the world, and its income from exports is less than the cost of servicing the debt. Open and concealed unemployment affects half the labor force. Even in Costa Rica the ingredients for a social explosion are present.

The Changing Role of the Church

The Roman Catholic Church came to Latin America as a department of the Spanish state, the bishops and higher clergy named and paid by the state. The function of legitimating the civil power continued in the postcolonial period, with the result that the institutional church—with outstanding but few exceptions—identified with the oligarchy and was little concerned for issues of social and economic justice. It was only in the 1960s that the Vatican Council and the Medellin, Colombia, meeting of bishops began to develop an awareness of the special needs and overriding claim of the poor, as a matter not of charity but of justice. This was called the "preferential option for the poor."

Some of the bishops have internalized this new understanding, the most notable being the martyred Archbishop Romero of San Salvador and his successor, Archbishop Arturo Rivera y Damas. Most bishops have not succeeded in breaking their emotional ties with the oligarchy. However, many of the priests, a majority of the nuns, and almost all the lay catechists have made the preferential option for the poor, combining works of charity with calls for justice. As a result they experience direct persecution at the hands of the military and the death squads. Seldom in the church's long history have we had so many martyrs witness to their faith.

Protestants, a minority of under 20 percent in Central America, have historically tended to be "otherworldly," focusing on personal salvation. Many have interpreted the violence around them as a sign of the imminent return of Christ. Some, nevertheless, have become more aware of the social message of the gospel and its implications for daily life around them. Where the church has been historically tied to state powers, we are witnessing the beginnings of a new alignment of Christians in Central America, as in all Latin America: socially-concerned Catholics and Protestants working together to speak and act the gospel imperative of justice as a basic ingredient to peace, and conservative Catholics and Protestants on the other side sustaining the policies of the local oligarchs, who increasingly rely on U.S. military support.

More noteworthy than the institutional expressions is the underlying Christian faith of the people. Fed by the Bible, which has become subversive literature and an organizing guide in the hands of exploited people, the Christian faith is alive and well in the hearts of the people of Central America. From the Jewish prophets and the life and teachings of Jesus, they have learned that human misery is not God's will, but rather the result of the greed of a few, that they are called to work as a community to liberate themselves from this slavery. Many have concluded that to defend their rights against the institutionalized violence of the state, they must form clandestine political groups and take up arms themselves. They bring their Christian principles and discipline with them into the struggle, rejecting the state's politices of torturing, maiming and killing—in short, terrorizing—innocent civilians.

Recent U.S. Policy

President Reagan in July 1983 named a commission headed by Henry Kissinger, not to seek new policy guidelines for Central America but to justify existing policy.

The Kissinger Report is, in the words of the *New York Times*, "an inconsistent hodgepodge." It recognizes the indigenous roots of the unrest in the appalling poverty, concentration of wealth, and gross violation of human rights. To correct this situation, it calls for major improvements in health, education, and social welfare, and a substantially improved distribution of income and wealth, to include land reform. In the next breath, it ascribes the success of the opposition forces not to these intolerable conditions, but to external support, with propaganda, money, sanctuary, arms, supplies, training, communications, intelligence, and logistics supplied from Cuba, Nicaragua, and the Soviet Union.

The report proposes a massive increase in U.S. military involvement to enable the oligarchic regimes to destroy the opposition forces, the solution that was tried and that failed in Vietnam. The Commission would have us believe that the victorious armies of the oligarchs would then reform themselves, ending what the report acknowledges is "brutal behavior" and "indiscriminate murder of suspects." Further we are to trust that the oligarchs, restored to firm control, will use massive U.S. aid to reform their economies and societies, thus ending the misery they caused in the first place.

A spokesman for Archbishop Rivera y Damas of San Salvador

condemned the proposed "military solution" as a grave error. "Mr. Kissinger has erred completely by ignoring the Christian sector," he commented. "It is a vital force in this country. He has excluded the possibility of dialogue which the archbishop had proposed. He has not listened to us. We have been very clear in our opposition to military aid."

Here we are facing the central ideological issue in all Central America. Reagan and Kissinger see the popular forces as puppets of the Soviet Union blindly committed to an evil system (Marxism-Leninism) with which no accommodation is possible. Archbishop Rivera y Damas, like his predecessor, martyred Archbishop Romero insists that the dominant inspiration is the preferential option for the poor to which the Church committed itself at Medellín and again at Puebla in 1979. For Reagan and Kissinger the opposition consists of a small clique of ultra-leftists, when in fact the opposition embraces the entire spectrum of public opinion from left to center, standing against the minority of the ultra right. It is the U.S. policy of resistance to inevitable and desirable change that builds support for Marxism.

True independence of the countries of Central America, and the people's determination to create a more just social order do not threaten U.S. national interest. On the contrary, the principles which guide those opposed to the repressive regimes, primary among which is the gospel, are the moral values on which the U.S. was founded. Current U.S. policy seeks to undermine the popular government of Nicaragua, and defends the interests of a tiny minority in El Salvador, Honduras, Guatemala and Costa Rica. It thus rejects the rights, principles, and aspirations of the vast majority of the American people, in both Central and North America.

Glossary of Spanish Words and of Acronyms

Spanish words:

aldea—a village or hamlet, but without the social structure such as stores, gas stations, and meeting halls which we usually associate with "village."

anciano—an elderly person.

campesino—literally means "one from the *campo*," or countryside. Two unfair translations are "farmer," and "peasant." In Central America this label encompasses all those with roots in the land, even if they are landless.

cantina—a local bar or pool hall; any store which sells beer or other liquor.

caserio—comes from the word *casa*—house. A *caserio* is a small cluster of houses fairly near an *aldea* but far enough away to warrant a separate name.

colones—the Salvadoran currency. The 1981 exchange rate was $1.00 = 3.5 *colones.*

Guardia—refers to the *Guardia Nacional*, the National Guard. This is one of the many branches of the armed forces in El Salvador.

lactario—has the same origins as the word "lactation" referring to milk. This was the name of the project to give each child a daily glass of milk.

lempira—the Honduran currency. The 1982 exchange rate was $1.00 = 2 *lempiras.*

muchacho—literally means "boy," but refers affectionately to "the boys" who lead the fight for liberation, i.e., the guerrillas.

orchata—a drink made of finely ground raw rice and sugar.

padre—Father. Used here in reference to a priest.

pupusa—a tortilla with beans or cheese folded into the middle before baking. This is a unique Salvadoran food.

ranchito—a grass hut built by the refugees.

Acronyms:

Caritas—An international Catholic organization for social and economic development. It operates in emergency situations like natural disasters or war to help those in most need. Caritas functions through local parishes under the direction of the priests and bishop of the diocese. Leadership and self-help promotion have been important elements of the program since Vatican II.

CEDEN—Evangelical Committee for National Development and Emergencies. CEDEN is the Honduran coalition of Protestant church aid and development which the Honduran government chose to coordinate the refugee work under the UNHCR administration. It was largely believed that the government chose Protestants to work with a largely Catholic population as a slap in the face to Caritas after it made public the Sumpul massacre.

CONCERN—an international, secular relief and development organization whose U.S. office is in Santa Ana, California.

DNI—National Department of Investigation (Departamento Nacional de Investigacion); the Honduran secret investigatory organization.

NCC—National Council of Churches of Christ.

OAS—Organization of American States.

ORDEN—Organization for National Democracy. It is a right wing paramilitary death squad which operates largely in rural El Salvador. Its dissolution has been a stipulation for continued U.S. military aid, but ORDEN continues to function openly in the outlying, more isolated areas.

OXFAM—Oxford (England) Famine Relief, established in 1946, now has branches in Canada, the U.S., Europe, and Australia. It is a privately funded, nonprofit organization which engages in relief and development work in many areas of the world.

UNHCR—United Nations High Commission on Refugees.

Suggested Additional Reading

Argueta, Manlio. *One Day of Life*. St. Paul, Minn.: Aventura/Vintage, 1983. A Salvadoran novel about the daily life of Salvadoran peasants as viewed through the eyes of the women of one family. A dramatization of the relationship of peasants to both the church and the state.

Armstrong, Robert and Janet Shenk. *El Salvador: The Face of Revolution*. Boston: South End Press, 1982. One of the most complete reviews of the history of El Salvador and the roots of the conflict.

Berryman, Philip. *What's Wrong in Central America*. Philadelphia: American Friends Service Committee, 1983. A short, concise history and analysis of the current Central American situation and the role played by the U.S.

Brockman, James R. *The Word Remains: A Life of Oscar Romero*. Maryknoll, N.Y.: Orbis Books 1984. A richly documented biography of San Salvador's martyred archbishop written with sympathy and firsthand knowledge of Romero's prophetic role.

LaFeber, Walter. *Inevitable Revolutions: The United States in Central America*. New York: Norton 1983. A thorough examination of the area by a Cornell historian demonstrating why the dependency system has turned back upon itself, making revolution inevitable.

Lernoux, Penny. *Cry of the People: The Struggle for Human Rights in Latin America*. New York: Penguin 1982. Possibly the greatest contribution to the American public's understanding of the role of the church in the conflict in Latin America.

Levine, Daniel H. editor. *Churches and Politics in Latin America*.
287

Beverly Hills, Calif., 1980. A compilation of essays on the development of liberation theology.

MacEoin, Gary and Riley, Nivita. *No Promised Land: American Refugee Policies and the Rule of Law*. Boston: Oxfam-America 1982. More than half a million Salvadoran and other Central American refugees live precariously in the United States, under constant fear of deportation to death or persecution. This book explains their right to political asylum under international and domestic law and details widespread violation of these rights by the U.S. immigration authorities.

Montgomery, Tommie Sue. *Revolution in El Salvador*. Boulder, Colo., 1982. A detailed account of the growth of the conflict and the active participation of the church.

PACCA (Policy Alternatives for the Caribbean and Central America). *Changing Course: Blueprint for Peace in Central America and the Caribbean*. Washington, D.C.: IPS 1984. The outline to an alternative approach for U.S. policy toward the region.

Pearce, Jenny. *Under the Eagle: U.S. Intervention in Central America and the Caribbean*. Boston: South End Press 1982. A comprehensive and highly informative account, weaving together the histories of the area and the preponderant role played by the U.S.

A number of Protestant denominations have published study packets on Central America. They provide excellent overview articles, study and reflection guides, and more detailed resource lists. Order them from denominational headquarters.

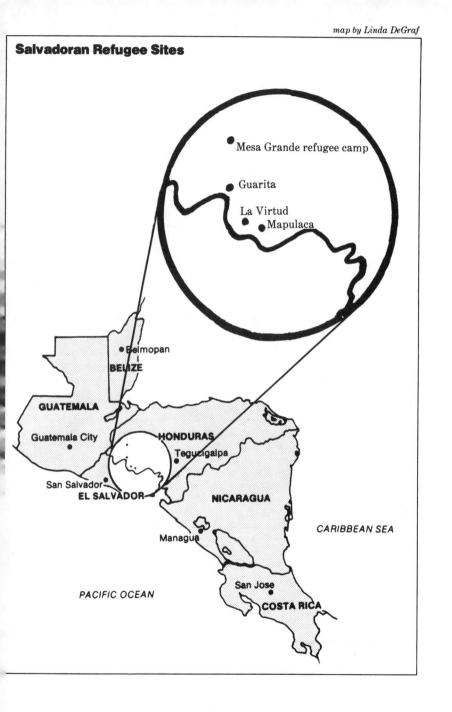

map by Linda DeGraf

Salvadoran Refugee Sites

Mesa Grande refugee camp

Guarita

La Virtud
Mapulaca

Belmopan
BELIZE

GUATEMALA

Guatemala City
HONDURAS
Tegucigalpa

San Salvador
EL SALVADOR
NICARAGUA
CARIBBEAN SEA

Managua

PACIFIC OCEAN
San Jose
COSTA RICA

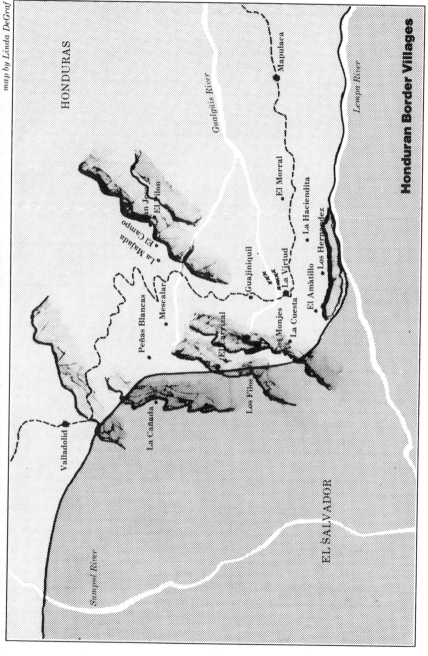

map by Linda DeGraf

Honduran Border Villages

Photo by Steve Stephens

Yvonne Dilling's interests in social justice, the Christian faith, and Latin America took her from her hometown of Fort Wayne, Indiana, to Honduras in late 1980. Yvonne, 29, had lived for two years at Tabor House, located in a largely Hispanic and black neighborhood in Washington, D.C. Tabor House was inspired by the model of base Christian communities in Latin America, where the praxis of biblical reflection and social action is at the core of daily life. The community was characterized by worship, economic sharing, hospitality for needy Hispanics, and actions against injustice both in the U.S. and in Latin America.

Yvonne initially became interested in Latin America during her college years at Manchester College in Indiana, from which she earned her BA in Peace Studies and Conflict Resolution in 1979. She studied Spanish, Latin American history, and took advantage of several travel-study experiences in Latin America and the Caribbean.

On the day after Christmas, 1980, Yvonne left home to travel through Central America. This book is a result of the experiences there which dramatically changed her life. Serious illness forced her to return home in the summer of 1982. While writing this book, Yvonne underwent a year of successful chemotherapy treatments for lymphatic cancer. Yvonne's sense of mission once again called her from her family home in Indiana to Washington, D.C.

She is currently offering her experiences from one Central American border to an ecumenical project focused on another border, northern Nicaragua. Yvonne serves as Nicaragua coordinator for Witness for Peace, a group which maintains a continuous nonviolent, prayerful presence of U.S. citizens on the Nicaragua-Honduras border, where CIA-backed mercenaries, many of them former Somoza National Guardsmen, carry out brutal attacks against Nicaraguan towns and villages, intending to destablize and overthrow the government.

Yvonne is a member of the Church of the Brethren.

Ingrid Rogers is a writer, pastor, and teacher. She has served on the faculties of Simmons College, Boston, and Manchester College, Indiana, and is presently pastor at the Akron Church of the Brethren in Indiana. She holds a PhD in English from Marburg University in her native country, Germany. Her publications include a collection of plays (*Swords into Plowshares*) and songs (*Peace Be unto You*) as well as numerous articles in church-related periodicals.